S. R. Keightley

The Crimson Sign

A Narrative of the Adventures of Mr. Gervase Orme, sometime Lieutenant in

Mountjoy's Regiment of Foot

S. R. Keightley

The Crimson Sign
A Narrative of the Adventures of Mr. Gervase Orme, sometime Lieutenant in Mountjoy's Regiment of Foot

ISBN/EAN: 9783337177409

Printed in Europe, USA, Canada, Australia, Japan

Cover: Foto ©ninafisch / pixelio.de

More available books at **www.hansebooks.com**

THE CRIMSON SIGN

*A Narrative of the Adventures of
Mr. Gervase Orme, Sometime
Lieutenant in Mountjoy's
Regiment of Foot*

BY

S. R. KEIGHTLEY

AUTHOR OF "THE CAVALIERS"

WITH ILLUSTRATIONS

NEW YORK AND LONDON
HARPER & BROTHERS PUBLISHERS
1898

BY THE SAME AUTHOR.

THE CAVALIERS. A Novel. By S. R. KEIGHTLEY. Illustrated. Post 8vo, Cloth, Ornamental, $1 50.

"The Cavaliers" is healthy in tone, spirited in treatment, and written in a manner calculated to attract lovers of historical adventure.... A capital book.—*Academy*, London.

PUBLISHED BY HARPER & BROTHERS, NEW YORK.

CONTENTS

CHAPTER		PAGE
I.	OF WHAT BEFELL ON THE ROAD TO ENNISKILLEN	1
II.	OF THE ENTERTAINMENT THEY HAD AT THE INN	28
III.	OF THE WAY MY LORD GALMOY SAT IN JUDGMENT	44
IV.	OF HOW THE VICOMTE PAID HIS DEBT	54
V.	OF A MAN'S MEMORY	69
VI.	OF HOW THE HEROINE COMES UPON THE STAGE	81
VII.	OF THE RESCUE FROM GREAT PERIL	101
VIII.	OF THE RETURN TO THE CITY	130
IX.	OF HOW CAPTAIN MACPHERSON FULFILLED HIS TRUST	151
X.	OF THE STAND IN THE TRENCHES	159
XI.	OF A SERIOUS COMMUNICATION	184
XII.	OF A WARM MORNING'S WORK	195
XIII.	OF A STRATAGEM OF WAR	208
XIV.	OF A GAME OF CHANCE	222
XV.	OF HOW THE VICOMTE WAS BROUGHT BACK TO LIFE	245
XVI.	OF A DEED OF TREACHERY	259
XVII.	OF A GREAT ADVENTURE	280
XVIII.	OF HOW GERVASE REACHED THE SHIPS	304
XIX.	OF A STORMY INTERVIEW	313
XX.	OF HOW THE GREAT DELIVERANCE WAS WROUGHT	325
XXI.	OF HOW THE VICOMTE MADE HIS GREAT RENUNCIATION	336

ILLUSTRATIONS

"GERVASE DROPPED NOISELESSLY INTO THE WATER" . . . . *Frontispiece*

"THE STRANGER CAUGHT HIS HORSE BY THE REIN" . . . . *Facing page* 62

"SHE STOPPED SHORT AND LOOKED ROUND HER CAUTIOUSLY" . . . . " 188

"JASPER BUCKLING HIS SWORD ABOUT HIM" . . " 254

THE CRIMSON SIGN.

CHAPTER I.

OF WHAT BEFELL ON THE ROAD TO ENNISKILLEN.

In the year of grace 1689 men were not a whit more long-suffering nor more patient than they are to-day. The choleric captain who had been pacing the guard-room for a quarter of an hour showed evident signs that he was fast losing what temper he possessed. As he marched with a hasty stride up and down the oaken floor, and wheeled with military abruptness on the broad stone that formed the hearth, the rafters of black oak rang with the clank of his sword and the jingling of the spurs on his heavy jack-boots. He pulled with a gesture of impatience at the grizzled white moustache that concealed his mouth, and muttered anathemas which, had they been heard in the pious city of Londonderry, would have been deemed little in keeping with his reputation. Nor did he seem a man with whom others would take unwarrantable liberties, or keep dangling upon their careless will and pleasure.

At first sight there was no mistaking him for anything but a soldier, and one who had seen lengthened service where hard blows had been struck and long marches had to be made. His lean face was brown and seamed with lines, each of which had in all likelihood its history; and a great scar, half concealed by his broad beaver, ran from the temple almost to his chin. His mouth was firm and resolute, giving its character to a face that did not seem apt either to lighten in humour or to soften in pity. He wore his own hair, which was nearly white, and, though he must have been close on sixty, his carriage was upright and soldierly, with a certain stiffness, probably learnt in early life from the drill-master.

The Town clock struck five. Halting suddenly in his walk he turned to the door, and his hand was on the latch when a young man entered hurriedly and stumbled against him. When they recovered themselves, they stood looking at one another inquiringly for a moment. Then the young fellow, who wore a military uniform, drew back a step and saluted gravely. "You are Captain Macpherson, I think?"

"I was Captain Macpherson, sir," the other answered, "a moment since, but what I am now I hardly know till my wits come back. You have a strange way of forcing your company on your neighbours."

"Such sudden acquaintanceship was wholly unexpected, I assure you, sir," the young man answered, with a pleasant smile that lit up his handsome face. "I was directed to meet you here. My name is Orme."

The old soldier, without speaking, retired into the embrasure of the window followed by the younger man, and then turned round sternly.

"Mr. Orme, you must know it hath struck five by the Town clock. A soldier's first duty is discipline, and here have I, your commanding officer, for such I take myself to be, been awaiting your coming a full quarter of an hour. I have been in countries where the provost-marshal would have known how to deal with such offences. Cities have been sacked and great battles lost and won, by less delay than that."

"I have left the Colonel but now, sir. He said nothing of the time, but told me that I should meet you here."

"Very like, very like," growled the other. "I know the breed of old. Feather-bed soldiers who need a warming-pan in camp. They take no heed of time. I was brought up in a different school, and would have you know that while you keep me company, you must learn my ways. How long have you served?" He asked the question abruptly, bending on his companion a keen and penetrating look that nothing seemed to escape.

"I have carried the colours for nearly two years in Mountjoy's regiment."

"And never seen man stricken in fair fight, I warrant; that is before you and will come speedily. Hath Colonel Lundy spoken of the work we are about to take in hand?"

"Only that I was to receive my instructions from you, and place myself under your orders."

"That is well, at any rate. You are green and tender for the business, but you may show the right stuff when the time comes. Things are going crookedly here in Londonderry and elsewhere, Mr. Orme. We go neither back nor forward, but stand swaying like men who know not whether to turn to the right hand or to the left. We would fight but we dare not; we would flee but we cannot. And all the while there are stout fellows here who would handle a musket or trail a pike with the best troops in Europe, if there were a man to lead them. These cursed councils and divided plans breed nothing but failure. You will see Hamilton with his levies across the Bann and round the wall of Londonderry, before the month is out."

"I humbly trust not, but if we do never fear but we shall give a good account of ourselves."

The old soldier smiled dubiously. "There is plenty of talk and furbishing of weapons, but little of the strict drill and discipline that makes soldiers; I am but a plain man myself and I have spoken out plainly. The city is open as a village. There are ramparts to be strengthened, ravelines and fascines to be constructed, supplies to be furnished, and arms to be collected. We talk of standing a leaguer, as if these things would do themselves. But needs must when the Devil drives, and I know whither that carries. These councils have many tongues and no head. They put forth declarations and think all is done when they set their hands to paper with much spluttering of ink. I remember when Francesco de Mello and de Fuentes——But that is an old story and may be told again."

"I doubt not," said Orme, "you have ripe experience, but I would do my own work like a simple gentleman, and leave these things to those whose business they are."

"Fairly rebuked. You are right, my lad, and I am an old fool to stand prating of what hath no concern for you. But 'tis an old trick of mine to find fault where I cannot mend. Natheless, the onfall at the castle of Carrickfergus and the break of Dromore give me cause to grumble, and Rawdon and Beresford and the rest of them might have taken a lesson from a plain soldier like myself, that they might have profited by. They think me only good enough to fetch and carry, spaniel-like—and you say that Colonel Lundy hath told you nothing?"

"Merely that I should place myself at your disposal; nothing else."

"We ride pell-mell for Enniskillen; you and I and some dozen troopers, less or more, without drawing bridle or tarrying by the way. There is a precious cartel these Enniskilleners must digest forthwith, inviting them to leave the safety of their water-walls and, as I hear, good store of provender, to take their chance with us and fight it out behind these petty dykes and fences here. If they ask counsel of mine—but it is our business to see that it carries safely."

"I had hoped," said Orme, "that we might have seen some service; this doth not hold out much hope of that."

"Hear how these young cockerels are given to

crowing!" cried Macpherson; "I promise you this means no evening stroll upon the battlements, but a work of danger which may try your mettle. I mean not the gathering of the desperadoes who make war upon the defenceless, though these have stood to their half-pikes and other outlandish weapons ere now, but I am much mistaken if the royal troops be not on the roads and give us play enough. In this barbarous country we do not look for the courtesies of war, or even the interchange of prisoners; my Lord Galmoy and others, whom I hope to remember, have shown that a gentleman can play the hangman, and a soldier hath other trades than fighting. The journey is like to prove adventurous though it end in nothing. See that your horse be sure and fresh, and your pistols such that a man may place his life on them. I remember me when my life was placed in jeopardy once by a rotten girth. It was in Flanders in sixty-nine—but this gossip hath no interest for you. It were more to the purpose that I told you we set out at three in the morning with what secrecy we can observe, and that you meet me at the Bishop's gate. Hackett, who is, I am told, a sergeant of your company, and knows the country, will bring our horses to the gate. You know the man; of what character is he?"

"As true and loyal as any in the city—the best man, I think, in the regiment."

"And discreet? these good men are ofttimes inconsiderate."

"He is no babbler, sir," Orme answered, somewhat nettled by the tone of his companion, "though a pious man and God-fearing."

"I, Ninian Macpherson, like him none the worse for that, young gentleman," answered the other gravely, "Our religion hath placed you and me, I humbly trust, in arms this day, and sends us forth on this embassage to the no small peril of our lives. But the ways of grace are not always the ways of worldly prudence, and it behoves me who am answerable for our safety to act with diligence. Now, look you, Mr. Orme, I have watched you carefully, and I think you honest—dull it may be but honest, and I speak you plainly. I am suspicious of your colonel—I do not understand his ways. There is treason in the air, though who is free and who is touched I hardly know, but I who have lived among designing men for nigh on seven-and-fifty years think I know somewhat of honest work, and I was fearful this was but another trap."

"I think, sir, Colonel Lundy is honest and devoted to Their Majesties."

"I do not doubt you do, but we shall see. The citizens will give him a short shrift if they find him a rogue. But I had liked to see such zeal as befits one who commands a city, and would not be taken unprepared. When the regiments arrive from England they will find their entertainment of the poorest. If empty magazines and disordered companies are evidence of loyalty you might find a sign to hang up before every house in the city.

But Ulster hath a proud heart and a stiff neck and will fight when she is pushed."

"The Kingdom's safety and the Protestant religion depend upon her stoutness; she will die hard."

"It may come to that. Now, young gentleman, get you gone. He that would be early afoot should be early abed, and see that you get to rest betimes. Let there be no late revelling. We meet at three."

Gervase Orme who had been lately an ensign in Mountjoy's regiment of foot, had been quartered with his company in Londonderry, when his Colonel was appointed Governor of the City. Like other gentlemen of his faith he had not wavered in his allegiance or dreamed of taking up arms against the House of Stuart, till loyalty had become a crime and resistance an imperative duty. His own slender patrimony was in peril; his faith was threatened and in danger of being proscribed; his friends, whose safety and honour were his own, were placed at the mercy of their bitter and hereditary foes. Civil war was imminent, and he could not hesitate as to the course he should adopt. James had broken faith with his people; the native Celtic population, steadfast in this, while they were wayward and fickle in all else, were determined to drive the English garrison into the sea, and the instincts of religion and of race intensified their hatred of the dominant caste.

When Colonel Lundy took the oath of allegiance to William and Mary, Gervase Orme willingly followed the example of his Colonel, and embarked with enthusiasm on the impending struggle. To him it was the one course left open, and he felt, like the other simple gentlemen of his time, that when he drew his sword it was for fatherland, for faith, and even for life itself. Nor did he very much doubt the result. The descendent of a Saxon colonist he looked down on the men of Munster and of Connaught as a race fit only for hewing wood and drawing water, for Fontenoy and other stricken fields had yet to be fought in which the Irish proved their splendid qualities as fighting men. And he had the Saxon's profound faith in himself and his people.

Therefore it was when Colonel Lundy had directed him to place himself under Macpherson's orders, with some prospect of service, he had obeyed with alacrity, hopeful that their destination might be one of those towns upon the Bann where the Protestant forces were awaiting the coming of the Irish army which was rapidly advancing north. In this he had been disappointed, but he was glad to forsake for a time the comparative inactivity of garrison life, and almost hoped that Macpherson's anticipation of danger might be realized.

The night was raw and cold when he arose unwillingly from his bed, and his preparations being complete overnight, hurriedly dressed and endeavoured to partake of the meal his careful landlady had provided the evening before. When he reached the gate Macpherson was already there before him. The old soldier, wrapped in a long military cloak, was standing with his back to the wall, reading from a small volume in a loud monotonous tone, and the men were drawn in a circle round him, holding their horses by the bridle. One of the troopers held a lantern for the reader, who closed the book as Orme came up, and thrust it into his breast.

"You are close on your time, Mr. Orme. We have just been having our stirrup-cup from the Word, that, mayhap, will put us in heart for our cold ride. 'Tis an excellent morning dram. The sergeant hath seen to the arms and tells me they will serve."

"Both arms and men, sir," said Hackett, in a low tone, "I will answer for them with my life."

"'Tis well. Now open the gate and get to horse, for we must put many a mile between us and the city before daybreak. A mile at the start is worth two at the end."

Macpherson leapt with surprising activity on the grey charger that Hackett had brought down to the gate, and the little troop sat patiently on their horses waiting till the drawbridge had been lowered and the great gate swung open. With a solemn "God speed" from the men on duty, they rode silently out into the darkness, Hackett leading at a round trot over the rough and broken road.

For three hours they pursued their way in a silence broken only by an occasional word of command, or by a cry of warning from one of the troopers who had stumbled over some obstacle, or had floundered deep in the bog by the road side. They were all rejoiced to see the first grey streak of light that gave promise of the coming day.

The morning had broken red through the mists that lay thick along the valley as they gained the top of the hill up which they had been climbing. The road was already visible, winding through a deep gorge, and skirted by great masses of rock, green with ferns and bramble. Here and there scattered through the uplands lay a farm steading, surrounded by its stretch of tilth and orchard close. But no sound of morning labour could be heard. The fields were lying waste and untilled, and the homesteads stood deserted. The clank of the horses hoofs made a melancholy music in the silence. The life and movement of the little troop brought into still greater relief the desolation round them.

Macpherson halted on the top of the hill, and dismounting loosened his horse's girths. Then he removed the saddle and taking off his gloves, began to rub down the charger.

"That is my prince of steeds," he said, contemplating his task and caressing the glossy neck with pride and affection; "nearly four hours' hard riding and never turning a hair! An old soldier, my young friend," he continued, turning to Gervase, "learns a good many things on his rough journey through the world. He learns to weigh a prince's promises and favours, the strength of friendship and the worth of love. And he finds they are all vanity, even the vanity of vanities, as the Hebrew hath it. But he grows to love his horse. Together they have faced the scathe of the battle, and the privations of the march. Often and often this sleek skin hath been my pillow, and but for him these useless bones had been whitening on the sandy plains of Utrecht, or the rolling uplands of the Maas. And for beauty—you youths go mad for beauty—is there aught in the world to compare with him for comeliness? That little head and graceful neck, those swift strong legs and deep shoulders fashioned as if by a cunning sculptor—there is perfect beauty. And he is faithful even to death. He will carry me till he drops and leave a royal stable at the whistle of his homeless master. I tell you, young sir, there is nothing in the world like a noble horse and the joy of battle in a righteous cause."

"In truth," said Gervase, "you are proud of your horse with reason, but I trust there are other things in the world one may love with as good cause."

"Aye," answered the other bitterly, "you are young, and youth is full of hope and trust. The man you call your friend cajoles and tricks you, and the woman whose favour is the breath of your nostrils, deserts you at the first whisper of misfortune. These things are of the world and they endure for an hour; the son of perdition baits his traps with them, but the man whose hope is fixed, learns to shun them as a snare."

"I have been taught otherwise," said Gervase, "and I have had no reason to question what I have learnt. I have no trick of speech, but I hold by love and friendship."

"And I tell you they are but shadows. Here there is no abiding city, and these things but wean our hearts from the eternal. Seven-and-fifty years have been the days of my pilgrimage, and at eighteen I saw my first battle. The blood of the youth is hot, the lusts of the flesh are strong upon him, and he is slow to see the finger of God writing upon the tablets of the heart. Mine was a wild youth and a wayward, and like another prodigal I went forth to riotous living. Surely I dwelt in the tents of Meshech, but God hath seen good to open the eyes of his servant."

"Captain Macpherson," said Gervase gravely, "I do not ask you to vouchsafe me your confidence, and I leave theology to the parson. I serve God after the fashion of the Church of England, and will do my duty as becomes my name and manhood. In all other things I am at your service, but in this we cannot walk together."

He turned away and left the old soldier gazing after him earnestly.

The sun had already risen above the morning mists that had gathered themselves into fantastic shapes and were dispersing slowly down the valley— the promise of a lovely day in spring. The troopers had dismounted, and were making a frugal meal of dry rye bread and cold bacon, washed down by a draught of the spring water that trickled down the rock by the roadside. Weary with their long march, covered with mud and flaked with foam, the horses cropped the long grass that grew luxuriantly under the hedge of thorn. Gervase threw himself down on the grassy sward by the roadside, and watched the picturesque scene around him. Then, tired as he was, a heavy drowsiness overtook him, and the deep valley and the swelling uplands, and the horses, and the travel-stained troopers became part of a broken dream. Over his head he seemed to hear the jubilant notes of a thrush in the white thorn, and in a little while a deep voice reading one of the psalms that glow with the rapture of battle and thrill with the triumph of faith, followed by the loud "Amen" of the troopers.

Then he fell into a profound sleep. When he awoke the sunshine filled the valley, and Macpherson was standing over him with a smile on his rugged face.

"Is it time to march?" cried Gervase.

"It is time to be up and doing," Macpherson answered solemnly. "This day will try of what stuff the Lord hath made your sinews and fashioned your heart. Yonder is the enemy."

Gervase leapt hastily from his resting-place. Already the men were in their saddles and were examining the priming of their carbines. Far down the valley he could see a small body of horse, the sunshine glancing on their swords and steel head-pieces, and the dust rising thickly under the hoofs of the chargers. A little in advance were riding two officers, one of whom rode a grey horse and was conspicuous by the scarlet cloak he wore over his armour.

Gervase watched Macpherson with surprise and admiration. The old soldier seemed like another man under the inspiration of the coming struggle; his eyes flashed, his chest heaved, and his deep strong voice thrilled like a trumpet. Leaping like a youth into his saddle and laying his hand lightly for a moment on the restive charger's neck, he drew his sword from the scabbard. Then he placed himself across the road in front of the troopers and pointed with his sword to the enemy, who had already quickened their pace and were advancing at a sharp trot.

"Yon are Galmoy's Horse, gentlemen. They are nearly three to one, and I am told they can fight. What say ye?"

Already the troopers had caught the joyous spirit of their grim leader; his voice stirred them like a trumpet. They had caught the contagion of his hope, his faith, and his enthusiasm.

"We are doing God's work, sir," said Sergeant Hackett soberly, as he gathered up his reins and drew his hat tightly over his brow. "We will follow you, Captain Macpherson, even to the mouth of the pit. Not one of us will fail you."

"Then we will show the butchers what we can do. Remember, let 'no quarter' be our word this day. Do not crowd together until we have drawn their fire. Then give them a salvo steadily, and like brave men and careful. Thereafter in God's name, let them feel the sword's edge and the power of the true religion."

Macpherson had risen in his stirrups, his face glowing with the joy of battle. Already the enemy had shortened the distance between them, and a few minutes more would bring them within pistol shot. They could already hear the heavy trampling of the horses as they came galloping up the hill, the jingling of the bridles and the clank of the swords. As the little troop swept up the hillside it made a gallant show. Gervase felt his heart beat fast and loud; his hand trembled with excitement on the hilt of his sword, and his breath came quick. He found himself longing with feverish impatience for the word to charge, but Macpherson kept his men well in hand, trying their temper, and watching them narrowly like a wary soldier. Not a man showed sign of fear or indecision.

"You are a young soldier, Mr. Orme," said Macpherson, with a joyous laugh, "and young soldiers are ever rash and heedless. Let us give yon sons of Belial time to think of what they do. You will feel in good time the thirst to trample down and slay, and the Devil driving you to rend and to destroy. Wait till they come to where the road widens into the marsh. Yon fellow rides like a gallant gentleman—a Frenchman too, I think, and knows his work. Ha! here they come. Now, my children, follow me, and may God defend his cause this day!"

Macpherson put spurs to his horse, and his troopers followed in an orderly array at a hard gallop.

It was clear the enemy was uncertain as to their intentions, for immediately Macpherson had put his horse in motion, they drew up short and halted. But still the little troop kept on steadily, riding two abreast along the narrow road, and holding their carbines in readiness to fire. The young officer on the grey charger had thrown off his scarlet cloak, and was giving directions to his men with the point of his sword. Several of the troopers had dismounted and lined the roadside where a fence of loose stones presented a sort of low screen, or parapet.

And now barely a hundred yards divided the combatants. Already a shot or two had been fired, but as they came within range the dragoons, without waiting for further orders, fired wildly. Gervase, who rode in advance, turned to see if any of the men behind him had been struck; not a man moved in his saddle. Then Macpherson rose in his stirrups and shouted in a voice of thunder——

"Now, my gallant fellows, fire! Aim at the horses and let every shot tell."

For an instant, as it seemed, the little troop stood fast, and orderly as on parade, took aim and fired. Several horses went down, and for a minute all was confusion and disorder in the royal ranks.

That minute was the turning tide of battle. With a wild shout and a deep oath, Macpherson waved his sword above his head and gave the charge. Instinctively Gervase drove his spurs into his horse's flanks, and grasped the hilt of his sword with a tighter clutch. In another moment he was in the middle of the red-coats and almost without knowing how it was done, he saw his blade buried in the body of the dragoon who had first encountered him. As in a dream he saw the man catch convulsively at the horse's mane and fall in a heap to the ground. Macpherson was at his side, hammering on sword and head-piece. His voice could be heard above the clank and clash of steel and the shouts of the fighting men. "No quarter to the men of Belial. Strike home for the true religion. God's wounds! you must have it."

Two troopers had thrown themselves across his path; one he had charged so violently that his horse had stumbled and gone down, crushing his rider; the other parried his thurst and then turned to flee. But his doom was on him. Down came the deadly steel on the iron head-piece. Nothing could withstand that blow, but the sword was shivered at the hilt.

"The curse of Heaven light on the hand that fashioned thee!" cried Macpherson, hurling the hilt from him and drawing his pistol from the holster. His men followed close upon his heels, hacking and hewing with their heavy swords. No man failed in his duty that day.

Gervase saw the young officer before him gallantly striving to rally his men, and imploring them to stand. Quick as thought their swords were crossed, and Gervase saw his eyes light up with inexpressible hate. "Ah! canaille," he cried, "you will see at least how a gentleman can fight."

It was not a time for nice tricks of fence, and Gervase saw in a moment that his opponent was a more skilful swordsman than himself. He saw the flash of his opponent's blade and felt the warm blood streaming down his face, but he did not give him time to repeat the blow. Throwing himself upon him he caught him round the neck, and together they fell to the ground. It was indeed a miracle how they escaped beneath the hoofs of the trampling horses as they grappled with one another in the dust. Then the tide of battle swept past them, and they were left alone to fight it out. But the delicate Frenchman was no match for the stout young giant whose arms were as strong as an oak sapling. Gervase placed his knee upon his breast, and wrenched the sword from his hand.

"It is enough, Monsieur; I yield myself prisoner."

Gervase leapt to his feet and reached out his hand to assist his prisoner from the ground. But the other refused the proffered courtesy, and when he had risen, nonchalantly began to arrange his disordered dress, and to brush the dust from his clothes with an embroidered handkerchief. "Your arms, monsieur, are very strong, but I do not understand the fashion of your country. We do not fight thus in France. It is my regret that you should not see the end of this gallant affair."

There was a covert sneer in the tone that there was no mistaking.

"I have seen the beginning and the end, sir," Gervase said simply. "Your men do not seem to relish the fare we have provided for them."

"My men are not soldiers; they are poltroons Let us dismiss them. May I inquire into whose hands it has been my good fortune to fall?"

"My name, sir, is Gervase Orme, sometime ensign in Mountjoy's regiment, and now in arms for the Protestant religion and the liberties of the kingdom. I am very much at your service."

"You are very good, but Victor de Laprade, whom men call Vicomte of that name, seeks favour from none. I think," he continued, looking down the road along which the pursuit had rolled, "we are likely to be better acquainted."

"It is not to be doubted, sir: the skirmish is over and your men are wholly broken."

"Nay, Luttrel was a brave man; I am sorry for him, but the rest—let them go."

The moment that the Vicomte de Laprade had gone down in Gervase's grasp, the dragoons had broken and fled, followed hard by Macpherson and his troop. The pursuers were in no mood to give quarter that day. The atrocities of Galmoy some time before had filled their hearts with a thirst for vengeance; it was a sacred duty not to spare, but to slay, and slay without remorse or pity. Far down the road thundered the headlong flight, pursuers and pursued mingled together. De Laprade had seated himself on the fence by the roadside, and watched without apparent interest the incidents of the pursuit. It was impossible to tell from his face what his real feelings might have been.

"*C'est fini*," he said lightly, as the troopers halted and turned to retrace their footsteps to where the conflict had commenced.

Macpherson came up, wiping the perspiration from his brow.

"I saw you go down," he said to Gervase, "and feared it was all over with you. I should have been sorry to my dying day, for you have shown the right soldier spirit,—you have been touched?"

"A mere scratch, but we have gained a great success."

"A pretty affair. What popinjay have we yonder?" and he pointed to De Laprade.

"One of King James's new French gentlemen," said Gervase smiling, "who is the first captive of my bow and spear."

"One of the accursed race," said Macpherson grimly. "And the message hath come to me; 'no quarter,' was our word this day. His blood be upon his own head." He drew his pistol from the holster, and dismounted from his horse. Gervase saw the deep gloom gather on his brow.

"What would you do?" Gervase cried, catching his arm and placing himself between his Captain and the Vicomte. "In God's name, you do not mean to say that you would slay him in cold blood?"

"In cold blood, no, but in righteous vengeance for the evil that hath been wrought upon our people. Do you forget Dixie and Charleton? I have taken a vow before the Lord this day that not one of them shall escape me. The blood of Abel is crying from the ground, and shall I, the least of his servants, suffer that cry to go unheard?"

"While I live you shall not injure one hair of his head. The lessons that you have learned in the school of Turenne we will not practise here. No prisoner shall be slain in cold blood while Gervase Orme can wield a sword to defend him."

Macpherson turned away and replaced his pistol in the holster without a word, and stooping down began to examine the forelegs of his charger. While this scene was being enacted on which his life depended, the Vicomte continued sitting upon the fence, flicking the dust from his riding boots with his handkerchief and smiling an easy smile of apparent indifference. He seemed to be the only one who had no interest in the issue of the quarrel. Then he rose, and going over to Gervase held out his hand.

"However you may yet decide this trivial affair," he said, "I thank you for your courtesy. I declined to take your hand; I beg your pardon. You are a brave man and a gentleman. But it is a matter of regret that you should quarrel with your friend on my poor account."

"There is no quarrel, sir," said Macpherson, who had overheard his words, raising himself to his full height, and looking steadily as he spoke. "This young gentleman was right, and I was wrong. He had given you quarter, which matter he may yet live to repent, and you were under his protection by the laws of war. I might have shot you down in the melee but I left him to deal with you. He hath seen good to spare your life, and in your presence, sir, I now ask his pardon, which will not be denied me."

"I cannot pardon where there is no offence, Captain Macpherson," said Gervase. "It was my good fortune to fight on the side that can afford protection, and had it been otherwise I am certain that M. de Laprade would have rendered me the like service."

The Vicomte bowing low, raised his hat with a grand air. Then he said, addressing Macpherson, "Monsieur le Capitaine appears to regret that he did not shoot me. It is not yet too late to try his skill. By the kindness of this gentleman I have still my sword, and if you, sir, do not think it beneath your dignity to try a pass with a poor soldier and gentleman like myself, I shall be happy to give you the opportunity you desire. Here is a pretty piece of heath—how say you, sir?"

"I say that I fight only in the way of my duty, but at another time when public necessity may give way to private entertainment I shall have no objection to oblige you either with sword or pistol, on foot or horseback. No man that knows him will say that Ninian Macpherson declined a duello because he feared the thrust of a rapier or the shot of a pistol. When our journey is ended and the business now on hand completed——"

"Be assured I shall afford you what you are pleased to call your entertainment. And now may I ask whither you purpose to carry me?"

"We shall carry you, sir, as far as Enniskillen, and, mayhap, if you so desire it back to Londonderry."

"I have no desires; I have learnt the uses of adversity."

"Then you have learnt the last lesson a man can learn," answered Macpherson, abruptly turning on his heel, and joining Hackett who was looking after one of the men who had been wounded.

The skirmish had in every sense been a complete success. Only one man had been slightly, and another severely wounded, and these raw and undisciplined yeomen had shown a wonderful steadiness and gallantry. When the horses of the dragoons had been collected, for Macpherson believed in gathering the fruits of victory, they were ready to start on the march.

"The prisoner is in your charge, Sergeant Hackett," he said. "Shoot him through the head if he tries to run away."

De Laprade shrugged his shoulders. "Bah!" he said, "your Captain eats fire. Whither would he have me run?"

"Not outside the reach of my carbine," said Hackett drily.

Gervase had fallen into the rear, where he was

presently joined by Macpherson, whose passion had apparently died away, and left his face pale with an almost ghastly pallor. They rode side by side, neither speaking a word. Macpherson's head was bent on his breast, and Gervase could hear him muttering to himself in a low tone, but he could not catch the meaning of his words. He was evidently struggling with some violent emotion. Then he seemed to wake up from the profound reverie in which he had been sunk, and laying his hand on the arm of his companion, said in a low voice,

"Mr. Orme, thou art a well-conditioned and, I think, a godly young man, and though it does not beseem one of my gray hairs and length of years to open his heart to one young and lacking in experience as thou art, yet the spirit within me prompts me to speak."

Gervase was silent.

"There are times," he continued, "when the Spirit of the Lord is upon me. Then I can hear the strains of a rich and heavenly minstrelsy, and my soul is possessed with the joy of everlasting hope. Alas! I do begin to fear it is but the snare of the fowler. This day the evil one took possession of me. I relapsed into the gall of bitterness and the bonds of iniquity. I sware evil oaths; I rejoiced in the shedding of blood, nor was it the cause of the Lord that I followed this day, but the promptings of my own carnal heart. Can the Lord of Righteousness and the Prince of the powers of the air dwell in the same breast?"

"I do not know how these things may be," Gervase answered, "but I know that you have done your duty this day like a good and valiant soldier. It may be that old habits are strong upon you, and an old warhorse like yourself lifts his ears at the sound of the charge."

"The hearts of the elect are purified, and old habits cannot draw the soul from God."

He looked at Gervase with a look of profound sadness in his eyes, and there was an undertone of despair in his voice. It was impossible to doubt his sincerity. Spiritual despair had seized upon him, and his narrow creed had no word of consolation to offer him in his hour of doubt. He had drawn aside the veil that concealed the workings of his heart.

"All the days of my youth were vanity," he continued; "I squandered my substance in riotous living, and spent my strength in the lap of harlots. Then the Lord found me in the wilderness, and for ten years I have walked in the narrow way, till now mine enemy has found me this day; nay, not this day, but the hour I girt this sword on my side. I am the same man that fought at St. Gothard, and walked up the breach at Philisbourg."

"And may I never fight by the side of a better soldier," cried Gervase with assumed gaiety. "The Protestant cause could ill afford to lose an arm like yours. But for you we had never charged this day.

"Ah! it was a gallant onfall;" said the old soldier

meditatively, "I have seldom seen a brisker, but it is vanity, vanity." He sighed, and relapsed into silence, nor did Gervase venture to address him again till they rode into the village where they intended to pass the night.

CHAPTER II.

OF THE ENTERTAINMENT THEY HAD AT THE INN.

At the door of the inn Hackett dismounted, and unfastening the latch with some difficulty entered the kitchen. A fire of peat was smouldering on the hearth, and the remains of what was evidently a hurried meal were scattered on the table. A number of pike heads and scythe blades were piled in a corner. There was no one in the room. He rapped loudly with the hilt of his sword on the table and presently a woman made her appearance from one of the inner rooms. She seemed greatly alarmed at the unexpected arrival of her guests, and as she entered she cast a look of fear and expectancy round the kitchen. Her eyes fell on the weapons in the corner and she stopped short.

"We want food and lodgings for the night," said the sergeant, who had been examining one of the pewter mugs carefully, "lodgings for the men and horses. Bacon, I see, you have in plenty. Is there hay in the stable?"

"Ay," she answered nervously, "but my man is from home and I cannot serve you."

"Oh, for that we will just wait upon ourselves

and be beholden to ye all the same. Your man, I doubt not, has taken to another trade, and belike it were as well we did not fall across him. And for what do ye keep these toys?" he asked, kicking the heap of weapons with his jack boot. "These are not tools an honest man would willingly handle, but we will inquire further thereinto."

So saying he went out to make his report to Macpherson, who was awaiting his return with undisguised impatience. "Things have an ill look, sir," he said, with a stiff salute, "and I doubt not there is mischief brewing hereabouts; but there is a can of ale for ourselves and fodder for the beasts."

"We can go no further if we would," said Macpherson, "there is not another mile in the horses. And," he continued, glancing at the capability of the house to withstand an attack, "we can make good this place against a hundred. Let the horses be looked to carefully. I myself will examine the stable. Come, sweetheart, thou hast done a good day's work and hast well earned a night's repose."

Gervase and the Vicomte entered the house together. The woman had replenished the fire and was busily engaged making her preparations for the reception of her unwelcome guests. As De Laprade came in she gave a start of surprise, but the look of recognition, which for a moment lighted up her face, immediately gave place to the dull, stolid expression she had worn in her interview with the sergeant. She continued her work apparently unconscious of the presence of the two strangers. The Vicomte threw his hat and sword on the table and sat down on a stool close to the hearth.

"I am destined to see Madame again," he said, stretching out his hands towards the warmth of the hearth, for the evening had grown chilly. "And how is la belle Marie?"

As he spoke a tall girl of eighteen, barefooted and bareheaded, entered the door, tall and straight as a young poplar, lissom and graceful, with the deep blue black eyes and low broad brow that one meets again and again among the peasants of the West country. Here is the pure Greek, instinct with life, but touched with a certain grace of sad and pensive beauty. She also started with surprise when her eyes fell on the young Frenchman.

"I thought, mother," she said hesitating—"I thought—"

"Have done thinking and help me with the supper," her mother answered, with a glance of warning. "The gentlemen have ridden far and will stay the night."

"Madame does not recognize her old friends, ma belle," said De Laprade lightly, "but you will not be so cruel. When we parted this morning, I did not dream that we should meet so soon, but it is the fortune of war."

"And the rest," cried the girl eagerly, "are they also—"

The woman looked up anxiously for a moment. "Poof!—they are gone—*ecrasés;* they need no roof over their heads to-night, nor a pretty maiden to wait on them. They drank too deep last night to have cool heads this morning, and now they will never hear the reveille sound again. It is a great pity, but the fortunes of war—"

"I don't understand," said the girl. "What has become of them?"

"They are lying yonder by the roadside and will waken never again."

The woman threw up her hands with a loud cry and fell on the floor.

"These barbarians have then some touch of humanity," said De Laprade softly, while Gervase ran forward and raised her head upon his knee, and the girl seized a water can which stood on the table and bathed her cheeks and forehead. In a few minutes the woman recovered consciousness and looked round her wildly.

"It is not true," she cried; "'tis a lie. My beautiful boy that left me singing this morning with the lovelight dancing in his eyes is not dead. The sword was never sharpened that could slay him. I care not for King James or King William and for— why should they not leave me in peace? Tell me, for the Holy Virgin's sake, that it is not true." She rose and staggering forward threw herself at De Laprade's feet and caught him round the knees, with streaming eyes and a look of wild entreaty in her face.

He endeavoured ineffectually to disengage himself, but she clung to him with desperate earnestness.

His look of placid indifference gave way to one of profound pity. "It may be," he said, gently endeavouring to raise her to her feet, "it may be that I was wrong and your son is not dead. I remember me he was our guide and did not carry arms. He may have escaped the fate that befell the others, but one of these gentlemen will tell you."

At this moment Macpherson, accompanied by the sergeant, entered the house.

"What pother is this?" he said roughly. "If you are unwilling to serve us we will even wait upon ourselves. We do not make war on women, but they must not hinder us."

Gervase drew him aside by the sleeve, hastily explaining how matters stood; but there was no comfort or hope in his answer. He had not seen the boy, but there might be good reason for that; the woman should have kept the lad at home if she was unwilling he should take his chance, and no one could be blamed if he went down with the rest. One more or less, what did it matter?

The girl stood listening to their brief conversation with flashing eyes, and then took her mother by the arm, and drawing her into the inner room closed the door behind them.

Macpherson was in the enemy's country and accordingly made himself at home. Under his direction a meal was soon prepared, and a cask of home-brewed ale that had been discovered in a recess, was rolled into the middle of the floor, and the men helped themselves. They were too tired for much speech and devoted themselves to their repast in silence, addressing one another occasionally in undertones, and making huge inroads on the rashers and coarse bread that rapidly disappeared before them. Macpherson sat moodily apart, eating and drinking but sparingly—a marked contrast to De Laprade who seemed to forget that he was a prisoner, and laughed at his own conceits with light-hearted gaiety. He had divested himself of his peruke and riding boots, and stretched himself along the rude settle that stood near the hearth. He appeared to pay no attention to the stern leader who scowled more and more deeply as the Vicomte's laugh grew louder, and the tone of his conversation assumed a more unbecoming levity. Gervase could not help feeling interested, for the type was altogether new to him—there was a life and colour about the stories to which he was a stranger; it was a little bit of Versailles, brilliant and careless, set down in the wilds of Fermanagh.

"Pardieu!" said the Vicomte, "it was play that did it; there was nothing else left. My creditors will miss me, I do not doubt, but they were troublesome and I hate trouble; so I hastened to seek glory—bah! it is a greater trouble than the other. Where is the glory when your soldiers will not fight, and your king is a poltroon? There is no music like the rattle of the dicebox, when fortune, the beautiful goddess, is smiling like a lover. Love and play are the two things that make life worth living."

"Of love," said Gervase, "I know nothing, but for play—I leave that to the fool and the knave. Nay, I mean not to say that men of honour have not ere now given themselves up to its strange fascination, but it was their weakness. For me, I like rather to hear the yelp of the otter hounds when the morning is young and the spring woods are full of life and beauty, or the cry of the beagles when the scent is lying strong. You have never seen the brown trout in the freshet?"

"There were no fish in the ponds at Versailles," said the Vicomte drily, "but when a great lady dropped her fan——"

Macpherson rose to his feet and drew out the small leather-bound volume that Gervase had seen him use before. "There has been enough of this untimely jesting," he said. "These are not manners that suit our station or our work, and if you, sir, care not to join in the devotions of Christian men, I shall not compel you to remain, but you may retire to your repose. But as for us, we will thank God for His watchful care this day."

"Your devotions, sir, will interest me beyond measure."

"Hackett, give me the light," said Macpherson, looking for a moment sternly at the speaker from under his heavy eyebrows. The sergeant went to the hearth and taking up a blazing piece of resinous fir held it up to his leader, who opened the book and began solemnly to read one of those Psalms that breathe forth vengeance and savage triumph.

"Plead my cause, oh Lord, with them that strive with me, fight against them that fight against me. Take hold of shield and buckler and stand up for my help."

Then he closed the book and dropping on his knees (an example which was followed by all the company except the Vicomte, who was apparently fast asleep) he prayed loudly and fervently. His prayer was to some extent a repetition of the verses he had been reading, clothed in more homely language. He prayed that God would lead His people forth in safety through the perils and dangers that encompassed them; and that the wicked oppressor might be taken in his own toils and destroyed utterly. Then from the language of supplication he passed to the enthusiasm of prophecy. The day was at hand when a great deliverance would be wrought for the people of God. The scarlet woman, sunken in her adulteries and witchcraft, would pass into the darkness of Tophet; they who lived by the sword would perish by the sword, and the Protestant cause would triumph over all its enemies. When he had finished, and his loud Amen was repeated by the kneeling men around him, he remained for some time on his knees apparently engaged in private prayer. Then he rose to his feet with the prompt alacrity that distinguished him, and gave the few necessary instructions for the night.

"We march at three," he said abruptly. "Ralston will do duty at the Bridge, and Given will take the church at the upper end of the village. In three hours they will be relieved. There must be no sleeping on sentry duty, my lads," he added, with additional sternness in his tone, "for we do not want our throats cut while we sleep. This is not child's play, and if you fail in aught be assured you have a man to deal with who knows how to punish laggards."

With these words he left the room abruptly and the men, with the exception of the two who had been selected for duty, settled themselves on the earthen floor of the kitchen to snatch a brief repose. Gervase had secured for himself a small room at the end of the house in which there was a rude bed, and which he had proposed to share with the Vicomte who, however, had declined his offer. The door of the room, which was of oak, was secured by a heavy bolt and this he fastened carefully behind him when he entered the apartment. The moon was shining bright and the sky was full of stars. From the little window Gervase could see the church tower standing square and black in the soft yellow moon-light, and the little river winding down the valley like a tangled silver thread. Placing his sword within reach and his pistols under his pillow, he threw himself on the pallet. But for some time his mind was too busy with the events of the day to allow him to settle himself to sleep. Half dreaming, half awake, he saw again and again in its deadly agony and unspeakable terror, the face of the man whom he had run through in the skirmish. He heard ringing in his ears the wild shouts of the charging horsemen, and his sword was raised aloft to strike, when his strength seemed suddenly to become as the strength of a little child, and his heart to die for fear within him. At length, worn out with the labour of the day, he fell into a profound and dreamless sleep.

It was long past midnight when he was awakened by the sound of the crashing and splintering of wood, the clash of weapons and the glare of blazing lights. Leaping, dazed and bewildered, from his bed, he caught up his sword, and placing his back against the wall, prepared to sell his life as dearly as possible. Already the stout oak panels had given way under the heavy blows that were being dealt from the outside. In another minute the door fell in with a crash, and the room was filled with flashing lights and a crowd of armed ruffians. At the sight of him standing with his weapon drawn, his assailants halted for a moment; then someone raised the cry: "Cut the throat of the heretic," and there was a simultaneous rush upon him. They were so crowded together that they could not effectually use their weapons, and to his own surprise Gervase was able to keep them at bay.

When the first shock of surprise had passed, and it passed almost immediately, he felt his eyes clear and his nerves steady themselves into a cool and deliberate resolve to die, if needs must, like a valiant fighting man. He realized at a glance the extreme desperateness of the situation, and his very despair gave him courage. His grasp was firm and strong on the hilt of his sword, and the pulses of his blood began to beat steadily. In after days he wondered that it should be so, and like a simple and courageous gentleman, he set it down to no heroism of his own, but to the inspiration and direction of a higher Power. In a moment standing there he knew what had happened. The sentinels had been surprised at their post, the men below had been taken unawares and overpowered without resistance, and the hostelry was completely in the hands of the enemy. For him there was no hope of escape, and he knew he need expect no quarter. Leaping upon the bed, he parried the blows that were dealt at him. Again and again his assailants came surging up, and again and again he cleared the deadly circle round him. Already two or three bodies lay on the floor below him: his sword streamed with blood from the point to the hilt. For a moment there was a pause—his courage and coolness had checked the first rush. Then with a deep oath one of the fellows sprang forward, and caught him round the knees with a grasp that he could not disengage, and another leaping on the bed beside him, sought to wrest the weapon from his hand. He thought that the end was come and that in another minute it would be all over. But he felt his strength the strength of ten. Dealing one of the fellows a tremendous blow fair and straight in the face, he shortened his sword and ran the other through the body; without a sound the man rolled over and fell in a heap on the floor. Again the circle cleared round him and he drew a deep breath. Then there was a sound of rushing water in his ears; the room swam round him; tottering and falling he clung to the wall for support. Through a blinding mist he saw, or dreamt he saw, the gleam of uplifted weapons round him ready to strike, and he wondered that they did not make an end of him; then the tall figure of De Laprade with his rapier drawn, striking up the weapons that were aimed at him; surely, too, that was the voice of the gallant Vicomte?—" What, cowards! would you slay the boy now that he is down, when you could not face him with his sword in his hand? Ah, *sang de Dieu!* you shall not touch him. I command you; I, Victor de Laprade. *Mille de Diables!* take up these carcases and see if there is any life left in them. He is a gallant gentleman, and you shall not injure a hair of his head."

To the reeling brain of Gervase all was wild tumult and disorder; the lights blazed round him; the flash of gleaming steel and the shadow of dark passionate faces came and went; the strident clamour of angry voices sounded as from immeasurable distances. And then his senses failed him and he remembered no more.

When consciousness returned he was lying on the bed with the Vicomte bending over him, while a little dark man in a shabby cloak and wig very much the worse for wear, was stanching the blood that flowed from a wound in his shoulder. The room had been cleared, but some fellows whose faces showed that they had been robbed of their spoil, were gathered round the door, and looked on with countenances that betokened little goodwill toward the wounded man. The little surgeon went on busily with his work and when he had finished, rubbed his hands with an air of satisfaction.

"A neat bit of work, Vicomte; as pretty a piece of accidental skilfulness as ever I saw in my life. The one hundred and twelfth part of an inch would have relieved this tenement of clay of its immortal soul, and being a heretic——" and he shook his head vigorously. "However, 'tis but a trifle to one who hath youth and vigour. This excessive bleeding will relieve him of sundry humours and affections that lurk in the veins of youth, and in a day or two at the furthest his natural strength will assert itself. He must avoid the use of intoxicating fluids. But I'm thinking," he added, with a twinkle in his eyes, "there will be little for him after my lord and myself."

Gervase opened his eyes and attempted to rise, but De Laprade, sitting beside him on the bed, gently restrained him.

"Be not in too great haste, my friend," he said. "My Lord Galmoy will want to see you presently and you will need all your strength for the interview."

"A very deadly disease for which there is no remedy known to the faculty," added the surgeon; "especially when he is in his cups."

"Monsieur le Medicin," continued De Laprade, "tells me your wound is not serious, and if you can listen I should like to give you a word of advice, though little accustomed to give it."

"I begin to feel better," Gervase answered. "The wound is a trifle painful and my head is somewhat dull withal, but I have strength enough left to thank you, Vicomte, for your help. I doubt not but for your kindly assistance I had now been past this gentleman's skill."

"I assure you, my friend, 'twas nothing. These wolves have a taste for blood, but they like their game better dead than alive and are easily shaken off. But the wolf—I mean the gentleman—who will presently be inquiring for you is altogether different. Him you cannot so easily satisfy. I should advise you, in all friendship, to answer his questions as fully as becomes a man of honour, and not needlessly to offend him. For myself, if I can be of assistance, you may rely upon me."

"I shall strive to do as you say. But for the others—what became of Macpherson?"

A smile passed over the Vicomte's face. "When la belle Marie brought my Lord Galmoy to the house, he made sure that all your party were within, and made your men prisoners before they could draw a sword or fire a shot. But your captain, for what reason I know not, was passing the night in the stable, and when he was discovered he was already armed and putting the saddle on his great horse. For a pious Christian who is given to long prayers, he swears strangely. But he is a brave man and can fight *sans doute*. It was beautiful to see him swinging his long sword and swearing great oaths that I did not wholly understand. They went down before him like the corn, and the others fled crying that it was the devil. For myself I admire brave men and did not care to help the cowards. I doubt not he and I will meet again; and we shall finish our little quarrel and one of us will return no more."

"Then he made his escape—on foot or on horseback?"

"The great horse is still standing in the bastle and your captain must walk far, Monsieur Orme, before he is at home. But you cannot kill such men; they do not easily die. If M. le Medicin will pardon me, I might suggest that we can now spare him, for I am assured that there are others who need his services."

"Faith," said the surgeon, "you are speaking the truth, Vicomte, for the mellow Falernian has been going round, and I can hear the gentlemen already in their cups. For you, sir, I hope to see you in the morning—though," he added, under his breath, "as like as not with a cord round your neck and your feet in the air."

"And now, my friend," said De Laprade, when the doctor had left the room, "I doubt not you have heard of what manner is my Lord Galmoy. It is best to speak plainly. He can feel no pity nor show mercy. He cares not for the laws of war. Every prisoner is only an enemy. Should you answer him boldly I think your death is certain; even I who have some influence with him could not save you."

"Have no fear for me," said Gervase, rising to his feet and feebly attempting to stand; "for I have little fear for myself. Life is sweet and I do not wish to die, but the dread of death will not make me a coward. I shall die as I have humbly striven to live—though," he added, with a faint smile, "hanging is hardly seemly for a gentleman. I knew poor Charleton, and they say he met his death like a man. I hope I may do the same when my time comes."

"These are but heroics," said the Vicomte; "we must not grumble at our cards but play the game, and yours—Well, sir, what do you want?"

A sergeant of dragoons entered the room and swaggered forward, "My Lord would see the prisoner, and I was sent to fetch him."

"Tell my Lord Galmoy he will be with him in an instant, and that he is badly wounded. I myself will attend him and you need not wait."

"Now, my dear Orme," he continued, as the man left the room with a doubtful nod, "take my arm and rely on my services; I have not forgotten yours. But act like a man of sense and forget your sermons until you are among your friends."

De Laprade gave him his arm, and Gervase painfully descended the crooked staircase, his heart beating loudly and his hand trembling from weakness and exhaustion as he leaned on his companion.

CHAPTER III.

OF THE WAY MY LORD GALMOY SAT IN JUDGMENT.

The character of Lord Galmoy had recently gained an unenviable notoriety by his barbarous murder of Cornet Charleton and Captain Dixie at Fermoy, nor were there wanting those who asserted there were still darker stains on his character as a soldier. Such a man, Gervase well knew, would not stretch the laws of war in his favour, and it was more than likely that this savage cavalry-leader would not be disposed to treat him as a lawful enemy taken in battle, but as a rebel and a spy. For such there was a short shrift and a long rope.

When they entered the kitchen, the scene was one of the liveliest disorder and confusion. The room was filled with soldiers attired in every describable costume, some smoking by the fire, some eating and drinking, and all endeavouring to make themselves heard in a perfect babel of tongues. Hats, cloaks, and swords were piled upon the table, at the furthest end of which was seated a small knot of officers, among whom Gervase recognized the little surgeon who had attended to his wound, now busily engaged in discussing the contents of a pewter measure. At the head of the table was an officer of superior rank, and near him stood Hackett, with his hands bound behind his back and a great gash on his forehead. He had evidently been under examination, and his replies had not been satisfactory to the officer who was cross-examining him. At a glance Gervase recognized Lord Galmoy. His wig was pushed back, showing the closely-cropped black hair that came low down on the forehead. His eyes were bloodshot and his lips trembled with passion. Yet the face was a handsome one, though marked by the signs of excess and unbridled indulgence; a face weak in its almost feminine regularity, with delicately marked eyebrows, regular nose, and rounded chin; his hands were small and white as those of a woman.

As De Laprade made his way through the troopers who turned to stare at his companion, Galmoy said to the men who were in charge of Hackett, "Do not remove him. I may have further questions to put to him. And now for this young cock who crowed loud enough to bring the barn down about our ears; I think we shall soon cut his spurs. How say you, Vicomte?"

"I am under obligations to the gentleman, my Lord," said De Laprade, "I trust your Lordship will not deal too harshly with him."

"Why, damme, we shall all be under obligations presently, but we shall see. And now, sir, what is your name?"

Gervase caught the eye of the Vicomte fixed on

him with a look of warning. "My name is Orme," he said, feeling weak and faint with the loss of blood and the great heat of the atmosphere.

"And your rank?"

"A private gentleman, now serving with other gentlemen of the North in defence of our liberties."

"And, prithee, who gave the gentlemen of the North commission to raise regiments or levy war on His Majesty's subjects? Do you know, sir, that being found with arms in your hand without lawful authority to carry them, 'tis my duty to string you up as a warning to other malcontents. His Majesty has shown too much long-suffering, and had he been wise we had stamped out this cursed rebellion in a month. There is one King in Ireland, and with the help of God and His holy saints one King there will be. You shall drink his health, and that, damme, in a bumper."

"That, with your Lordship's pardon, I shall not do," said Gervase, disregarding De Laprade's gesture of warning. "I have taken the oath of allegiance to William and Mary, and to do what your Lordship asks would be an act either of disloyalty or hypocrisy."

"We shall see," Galmoy answered, with a smile that was full of meaning. "Fill up a cup, Whitney, for no one shall say that we did not give this damned rebel a chance. And now, sir, whither and on what errand were you away when we interrupted your journey?"

"Our destination was Enniskillen, but for our errand, from answering on that matter I pray your

Lordship to hold me excused. My knowledge of our real purpose was but slight and would advantage you little."

"And do you refuse to answer a plain question, sir?"

"I have given your Lordship my answer."

Galmoy pushed his chair back from the table and his face grew purple with passion. Then he turned to the officers who were sitting round him, bringing his hand heavily down on the table. "God's blood, gentlemen, what think you of that? I have been blamed by those who should know better, for the practice of a little just severity, and His Majesty would pet and pamper these rebels and treat them as faithful subjects who had been led astray. And here you have the issue. Every peasant and scurvy citizen struts about with armour on his back and a weapon in his hand, as if by the grace of God he had divine right to use the same. These are airs that will find no countenance while I am master of ceremonies."

"This young gentleman should know better," said one of the officers with a sneer, "for if I mistake not I have seen him before. Pray, sir, have we not met in Dublin when you were of Mountjoy's regiment?"

"You can do what you please," said Gervase, forgetting the caution he had promised himself to observe; "I am in your hands, but I will answer no questions; and if it be your good pleasure to murder me, on your heads is the infamy."

"We will answer for ourselves whatever we do," Galmoy answered. "But remember, the toast is waiting, and no man in my presence will refuse to drink to the health of His Majesty."

"I will not drink it, and no man living will force me. I have already given you my reasons."

"In good time," said Galmoy, "we shall see. How say you, Major? Do you recognize this stiff-necked Whig as being lately in the service of His Majesty?"

"On that head," was the answer, "I have no doubt. He was lodged at the Bunch of Grapes hard by the Castle, and though we were not intimate, I have seen him too frequently to be mistaken."

"Then, by Heaven, the cup of his transgression is full and the provost-marshal must see that he drinks it. I will take the matter on my own shoulders and answer for it to whomsoever may question me. Look you, sergeant, take the prisoner without, and see that he drinks that measure of wine. A lighted match, if properly applied, will bring him to reason. In the morning you will see that he is shot before the door an hour before we march, for I do not like these things arranged hurriedly. For the other 'twere a pity he should not bear him company. Let them both go together."

Weakened as he was by the loss of blood, and unstrung by the ordeal he had just passed through, Gervase tottered and fell on the bench beside which he had been standing. The room swam round him, and though he strove against it he felt that his senses were rapidly failing him. He would have fallen upon the floor, but De Laprade springing forward and placing his arm round him, supported him on the seat.

Then the Vicomte turned to Galmoy. "I have said nothing, my Lord, because I did not wish to interfere, as I thought your Lordship would have treated this gentleman as a fair prisoner of war. It is now my duty to speak; I trust your Lordship will hear me."

Galmoy had now recovered his temper and answered De Laprade with a show of courtesy. "Certainly, my dear Vicomte, there is no one to whom I listen with greater pleasure. But I trust you will not ask me to alter this little arrangement."

"You will pardon me; I have told you that I am under an obligation to this gentleman, and but for that obligation I should have been lying beside Luttrel on the high-road. I always endeavour to pay my debts of honour, and if need be I borrow from my friends to discharge them."

"Faith! my creditors will tell you that I find it hard enough to discharge my own."

"When the fight was over, the captain who has escaped showed a great mind to pistol me, when this Monsieur Orme, at great peril to his life, for I apprehended a pretty quarrel, stepped between us and compelled him to forbear. To him I owe my life, and I should be wanting in gratitude if I failed to avow the service he has done me."

"There is not a traitor or a rebel in the country

who has not a loyal subject to plead for him. God's wounds! Viscount, you forget that he first attacked you on the high road, and that he has worn the uniform of His Majesty, whom Heaven preserve."

"But, my Lord, I do not forget. These rebels have not saved my life and I do not intercede for them. I have lent my sword and service to the King of England, but I do not forget that I am a gentleman and a man of honour. In France we do not put our prisoners to the torture, nor will I fight in the company of those who do. Rather would I break my sword across my knees and disown the name I bear."

"The Vicomte de Laprade is right, my Lord," said the officer who had recognized Gervase. "Gratitude is a most estimable virtue, and exceedingly rare. In return for his services perhaps your Lordship will pretermit the young gentleman's drinking the health, and merely give him his dry quietus in the morning."

"With you, sir," said De Laprade coldly, "I have no dealings now nor at any future time. I ask you, my Lord, for this gentleman's life. 'Tis the only return I am likely to receive, and indeed it is all I ask."

"I regret, my dear Vicomte, that I am unable to do your will in this matter, but we must hold out a warning to others. However, as Butler has suggested, he need not dance to-night. Sergeant, you need not apply the thumbscrew. And for you, sir, you can make up your mind to set the example you hinted at. As it is, you may thank Viscount de Laprade that you have escaped a dram that was like to prove bitter enough, but had I had my own way, you should have had both the dram and the halter for a renegade deserter."

"Am I then, my Lord Galmoy, to understand that you refuse to accede to my request? and that the gentleman in whom your Lordship sees I am so deeply interested must die in the morning?"

Galmoy nodded and motioned to the officer who sat nearest him to pass the wine.

"I know not," De Laprade continued, drawing himself up haughtily, "whether it is because my sword and friendship are of so little value and are held in so slight esteem, that this simple favour is denied me, or because in this country gentlemen are deaf to the voice of expediency. But I know that the brave Luttrel, and a braver man never drew a sword, met his death because you, sir, have seen good to bring in the executioner where the soldier fails."

"Bah! we will not quarrel, though I will not answer for my temper should you provoke me further. You do not understand these matters, but for my part I hold it a safe rule to let every country manage its own affairs according to its own customs. Damme, man, this is not the court of Versailles, but the country of Whiggery and pestilent traitors, where every Jack-pudding is up in arms against his king and master. In a few months you will have learned not to be so whimsical."

"I trust that I shall never learn to forget that I am a gentleman."

De Laprade's manner was so pointed and his tone so full of fine, studied disdain that Galmoy, who could not fail to see that an insult was intended, leapt to his feet and drew his sword. In an instant his example was followed by the Vicomte. But they were not permitted to fight out their quarrel, for several gentlemen threw themselves between them, and succeeded in disarming them both; not, however, without difficulty in the case of Galmoy, who seemed almost to have been deprived of his reason in the excess of his passion. In vain they endeavoured to assure him that no insult had been intended, and that he had misinterpreted the Vicomte's words, while the Vicomte himself stood looking on with a smile playing round his lips, cool and unconcerned as was his wont.

In the midst of the confusion Gervase was removed from the room into the open air. His guards permitted him to sit down on the stone drinking-trough outside the door, while one of them went to prepare a place in which he might pass the night securely. Bending down till his forehead touched his knees, he endeavoured vainly to collect his thoughts and to realize what had happened, for his mind was still confused and weak. He knew that he was about to die, but it seemed to him at that moment as if it were another and not himself who had taken part in the drama that had just concluded. For himself, he was drifting blindly among shadows that grew thicker and darker as he sought to dispel them. The voices he had heard were still ringing in his ears; the faces he had seen were still coming and going. Then he heard the voice of Hackett and looked up. The old sergeant was standing beside him with his hands still bound behind his back, and his grey hair hanging, matted and stained with blood, about his face.

"Be of good cheer, Mr. Orme, it will soon be over, sir," he said, with homely dignity. "I am proud to think that you bore yourself bravely, and showed them that a gentleman and a Christian does not fear death. I should have liked, if it had so pleased the Almighty, to have died on the field of battle, but since 'tis His will, then His will be done. It is not for us to complain or dispute the great decrees. I will see you in the morning, sir," he added, as his guards prepared to lead him away, "and it may hap that we shall enter the Kingdom together."

Gervase was conducted to a low outhouse where a quantity of fresh straw had been spread for him, and one of the troopers, with rough goodnature, threw a horse cloth over his shoulders, for the night had grown chilly and he was shivering with cold. Then they withdrew, locking the door behind them, and left him to await the arrival of the provost-marshal in the morning.

CHAPTER IV.

OF HOW THE VICOMTE PAID HIS DEBT.

ORME lay for a considerable time in a dull stupor, unable to collect his thoughts, but by degrees his senses came back, and he awoke to the situation in which he was placed. He believed that it was idle to hope for mercy; he was in the hands of a man who was not likely to trouble himself further about his fate. He felt that he must die, and that he must face death with what courage he could command. He had never thought much about it before, but now when he stood face to face with death, it became so real and so terrible that for a time he stood aghast at the contemplation. He saw with awful vividness the preparations of the morning, and he thought of the moment when his soul and body would part company for ever. He was young, and the great mysteries of life and death had never troubled him. The path of his duty had been simple and plain; to stand by the truth, to show himself modest and pure and valorous always, to betray no trust, and to worship God according to the custom of his fathers—this was his creed and his plan of life; according to this he had sought to live and die. He had no desire for the martyr's death and the martyr's crown; he loved life and clung to it, and now all the more when he was in danger of losing it. Men like Hackett might find consolation and support in religion at a time like this, but for himself it could not lift him superior to the fear of suffering and the dread of death. There was, however, some consolation in the thought that he had striven honestly to do his duty, and that he had not begged in any unmanly way for life. Then his thoughts took another turn, and his whole past life unrolled itself before him. Incidents of his boyhood that he had long forgotten came fresh into his mind. He saw the stream and the stepping-stones where he had been used to fish, and the patches of sunshine glinting on the water through the willows; the old stone house and its tall chimneys lifting themselves among the oaks and firs; the dark wainscoted room where his father had taught him from Tacitus and Cæsar; and he longed with a great longing for life.

He raised himself from the straw and stretched out his hands in the darkness. The walls of the shieling in which he was confined were of wood, and he did not doubt that had he not been disabled he could have forced his way out. As it was escape even yet might be possible. To feel again the fresh wind blowing across the hillside and see the clear light of the stars, and the dark green fields stretching under them—the thought gave him strength and courage. Feeling carefully along the walls of the shed, and searching for a loose plank he came to the door which opened from without. He stood listening for the tread of the sentry's feet, but there was no sound audible but the beating of his own heart that throbbed wildly with the hope of escape. The door was not guarded. The planks of which the door was made, were light and had been roughly put together, but he found it impossible to make any impression upon them, though he strained and pulled till his wound broke out afresh. In the darkness he searched for a weapon that might assist him, but he could find nothing suited to his purpose. Again he followed the walls of the shed with his hands, searching carefully for a weak place in the timbers, but again he was unsuccessful. Then the great wave of hope subsided, and he threw himself once more upon the straw to compose his mind to meet with resignation the fate that was before him. There seemed to be no hope of escape left. By degrees he grew calm, and from some odd corner in his brain there came to his mind the lines—

> "Stone walls do not a prison make,
> Nor iron bars a cage;
> Minds innocent and quiet take
> That for an hermitage."

Again and again they repeated themselves until they seemed almost to lose their meaning for him; but the feeling remained with him, and by and by he found himself looking forward to the morning with resignation.

Suddenly in the unbroken quiet he heard the

sound of footsteps on the causeway without; then the door of the shed was opened, someone entered, and the flash of a lantern for a moment dazzled his eyes. It was De Laprade, flushed with wine and somewhat unsteady in his gait. Closing the door behind him, he looked round and saw Gervase lying in the corner.

"Eh, mon ami!" he said, laying down the lantern and removing his cloak, "but you have had a bad quarter of an hour. It was my fear that they would hang you at once, for these gentlemen are not nice in their manners nor long in their grace. It would give me much delight to measure swords with Galmoy, but the barbarian will not fight save when he is drunk, and then I am generally far from sober myself. These are not comfortable quarters," he added abruptly, looking round him and shrugging his shoulders.

"They are good enough for a dying man who has but a few hours to live," said Gervase gravely.

"For that we shall see," was the answer. "They have succeeded, not without difficulty, in putting my colonel to bed, and his condition is such that he will be hard to awake. I, Victor de Laprade, will now proceed to arrange matters for him. Are you able to stand?"

Gervase caught a glimpse of his meaning and again a wild hope arose in his heart. But reflecting for a moment, he felt that he could not take advantage of the gallant Frenchman's generosity, and he shook his head. "I cannot allow you," he said, "to undergo further risk for me; I cannot do it; already you have far more than repaid any kindness I was able to render you."

"Have no fear for me; I am able to answer any man who may dare to question me in what I do or leave undone. You do not know me, Mr. Orme. No man shall prevent my paying my debts of honour, whether they be debts of friendship or enmity. And shall I refuse to give him his life to whom I owe my own, when I have merely to turn the key in the door and say, 'Friend, that is your road'? It is impossible."

"But you do not recollect——"

"I recollect perfectly. Let us not enter into heroics, my friend, for this thing is simple and easy. Galmoy shall not know that to me you owe your escape; indeed it is probable that in the morning he will have forgotten you altogether, and remember only his headache. I have already provided you with a horse; your captain's great beast is the best in the stable; and for a passport, this will have to serve your turn, though it will be best that you should avoid showing it too frequently. The name of De Laprade will not carry you far in this barbarous country. But, in faith, the signature might pass for that of His Majesty King Louis himself, or for that matter, of my Lord Galmoy. The handwriting is hardly as sober as I could wish—indeed, it is cursedly tipsy. When we next meet it may be at the sword's point, in which case it were well to forget this interlude of Corydon and Strephon and try what yesterday we failed to finish. I have a pretty thrust in tierce that I should like to show you."

"If we meet I hope it will never be as enemies," said Gervase with warmth, "for I can never forget how much I owe you. I fear you undergo great risk in thus serving me."

"Find yourself safe on shipboard or within the walls of Londonderry, and trouble not yourself about any danger that I may run. I can protect my reputation and my honour with my sword, and for this act if need be I shall answer to the king himself, though I fear he has not the nice sense of honour. I knew him in Whitehall; he is no king, but a priest in the purple, and a priest without piety. Your William is cold, but he is the better man. There is but one thing more. Should you again find your captain, tell him that I have not forgotten his promise, and that I look forward with eagerness to our next interview. I have crossed swords with Lauzun and Hamilton and will teach the clown to threaten a gentleman. That is finished, and now to horse."

Raising Gervase from the ground, he supported him to the door, in the meantime wrapping his own cloak about his shoulders and warning him that the night air was bad for a green wound. Then he left him for a minute and returned almost immediately with Macpherson's grey charger, already harnessed. The windows of the tavern were still aglow with light, and the sound of loud and uproarious laughter rang on the quiet night as he helped Gervase into the the saddle. There was little likelihood of pursuit, for it was clear that no precautions had been taken to guard the prisoners, and before Gervase was missed he would have put many a good mile between himself and his pursuers. The only fear was, that weak and exhausted as he was, it would be impossible for him to continue his journey for any length of time. Still, there was the sense of the removal of a great dread, and a feeling of joyous freedom that gave him new heart and strength. He gathered up the reins in his hands and at that moment the recollection of Hackett flashed upon his mind.

"It was selfish and cowardly of me to have forgotten," he said. "Is it not also possible to save the sergeant? I feel that I am deserting a comrade and I should not like to leave him."

"What can you do for him," said De Laprade, "but make one more for the hangman? Your remaining will not save him; your going cannot harm him. I cannot do more than I have done, but I tell you to be of good courage regarding his safety, for I give you my word of honour that I will do what I can for the psalm-singing rogue. Be of good cheer. And now you will find a pistol in your holster which may be of some use. It may be we shall meet again. Farewell!"

Gervase wrung De Laprade's hand in silence and giving his impatient horse the rein passed through the yard, and found himself in the village street which lay quiet and dark before him. The tower of the church was darkly outlined against the starlit sky, and from a distance the murmur of the little stream stole with a hushed and solemn music through the night. Nowhere was there sight or sound of life; to the ear of the rider the hoofs of the horse rang upon the road with startling distinctness, though he walked him slowly past the sleeping houses. Then he came to the bridge, and on the bridge the the horse started suddenly and sniffed at something lying at his feet. The night was dark with the moon lifting faintly through a bank of cloud, but Gervase saw on the road the body of a man lying on his back with his arms outspread. He dismounted with difficulty and stooping down, saw it was Ralston. The body was already cold and the pulse had ceased to beat. It was evident that he had been surprised at his post, for his carbine lay undischarged at his side, and the long sword he had carried lay under him, unloosed from the scabbard. This was the young fellow whose merry song had disturbed Macpherson in the morning—his lips were silent enough now. Gervase bent down and touched the cold forehead. As yet he had not grown callous to the sight of sudden death, and it was with a lump in his throat and a mist before his eyes that he again set out on his perilous journey.

The road, a mere cart-track, wound for several miles up the hill, climbing for the most part through a dense growth of stunted firs, but here and there winding through the open bog and hardly to be distinguished from it. But the great horse seemed to have a natural instinct for the beaten track, and put his generous shoulders bravely to it. So steady he was and so footsure, that his rider let the reins fall upon his neck and left him to choose his path as he pleased. A small rain had begun to fall and there was a sharpness in the wind blowing down the mountain-gap. But Gervase heeded neither the rain nor the wind. For a time the sense of deliverance swallowed up every other thought, but presently he began to consider what fate was in store for him. It was hardly likely that he could reach Londonderry in safety, for the enemy would by that time no doubt have completely invested the city; and there was only a remote chance of his finding a ship in Lough Foyle, could he get so far. He had now no doubt that the enemy held possession of the roads; should he be fortunate enough to meet with part of the regular force he did not much doubt that as a prisoner he would receive honourable terms, but should he meet with a body of those marauders who hung on the skirts of the regular army and whose main business was robbery and murder, there was little hope of his life. But, after all, was it not idle to hope to escape at all? Wounded as he was he could not long continue his journey but must inevitably sink from weakness and exhaustion.

The road began to descend once more into the valley, and under the grey light of the early dawn he could see the fields and hedgerows sloping down to where the little river ran through clumps of hazel and osier. As he drew towards the river the sound of running water was pleasant to hear in the unbroken

"THE STRANGER CAUGHT HIS HORSE BY THE REIN"

silence—a sign of movement and life. After a while the road grew narrow and ran through an arch of tall poplars, through which he could see the dull red light of the rising dawn at the further end. On one side of the road was a sluggish pool of water and on the other a high hedge of thorns. He had ridden half way through this dark colonnade when he saw the figure of a man standing in the shadow, apparently awaiting his approach. He could not see his face but he could see that he had a weapon in his hand. He instinctively drew from his holster the pistol with which De Laprade had provided him, and was about to drive his spurs into the charger's flanks, when the stranger sprang forward, caught his horse by the rein, and placed the point of a sword at his throat. Gervase presented his pistol at the head of his assailant and fired point-blank, but the hammer snapped ineffectually on the flint. Then he drave the spurs deep into the horse's sides, but he stopped short and refused to move.

"This has come as an answer to prayer," said a deep voice. "Dismount, sir, and that speedily; I have business to do that will not brook delay and your necessity, however pressing, must yield to mine."

In a moment Gervase recognized the full sonorous voice as that of Macpherson. The horse, too, had recognized his master, for he gave a joyous whinney.

"Use no force, Captain Macpherson," said Gervase; "right glad am I to see you, for I had begun to fear that we should meet no more."

"It is Mr. Orme," said the old soldier, lowering the point of his weapon and placing his hand on the horse's neck. "I knew not what withheld my hand that I did not strike, but now I know. Little did I think as I heard the sound of the horse's feet far down the road that I was listening to the tramp of my brave Bayard, or that it was for you that I held my sword and prepared to strike hard and deep. It was God's mercy that my pistol was left behind or I should have brought you down like a laverock on the wing. And how have the others fared?"

Gervase told him briefly what had happened, explaining how he owed his life to the kindness of De Laprade, and how Hackett had been left behind, with the prospect of a violent death before him.

Macpherson interrupted him with many interjaculations, and when he had finished exclaimed dejectedly:

"My fault, my fault! that comes of sending a boy to do a man's errand. The lad fell asleep and the villains stole a march on us. There is no use crying over milk that is spilt, but I would that I had arranged it otherwise. And old Hackett—I saw he was made of the right stuff; they may break but they will not bend him. I will yet make them pay for it. And now let us hold a council of war, for in no case can we let the grass grow under our feet."

"I fear," said Gervase, leaning forward on the horse's neck and feeling faint and ill, "that I am not in a condition to travel with much expedition. I have lost some blood though I do not think the wound is serious."

"Hell's fury! man, why did you not tell me that you had been touched? Here have we been talking like a pair of garrulous gossips, while haply in the meantime your wound needs that I should look to it. A hospital hath been made ready to our hand, and if needs be we can pass a day or two here in safety, for I do not think the enemy will trouble us. I had already made my bivouac, when I heard Bayard on the road, and turned out to see if I could not better my fortune."

Taking the horse by the bridle he led him a short distance down the road, and then turning abruptly up a path to the right through a small plantation of oaks and poplars, came upon an open space, lately used as a farm-yard, before a low thatched house built of stone and roughly plastered over. The roof had been fired at one end, but the oak rafters were still standing blackened and charred; at the other, where the thatch had not ignited, the roof was still intact. The door lay open, through which shone the glow of a hospitable fire that burned in the open hearth. Macpherson had fastened his cloak against the open window to shut in the light and prevent it being seen from the outside. The greater portion of the simple furniture still stood as the owner had left it—a high-backed oak chair drawn up to the hearth, the rough earthenware ranged upon a dresser against the wall, a bed, known as a settle, in a corner, and a small table roughly put together, under the window.

Macpherson helped his young friend off the horse and gently supported him into the kitchen. "We will look to your wound presently," he said, "but first it behoves us to set our guard and prepare against the approach of the enemy. Howbeit they will not trouble us here; we may lie *perdu* for a week if needs must, though it were well we should be astir as soon as you think you can travel."

"A day's rest will set me on my feet, I doubt not," said Gervase wearily, "but we cannot live without food, though the bullet they have bestowed on me has somewhat robbed me of an appetite."

"Be not troubled on that score; I am too long campaigning not to have an eye to the commissariat, which matter is too often neglected by the great masters of strategy; 'tis half the art of war. There are several measures of meal in the chest yonder; there are some lean fowl roosting in the byre, and I heard the lowing of a cow in the little meadow at the foot of the orchard, though I cannot understand why her owner should have left her behind, unless, as I take to have been the case, his flitting was of the speediest. But why the rogues should have overlooked spoil so much to their mind passes my comprehension."

"Perchance," said Gervase, with a wan smile, "'tis *vox et praeterea nihil.*"

"A vox that runs on four legs, and will furnish us with some excellent beef when I have passed my sword across the throat of the same. I remember that such a beast furnished five of us with excelient, if scanty, sustenance for a month, until we fell out over the horns and hoofs, and two of us were removed thereafter from all need of earthly provender. But 'tis not likely that thou and I will come to such a pass," he added, holding out his broad brown palm, while a gleam of kindly humour lighted up his rugged face.

"I am but fit for the hospital, and am like to be a heavy burden on your hands."

"Tut, tut, man, never despair till the last shot is fired, and the garrison has hauled down its ensign in token of surrender. I had been a passable leech had I not rather cared to break heads than to mend them, whereby it seems to me the two trades are but complements the one of the other. In a day or two at the furthest you will be able to hold your own with any cut-throat rascal who cries for James Stuart. For that you may trust Ninian Macpherson."

The old soldier had a good many sides to his character; as yet Gervase had only seen the praying and the fighting sides. He was now to see him as a loyal comrade, ready to cheer him with words of comfort; helpful as a brother, tender as a woman. In half an hour he had looked to his wound, which had opened afresh and bled considerably, had prepared a meal, and had stretched a bed for him along the hearth, which though rough and hard, was very acceptable in his present condition. Then Bayard was stabled at the further end of the building, and the day had already risen broad and clear with the singing of birds and the whisper of the soft spring wind, as Macpherson wrapped himself in his cloak and with his saddle under his head, gave himself up to sleep.

CHAPTER V.

OF A MAN'S MEMORY.

FOR upwards of a week Gervase was too ill to travel, though he rapidly recovered under the care that Macpherson bestowed upon him. No woman could have nursed him with more tenderness and solicitude. Every want that he had was anticipated, and during the tedium of the day the old soldier beguiled the time with stories of the camp and battle-field. He seemed to have no care or thought for his own comfort but waited assiduously on his wounded comrade with a simple kindness that touched Gervase deeply. The darker side of his character seemed to have disappeared completely; even his devotions he conducted in private, and it was only at Gervase's request that he read from the little volume that he carried about with him continually.

They were left undisturbed in the farm-house, though they heard on two occasions the jingling of bridles, the clank of weapons, and the tramp of marching men upon the road, bound apparently for Londonderry; and upon one occasion they were upon the point of being discovered. Gervase was alone in the house when he heard the sound of voices without, and going to the window, he saw half a dozen dragoons drawing water from the well in the farm-yard. They evidently thought the house deserted, for they bestowed no attention upon it. At that moment Macpherson came swinging down the lane in the rear of the house, and was about to enter the yard when he caught sight of the steel head-pieces, and stopped short. Having filled their bottles, the fellows rejoined their comrades without suspecting the discovery they were on the point of making. Thereafter Macpherson was more careful, going out only when the twilight came down, and carefully avoiding the highway.

The chickens in the byre had gone the way of all flesh, and the cow in the meadow had been turned into wholesome beef, from which the old soldier concocted many a savoury stew. He was a rare hand at cooking, setting about the matter with sober and becoming earnestness, and mightily proud of his achievements therein. All the herbs of the field lent themselves to his purpose; he had studied their uses aforetime, and now he turned the knowledge to account. He knew something, too, of their medicinal qualities, and insisted with a solemn persistence on Gervase swallowing many nauseous draughts, which, indeed, the latter did rather from a feeling of good comradeship than from any liking for the dose. He greatly preferred the stories of Macpherson's earlier days when he carried a halbert with Turenne, or one of the ballads—of which he had quite a store—which he crooned in a low tone with a solemn shaking of the head. They were all of battles, sieges, and warlike fortunes, and touched not at all upon the lighter passions. "Mary Ambree" was a great favourite of his, and another whose refrain ran thus:—

"Then be stout of heart when the field is set, and the smoke
is hanging low,
And the pikeheads shine along the line to meet the advancing foe."

But chiefly he preferred to sing from the psalms in Francis Rous's version, especially those which speak of battle and vengeance, and the rugged metre and halting lines lost their homeliness, and were clothed with a fine vigour and glowed with inspired fervour as he followed the measure with the motion of his hand. So earnest he was, indeed, and so direct, with a touch of childlike simplicity, that Gervase was lost in continual wonder.

As a rule he was reticent regarding his past life and spoke of it in only a general way. On one occasion he had been more communicative. Gervase had become perfectly convalescent and was able to move about without being supported, the fever having entirely disappeared, and his strength having returned in some considerable degree. They were sitting together discussing the various plans by which they might reach Londonderry, and Macpherson's brows were drawn into a curious frown, as always happened when he was engaged in deep thought.

"Could we," he said, "come haply on a garron, the thing were as good as done; I doubt not we shall find one to our hand as we proceed, and in the meantime you will ride Bayard while I tramp as best I can. I have done as much before, and with a little strategy, which is just and necessary we shall be able to satisfy all civil inquiries."

"'Tis out of the question," Gervase answered. "Turn and turn will I take if you will; and it may be that this passport of De Laprade's will be of some service after all, though I do not think the rogues we may meet will care much for aught but a strong arm and the sword's point."

"'Tis a curious document," said Macpherson, spreading it out before him and laying his open palm upon it. "I am not a great scholar, but I think no man could tell in what language it was written, or what may be its purport. Even his name has so fallen to vinous pieces that 'tis impossible to pick up the fragments. But I think he hath a good heart, a very good heart."

"That I will answer for," said Gervase, "and I will answer for it also that you are rejoiced that you did not harm him. I was not brought up to understand his ways, but I know he is brave as a lion and true as steel; and what a handsome fellow he is!"

"Pooh! wax and paint. I have seen too many pretty fellows to care for the tribe. But he is as you say, I doubt not, though he be a Frenchman—for which latter reason I do not love him."

"Still, it is no reason why you should hate him."

"I know not that; the narrow seas divide us for

some wise reason, and we speak with different tongues for a purpose. I have lived too long with Frenchmen not to love my own country best. God forbid, however, that I should hate any, though it is permitted to hate their works. He is, as you say, a gallant fellow. I remember when I was of an age with him, I thought as little of the end whereunto all life tends, and wine and women were the gods I worshipped. The devil is a liberal paymaster but he pays in his own currency; I have a bagful of his ducats."

"Then you carry them easily," said Gervase, feeling that he was treading on tender ground.

"That do I not. Alas; memory will not die; we cannot slay it even with prayer, though we may fall back on that to help us to bear the pain. Why I should talk thus to you I know not, but the spirit prompts me, and 'tis ever safe to follow its promptings. I shall open for you one of the pages that I have striven to tear out of the book of my life, and failing in that, to blot out with the tears of penitence and contrition—haply in vain. 'Twas in '64, and the April of that year I was in the service of the Elector of Brandenburg, and we were quartered at Spandau. Our company was wicked enough, but I think none could touch me in all manner of iniquity. We drank deep, quarrelled and fought at will, and rejoiced greatly in fearing not God nor regarding man. I knew my work as a soldier, and men said I had some skill in the art of war. Howbeit I had got some preferment which I held lightly enough, as I cared but little whom I served as long as there was wine in the measure and women for the asking. One man I was drawn toward in a special manner, for we had both known better things and had some sorrow together when our cups were spilt, and the headache and heartache came in the morning. Jack Killigrew (for he was an Englishman, and well born, as I have since learnt) should have been a parson, but the devil set him trailing a pike and drinking deep as the rest of us. After a while I noticed a change in his ways, which change I could not well understand at first, but soon I discovered. He drank no more, foreswore the dicebox, would not beat up the town, and I shrewdly suspected took to saying his prayers in secret. Then one day he made his confession—I laughed loud enough thereat—that he was in love with the daughter of the Protestant parson outside the city gates. He would not rest satisfied until I had gone thither with him, and in an evil hour I consented. Beware, boy, of women; avoid them like the pestilence, and trust not the fairest. Delilah, Jezebel, and Herodias, these are but samples of the smiling, treacherous, beautiful devils that go up and down on the earth to catch men's souls in a silken snare. Annchen was of the same order but carried her wickedness more demurely. Poor Jack gave her all his heart, and the little vixen was not content therewith, but needs must have mine too. And mine she had, ay, and my soul too—all, all."

Macpherson rose and paced the kitchen with a

hasty stride, his long brown hands clasped before him, and his leonine head thrown back. His eyes were filled with the strange, wild light Gervase had noticed once or twice before; his voice thrilled with suppressed emotion.

"How she purred and ogled and slighted honest Jack, to whom she had plighted her troth, and whom she was to marry in a sennight! God help me! I was wicked and mad; I forgot my friend and robbed him of his mistress. Then the end came. Never, never shall I forgot it. 'Twas a moonlight night in the pleasant summer time; I was drunken with the passion of lust, and Annchen and I had forgotten the hours as we stood locked in each other's arms, under the shadow of the city's walls. Suddenly a tall form came between us, and a sword flashed out in the moonlight. I knew it was Jack Killigrew, and knew that either he or I must die for this deed. Our blades crossed, and while Jezebel stood looking on, my friend and I (and truer comrade had no man) sought each the heart's blood of the other. May God in His mercy forgive me, for I shall never forgive myself. Oh! we fought a bitter fight under the walls that June night, and he died hard. For I killed him; yes, I killed him. Do not start or turn away from me— his sweetheart did not, Nay, when he was down and his life blood was flowing from his breast, she threw her arms about me, and told me that I was a man, and she loved a man. You do not know what it is when love turns to hate. I flung her from me, cursing her, with anguish in my heart that I had not words to speak of. I never saw her again, but often I see the face of Jack Killigrew lying there turned up to the moonlight and frowning as he died. 'Twas the sin against the Holy Ghost, I sometimes think. An ocean of tears will not wash out the deed."

"'Tis a sad story," said Gervase, with emotion, "and better left untold. But I think not that all women are like Annchen, whom I cannot understand, else were life hardly worth living, and death better than life."

"That it is—that it is. Life is a burden we must bear as best we can—a heavy load for the back of the strongest. You are young and cannot yet understand the matter, but for me I would that my salvation was assured, as sometimes I have hoped it is, and that I were entering into my rest. But youth cannot understand this, nor will I compel you to listen to me."

"Nay," answered Gervase, "rather would I be by your side fighting in the good cause, for Heaven knows strong arms like yours are needed now, if need ever was. I cannot foresee how it will end."

"Have no fear for the end; Londonderry may fall, but Dutch William is stronger than a walled city. I know the Stadtholder of old, and I tell you behind that cold look and slow speech there is the power of many regiments. I have seen his eyes in the day of battle. He is one of a race that never knows when it is beaten. I think that he will not leave the men in Londonderry to die like so many rats. But, believe me, they are the stuff whereof fighting men are made, and will make a gallant stand."

"I would," said Gervase, "we were among them once more. By this time, I doubt not, if Colonel Lundy be a true and loyal man, Roaring Meg and her iron sisters have given joyful voice."

"Bah! How goes your burghers ditty?"

"'Scour me bright and keep me clean—
I'll carry a ball to Calais green.'"

"Your colonel is no true man, but a hypocrite and a coward, and I put no faith in the long guns, though they have their uses, but in stout and loyal hearts that will hold out in trial and privation. The Irish do not understand the practice of artillery; they may not batter down the walls or breach them, while there are men there to say 'stand back'; but hunger and disease are enemies that few can fight against: and hunger and disease Londonderry will have to face. 'Tis here the Protestant faith must make its last stand. Should the city fall before relief may come, then the end is far off, and the Stuart may yet wear the crown of his ancestors. Relief ever comes slowly—how slowly, only that man knows who, like myself, with wasted shanks and shrunken jaws, has kept his place on the ramparts, while women and children were dying indoors by the score, and brave fellows were struck down at his side by an enemy no man could see."

"But William of Orange is a soldier, as you say, and, being a soldier, will not leave the city to stand alone. Besides, the Irish cannot fight a stubborn fight."

"There you are wrong utterly, and here I speak of what I have seen and known. In the army of Louis is many a gallant gentleman of Irish birth, who has displayed a courage and devotion in a foreign country that he might not show in his own. These wild kernes want but the sergeant's drill and a cause to fight for to prove the stoutest soldiers in Europe. But they care not for James Stuart, and I think he has no general who can take their measure. Rosen is a foreigner, and Hamilton a man of few parts; while Sarsfield, of whom I have heard much, lacks discretion and temperate wisdom, else might he do greatly. 'Tis ever the general that makes the soldier—that is the difference between a rabble and a regiment. Tilly and Gustavus and Turenne, all of whom fought great battles, first put heart into their men, and then taught them to fight as if fighting were the easiest trade in the world."

"But in Londonderry," said Gervase, "we fight for all that men hold dear—for liberty, religion, wife, child, and even for life itself. If that does not give men heart and inspire them with courage, there is no general in the world can do it."

"You are right, and therein I rest my confidence. Religion is the best cordial in the world to tune the coward's heart. If all goes well, behind yon poor walls I look to see as bold a stand as ever was made in Christendom, even should England leave us to tread our own path—which Heaven forfend. But 'twere easy to succour the city. With the Foyle running close by the city walls, men and provisions were easily furnished. Heaven send a man with a wise head on his shoulders, for Providence never yet wrought through fools and cowards. Howsoever, it is for us to do as best we may, and I doubt not, my lad, you will do your part bravely."

"Mine is a small part and easily played," Gervase answered, "but how we are to get into the town, I see not, even were we so far on our journey."

"A way will be provided, I doubt not, with a little strategy. For you, that fine cloak and hat, even those riding boots, must be left behind, while like the stage-player, you must enact the rapparee and speak nought but the Irish speech, or what will pass for such, till you are behind stone walls. For myself, I think the story I shall tell and my knowledge of the French tongue, will carry me through. As David played the madman in the city of Achish, and as the spies went into the walled city of Jericho and abode in the house of the harlot Rahab, so shall we do with the like success."

"I hate all masquerading," Gervase said, "and had rather take my chance even as I am."

"Ay, and find a pikehead between your ribs for your scruples. We have Scripture precedent which it is ever safe to follow. In this you shall not thwart me. So to bed, for at cockcrow we must start, first having commended our lives to Providence, and put a new edge on this sword, whose late owner was a careless fellow and knew not how to care for a good blade."

CHAPTER VI.

OF HOW THE HEROINE COMES UPON THE STAGE.

It was an hour after dawn when they bade farewell to the farm-house and set out upon their journey, Gervase mounted upon Bayard, and Macpherson trudging sturdily upon foot. The latter had made his preparations for the journey with abundant care and forethought. The night before he had baked the little meal that remained, and cooked a portion of the meat, of which there was still a considerable quantity left, all of which he stored carefully in the saddle-bags. He then turned his attention to Gervase, and with very little trouble succeeded in transforming him into a formidable-looking desperado, whose attire owed nothing to the art of the tailor, but hung together merely by fortuitous circumstances. Macpherson had, with studied humour, turned the embroidered coat inside out and rolled it in the mud that lay round the well in the farmyard, and then considerately removed one of the skirts with the edge of his sword. His beaver was divested of all form and shape; and a rope of straw rolled round the jackboots, which Gervase had refused to part with on any terms, completed his nondescript costume. He was now a reasonable representative of any of those lawless marauders who were swarming upon the roads, or hanging upon the skirts of the Irish army, in the expectation of plunder.

Macpherson had refused to make any change in his own costume. His rôle was that of a French soldier on his way to Londonderry—in such a character De Laprade's passport would lend verisimilitude to his story, if there were any learned enough to read it, about which he had his misgiving. Gervase was to act apparently as his guide, and in such character the old soldier did not doubt but that with ordinary discretion, they might smuggle themselves though the Irish lines if the investment had been completed. If they failed, there was some chance that the stab of a pike or the end of a rope would put a stop to their further adventures in this world.

Notwithstanding, Gervase was in high spirits at starting. He was now completely recovered from his wound, and the eight days' confinement had made the anticipation of action and enterprise doubly welcome. He revelled in the fresh spring wind that blew softly across the bog and heathy mountain side, and could with difficulty restrain his horse to keep pace with Macpherson, who trudged at his side with a long swinging stride.

The hedges were green with verdure, and the sunshine touched with a warmer colour the bog myrtle and flowering blackthorn in which the birds were busy building. It was hard to realize that dangers were spread round them on every side, and that the entire country was up in arms in a quarrel that could have no end, till one of the combatants went down utterly. Even Macpherson, whose feelings were not easily moved, was affected by the brightness of the morning and the beauty of the scene. His emotions took their own method of expression. For a time he had been entirely silent, or replied only in monosyllables, as if engrossed in his own secret meditations, when suddenly he began to sing in loud resonant tones:

> "The Lord doth reign and clothed is He
> With majesty most bright."

When he had finished he threw up his beaver with an air of jubilant exultation.

"There, young sir, is a song for you to sing when you are merry; that eases the oppressed heart, and runs along the nerves and sinews, strengthening them to acts of endurance and valour. Were I a maker of songs these were the verses I should write—great words wherewith to hammer out a weapon."

"I cannot help thinking," said Gervase, "of the song poor Ralston was singing as we passed this way, hardly a fortnight ago. We little thought then that you and I should return alone."

"They did their duty," Macpherson answered, "and died in doing it; brave men want no more. I hope I shall not flinch when my time comes, as come it will, and that shortly. I have gotten the message and it doth not sadden me."

Gervase looked at him inquiringly, but he offered

no explanation of his mysterious speech and again relapsed into silence.

They continued their journey till noon, when they halted to refresh themselves, Macpherson asserting that if it were not for his great boots he would as readily walk as ride.

On resuming their march Gervase insisted on Macpherson taking his turn upon horseback, which the latter did very unwillingly.

"One horse to two is out of all reason," he said. "You are yet too soft for this work and your wilfulness will bring its own punishment."

And Gervase found his words come true. Long after his strength had exhausted itself, he found himself toiling by Macpherson's side, too proud to own his weakness and determined to keep on till he dropped from sheer fatigue. Macpherson watched him for a while in silence, with the flicker of a grim smile playing about his lips. Then he spoke;

"'Tis ever wise to confess your weakness in the ear of a friend—keep your bold looks and your wooden guns for the enemy. My dear lad, thou art but pickling a rod for thine own whipping, and that to serve no good or wise purpose. Thank Heaven, I am stout of limb, and nought can tire me; but for you, your bones are still soft, and I would not have you again a burden on my hands. There is no need for immediate haste, for we can accomplish to-morrow all that we might do to-day. Then mount, and let us proceed leisurely."

That day they made good progress, and by nightfall

were a considerable distance on their journey. By the next evening they hoped to reach the ford of the Finn. But in the meantime it was necessary to pass the night under the open sky, for the country was completely deserted, and nowhere within sight was there trace of a human dwelling-place—only broad tracts of rough uncultivated land, and rolling hills of wild heath and tangled wood. A few houses they had passed, but the roofless walls afforded neither shelter nor protection. Every dwelling had been given up to fire and destruction, and the inmates had fled elsewhere for refuge. A great curse seemed to have fallen on the devoted land; all was silence and desolation.

That night they passed under a thorn hedge, which proved, as Gervase found, a cold and uncomfortable lodging, and afforded little protection from the night dews and the wind that blew across the open with a shrewd and penetrating keenness. To Macpherson it mattered not at all, for, rolled in his cloak, he slept the sleep of the just, and did not awake till the morning was some way up. But Gervase could not sleep. Above his head the jewels in the sword-belt of Orion flashed with a bright and still a brighter lustre, and the wind seemed to call with almost a human articulateness from the distant hills. The lonely night with its mystery and silence, was instinct with life. In such a presence his own fate seemed to dwindle into infinitely little importance, and all human endeavour appeared of no greater moment than that of the ant or the mole in the ditch hard by. Gervase was not given to talking sermons nor to much introspection, but he felt these things in his own way. He was glad when he saw the morning coming up; and when he arose from his damp uncomfortable couch, felt little inclination for a day's hard work. But when he had bathed his face and hands in the neighbouring rivulet, and partaken of the breakfast Macpherson insisted on their making before they started, life assumed a somewhat brighter outlook, and his flagging spirits revived a little.

Macpherson's spirits were keen and high. The prospect of danger ever acted upon him like wine, and Gervase saw his eyes kindle, now and again, under his rugged brows, with that sudden flashing light he had seen in them before, in the time of peril. He had loaded his pistol afresh and carefully looked to its priming.

"We may fall in with the enemy now at any moment," he said, "and it behoves us to be ready either for peace or war. Peace I should prefer, but if, haply, the rogues number not more than half a dozen, a skirmish were not out of place to afford us a little amusement. A young soldier requires practice, and cannot have his hand in too often."

"Faith!" said Gervase laughing, "fighting would seem to be meat and drink to you, but I have not yet acquired such relish for the fare that I cannot do without it. I fear you are like to prove a troublesome companion for all your boasted diplomacy."

"Tut, man, do not fear. We are not an army, nor even a troop, and may not carry things as we would. But a little fighting is a wonderful medicine, and clears the humours better than any elixir. I mean but that when we can we may as well be honest, and keep our stratagems for such times as we shall be hard pushed, and must employ them, will we, nill we. D'ye see?"

"Oh! 'tis not easy to mistake your meaning. You give it just emphasis with that long sword and pistol handle. But I had rather you were less inclined to violence; there were more chance of our reaching Londonderry in safety."

"All in good time, we shall see. By evening we shall arrive at the ford, which we had better cross in the dark. One pair of legs will then be worth two pairs of hands, even with toys like these in them;" and he touched the sword he carried with a smile. Then after a pause he went on, "Who knows what may have befallen since we left the city last? There are brave hearts within the walls, but there are traitors and cowards too; and the latter have sometimes the best of it in this world. Still, I think not, and will wager that the Protestant cause goes bravely on. They are a stiff-necked race, these men of Ulster; bend they cannot and break they will not. I have watched them narrowly; if they did break at Dromore it was because they were fearful of the treachery of their friends, not of the violence of their enemies. But I know not what Colonel Lundy means—if he be not a traitor and a knave at heart, I know not what he is."

For the greater part of the day they continued

their journey without adventure. Several small parties of the enemy they met with, but were subjected to no very rigorous cross-examination. Their replies proved perfectly satisfactory. The story Macpherson told was eminently plausible, and about Gervase they did not trouble themselves. There were many French gentlemen in the Irish army, and it was not a strange thing to find one on his way to head-quarters accompanied by a guide. One troop of dragoons had, indeed, stopped them and put several questions to Gervase, but he managed, with the voluble assistance of Macpherson, to disarm their suspicions. Fortunately his questioners spoke English only, and the fragments of the Irish tongue that Gervase had acquired, stood him in good stead.

It was now two hours to sundown, and they anticipated that another hour's travel would bring them to the ford. They were toiling uphill, Gervase a little in advance mounted upon Bayard, and Macpherson stepping out sturdily in the rear. On the top of the hill Gervase halted, reined the horse back hastily within shelter of a clump of hazel, and called out to Macpherson, who hurried up and joined him where he stood. Together they looked down the valley.

"What is the matter yonder?" Macpherson asked, instinctively placing his hand on his pistol-butt.

"I know not," said Gervase, "but I think it is robbery and murder."

"Then, my young friend," said the other, laying his hand on the horse's bridle, "it is not our business, and we have cares enough of our own without taking on us the troubles of others. But how is the day going?"

A quarter of a mile down the steep road lay a post-chaise overturned: one of the horses lay dead in the ditch, the other was flying with broken traces over a neighbouring field. A man with his back to the coach and a sword in his hand, was valiantly striving to keep at bay half-a-dozen wild-looking fellows armed with half-pikes. Two bodies lay at his feet, another a little distance away, and outside the ring of assailants that surrounded the solitary swordsman, a young woman was kneeling in an agony of distress over the prostrate body of a man. The man with the sword fought with skill and strength, but the odds were terribly against him. In the end he must succumb.

"By the living God, it is a woman," said Gervase, grappling blindly and eagerly at the holster.

"Softly, what would you—what have we to do with women?"

"Follow me, follow me, for God's sake, as speedily as you can," Gervase cried, dashing his unarmed heels into the horse's flank, and giving him free head.

Away went the brave steed thundering down the steep road, as Gervase gave a great shout and flourished the long pistol above his head. Macpherson watched his breakneck career down the hill for a few seconds, and then proceeded to follow him with the best speed that he could make.

"I would not lose the youth or my good horse for all the women in Christendom. This is but the beginning of trouble, and it begins with a woman."

Hearing the shout, the swordsman had turned his head for a moment, and at that instant one of his assailants sprang within his guard, and plunged his skene deep into his breast. With one last convulsive effort the wounded man struck his opponent fair in the face with the sword hilt, and they both dropped on the road together. Seeing Gervase approaching, the ruffians appeared to doubt whether they should take to flight or await his attack, but while they were making up their minds, Gervase was on the top of them.

Reserving his fire until he was among them, he discharged his pistol pointblank at the head of one fellow with deadly effect, and riding down another, wrenched the half-pike from his hand. Then they were utterly panic-stricken and fled right and left, leaving Gervase master of the situation.

Meanwhile the young lady had risen to her feet, and was standing looking in wonder at her unexpected deliverer, who had reined up his horse, and was watching the fugitives as if in doubt whether to follow them or to allow them to depart unpursued. Then Gervase turned towards her and raising his hat, was silent for a moment.

She was only a girl in years, but of a sweet and

stately figure and striking beauty. Her abundant hair loosed from its confinement, streamed in disorder over her shapely shoulders, and fell in thick folds to her waist. Her lips were trembling and her cheeks were blanched and colourless, but her great, dark eyes looked with a steady and courageous glance. There was no sign of fear in the sweet face—only a high, resolute courage. Her scarf had been torn from her shoulders, and showed too much of her white and heaving bosom. Instinctively she put up her hand to cover it.

"I fear," said Gervase, hat in hand, "that I have come too late to save this gallant fellow from these wretched cowards. But I am glad that I was still in time to render you some service. Haply," he continued, dismounting from his horse, "the wound may not be fatal, and something may still be done."

The girl looked in great surprise at the strange figure before her, and was evidently lost in wonder at hearing her wild-looking and ragged champion deliver himself in such excellent English, and with such a well-bred air. To outward seeming he was as much a cateran as any of the scoundrels he had lately put to flight.

"I thank you, sir," she said simply. "It may be poor Martin is still living."

She knelt down by the side of the fallen man and raised his head upon her knees. But the skene, driven with great force, had passed beneath the breast-bone and had penetrated the heart—the man was dead. A glance was sufficient to show that life was extinct. She allowed the head to remain resting upon her lap for some minutes, gazing at the rugged face of the dead man in silence, and then she looked up, her eyes filled with tears. "I have known him all my life," she said, "and never was there a braver or a kinder heart. Years ago he saved my father's life, and now he has died to save mine."

Gervase had knelt down beside her, and had been endeavouring to catch some feeble sign of movement in the pulse. "Yes, he is dead," he said, "and we can do nothing for him, but it may be the other needs our help."

"My grandfather has not been injured," she said. "He swooned when they came round the coach, and though they used him roughly, I do not think he hath suffered from aught but fright. Still, he is an old man and very frail, and it may be—"

But the old man had raised himself on his elbow, and was looking round him with an expression of bewilderment, as though not yet able to realize what had happened. Then suddenly his eye fell upon the chaise lying overturned, and with a nimbleness that one could not have expected, he leapt to his feet, and walked with rapid strides to the vehicle.

"Dorothy," he shouted, "Dorothy, help me, girl! The rogues have stolen my treasure. Good God! I am a beggar—a beggar. Why the —— did they not take my life? The gold that I have watched growing and growing, and the precious stones that I would not have parted with for a kingdom! Oh God! I am a beggar, and will die on the road-side after all."

The old man seemed entirely beside himself with grief and rage, and began to pour forth such a string of oaths, wild and incoherent, that Gervase felt deeply for the girl who was in vain endeavouring to calm him.

"I think, grandfather," she said, "it is still safe, but I had thought the matter was of little worth—"

"Worth! Great Heaven! there were ten thousand pounds—" here he stopped short and looked at Gervase, whose appearance did not tend to reassure him.

"I am an old man, sir," he went on piteously, "and I know not what I say. These are but wild words of mine, and, I prithee, forget them. They meant nothing—nothing, and I ask you to let them pass. Would it trouble you too much to assist my servant?—Where the devil is Martin, the rascal?"

"Your servant, sir, is dead," said Gervase, losing his temper somewhat, "and this young lady and yourself are left alone, in great straits and peril. Therefore I would ask you to dismiss all thoughts of the trash from your mind, and let me know what you purpose doing."

But the old man had already clambered into the coach, and in a few seconds reappeared with a heavy, brass-bound box in his arms, which he clutched with every expression of delight.

At this moment Macpherson, who seeing Gervase completely victorious, had been strolling down the hill in a leisurely fashion, had come up.

"What is this Punchinello?" he said roughly, but as he saw the old man cower terrorstricken, he continued in a more kindly tone, "Fear hath turned his brain, and, haply, he takes me for one of those marauding rascals, of whom, I doubt not, we have not yet seen the last. And now, madam," he said, turning to the girl, "as you see, this gentleman and I are your friends and are bound to serve you, though I tell you plainly, I would it had fallen to other hands. We were even trying to bring ourselves to some place of safety, which is like to prove a matter of some difficulty."

"Then, sir," and here the girl's eyes flashed proudly, "I pray you do not trouble yourself further, or imperil your safety on our account. For the gallant service this—this gentleman hath rendered me and my grandfather, I give him our best thanks, poor as they are, but we would not be a burden to you, and therefore think not of us, but go your way."

"My friend," said Gervase, "speaks not as he means, nor will I let him do discredit to his own kind heart. The sword which this poor fellow drew to defend you, will still be used for that end in my hands, and if I cannot use it as well it will be the power and not the will fails me."

Macpherson turned away, muttering under his breath, "Humph! the young fool is caught already. I see that she hath him in the snare."

"We were on the road to Londonderry, and though my friend is somewhat rough and discourteous withal, I doubt not he will do his best to help you thither, if such be, as I imagine, your desire."

"We were on the way to the city when we were attacked as you saw. My grandfather, who is Colonel Carew of Castleton, refused to believe that there was any danger in remaining at home; but last night, hearing that the enemy was burning and plundering round us, he set off at midnight, and we have been travelling ever since; and now I think the terror has turned his brain, for I never saw him thus before. What we shall do I know not, but if we can trust you——"

"Appearances are against me, I admit," said Gervase, with a smile, and feeling, with perhaps excusable vanity, that he would have preferred to cut a gallanter figure. "Still, I hope that you will believe me when I say that I am a gentleman, and most desirous of serving you. I have carried the colours in Mountjoy's regiment and——"

"And I think that I can trust you," she said, holding out her hand, with a frank look in her eyes, and a sweet, sad smile upon her lips.

"In your service wholly," said Gervase, bending low over her hand, which he pressed with unnecessary fervour. "My friend is an old soldier who has a grudge against your sex for some reason known to himself, but I have cause to know that a more loyal and faithful friend there never was. He will scoff and rail, I doubt not, but believe me, he will serve you with the last drop of blood in his heart. He hath great experience in matters of danger, and I doubt not some scheme may be devised whereby we may convey you to Londonderry in safety."

"I care not for myself," she answered; "it is for my grandfather that I fear. He seems to have lost his reason."

The old man had carried the box to a distance, and had sat down before it, examining the contents eagerly, and talking to himself in a loud excited tone. From time to time he glanced round furtively to see if he was observed, and then went on with his examination. "Safe! safe!" he muttered. "That was the Spaniard's gold, and you wear bravely, my beautiful doubloons. How you shine, my beauties, and I thought you were gone for ever! It would have broken my old heart—I could not have lived without you. And my stones of price——What want you, sir?" he said, closing the box, and turning round savagely as Macpherson approached.

"I know not what devil's trinkets you have enclosed there," said the soldier, "but I would have you act like a reasonable man, and tell me what you purpose doing. Yonder lady is young and unprotected, and we would not willingly leave you, but this is no time to give heed to such trash as you have shut up there, when your life is in danger every moment."

"My life is here," answered the old man, "and I pray you, for God's sake, leave me in peace. I know you not."

Macpherson turned on his heel and rejoined Gervase and the girl. "His mind is gone utterly," he said, "and it is useless endeavouring to reason with him. My young friend, madam, has, I doubt not, told you how matters stand with us. If you will, we shall endeavour to carry you with us, and trust to the fortunes of war to bring you safely through. Another hour should bring us to the ford. I trust that you are able to ride, for the chaise is rendered useless, and were it not, we have not horses to draw it. In the meantime I had better secure your nag."

Macpherson went after the stray horse which was now quietly grazing at some distance, and shortly returned with it. "And now," he said, "I regret that we cannot give this brave fellow Christian burial, but if you, madam, will look after your grandfather, my young friend and I will even place him where he may sleep his last sleep decently, like a brave and honest man as I doubt not he was."

The girl went over to the dead man, and kneeling down kissed his forehead, and then rising without a word, but with a great sob which she bravely strove to repress, went over to her grandfather. Macpherson and Gervase carried the body into the field, and placing it in the ditch, cut a quantity of bramble with which they reverently covered it.

"Sorry I am that we cannot dig a grave," said Macpherson, "but it may be that is a pagan thought. He hath died like a man, and at the last day he will rise, knowing that he fell in the path of duty.

What does it matter for this poor carcase what becomes of it? 'Tis for the living, not for the dead, that we should mourn. And now look you, Gervase Orme, I love you like a son, and would not willingly see you come to evil. Yonder damsel is goodly to look upon and hath the tender ways of a woman. I can see that you are already drawn towards her, and are ready even now to let her lead you as she will. Be warned by me, and shun the snare while you are still heart-whole and your wings are still unplucked. Nay, you are angry at the wise counsel of a friend; I speak only for your good, and will say no more. But I would that we had not met them, and would yet—"

"Surely," said Gervase, with warmth, "you would not leave this defenceless girl and the feeble old man, even if you might?"

"Nay, I said not that. In some sort they have been committed to our care, but it means for both of us, or I am much mistaken, either the length of a rope or the inside of a prison. I am older than you, my young friend, and think there is no woman worth the sacrifice either of my life or of my liberty. Now, go your way, and see her mounted upon Bayard, while I look after the old man, for I will have nothing to do with the wench. The rogues you dispersed will be looking for us presently. Before we meet them I should prefer being within sight of the Royal troops."

The old world laughs at Love, as laugh it may. And yet from generation to generation unheeding youth takes up the foolish old song, and dances to the ancient measure with a light and joyful heart. What though the roses wither and the garlands fade? These are fresh, and the morning dew is on them. What though the lips grow dumb, and the sound of the flute and the song is hushed and stilled? In the fresh and roseate morning as yet there are no shadows and no regrets; the heart is full of hope and joy. And so it has been since the lips of our first parents met in newly-awakened bliss, in the time when the world was young, and pain and satiety were unknown to mortals.

As yet Gervase was not in love, but his heart throbbed with an indefinable emotion as Dorothy Carew rested her hand upon his shoulder, and placing her dainty foot in his hand, sprang upon the great military saddle and thanked him with a smile.

"This is a dear old horse," she said, patting the charger's neck, and gathering up the reins in her hand. "We begin early to trouble you, and shall never be able to repay you and your friend."

"It were repayment enough," said Gervase, "to find you safe within the walls of Londonderry, and I am pleased to think that I have been able to serve you a little."

"That is the speech of a gentleman, after all," she said smiling. "I little thought you were a friend as you came shouting down the road; indeed, you would make a great hit at Drury Lane or Sadler's Wells; and what a figure you would cut at Saint James's!"

"I confess I do not make a very gallant show," said Gervase, "but these rags will serve their turn, and help us both, I trust, to better fortune."

The old man had been helped upon the second horse, and, with his box placed before him, followed them along the rough and broken road. He seemed wholly oblivious to what was taking place, and so long as his treasure was safe, seemed perfectly content to act as he was bidden. Macpherson, with his head bent, walked by the horse's bridle and listened with a frown upon his face to the conversation of Gervase and the girl. He had cast no glance in her direction, but after he had delivered his mind to Gervase, had busied himself about the old man with a rough kindliness.

"Thus we trudge on," he said, as if talking to himself, "as the world is doing everywhere. The old fool, at the end of his journey, thinking only of the pieces of gold for which he will have his throat cut in all likelihood before sunset. Heaven and Eternity are shut up in his box. The young fool, thinking only of the brown eyes and tender speeches of the wench, and willing to dare all things for her foolish sake, while the wench herself, woman that she is, baits her trap with honied words and draws the manhood out of him with the glance of her eye. And I—I must go where the Providence of God directs my steps, though avarice and vanity and the folly of youth be my companions and my guide. 'Tis a strange world and full of shadows, and these are of them."

CHAPTER VII.

OF THE RESCUE FROM GREAT PERIL.

COLONEL CAREW was the third in descent from the original planter who by right of conquest and the grace of James the First, had settled upon the broad lands of Castleton, and having swept the ancient possessors from the soil, had planted there a hardy race of colonists, and built himself a great house, half mansion, half fortress. The first Jasper Carew had looked upon himself as the instrument in the hands of Providence to civilize the land and found a family. He had ruled with despotic severity, and when he was laid in the family vault in the new church that he had built, left a name of undying hatred to the native Irish. The second Jasper followed in the footsteps of his father; he built and planted, and like a strong man armed, ruled his own demesne and showed neither mercy nor tolerance toward the ancient race. They were a God-fearing stock and showed no compassion nor kindly pity. Virtues they had, but only toward their friends, and never forgot that they had won by the sword's right and must continue to hold by its power. The present Colonel Carew had been wild in his youth, and had left the home of his fathers in disgrace. For a time he had entirely disappeared; there were vague rumours that he had prospered in the Virginias and had made a fortune there. However that might be, he had returned home on the death of his father, bringing with him an only son, and lived a moody, retired life in the great house, attended only by a servant who had shared his adventures abroad. His son had early obtained a commission, and served with distinction on the Continent. He had married against the wish of his father, a young lady of great beauty and slender fortune, the daughter of a Huguenot refugee, and when he fell at Senef some years afterwards, left an orphan son and daughter to the care of his father, who received the unwelcome legacy with little outward show of favour or affection. Colonel Carew had brought his grandson home, but permitted the girl to remain under the care of her relatives in London. Here Dorothy had remained until she was sixteen, when the death of her aunt compelled her to seek a home with her grandfather, who was unable to make any other provision for her, however anxiously he desired to do so. At Castleton, Dorothy Carew had spent two years of her life—not very happy or pleasant years, but her sweet and joyous spirit had broken down in some slight degree the barrier that her grandfather had raised between himself and all the world.

He was growing old and frail, and his mind seemed to have gone wholly back to the early years which he had spent in wild adventure and lawless wanderings. The care of his estate he had left to his grandson, who paid little heed to the old man, but went his way with the headstrong and reckless selfishness that was the characteristic of his race. The presence of his grand-daughter seemed to give him pleasure, but companionship between them there was none. He accepted her attentions, not, indeed, with an ill grace, but without any apparent sign of affection, though at times, as he sat watching her moving about his room, her figure appeared to arouse him from his fit of abstraction, and to awaken a chord of memory that was not wholly painful.

So she passed these two years at Castleton— dull enough for a girl of spirit and used to the excitement and life of a great city; and when the news of a great Catholic rising and massacre arrived, it found her alone and unprotected, with a number of panic-stricken domestics and a helpless old man looking to her for assistance and advice. Her brother had gone to Londonderry on business of his own, and there was no one near her on whom she could rely. The servants had remained at their posts for some time, but as the excitement deepened, and the tenantry fled to Enniskillen or to Londonderry for safety and shelter, they refused to remain longer, and while imploring her to join them in their flight, one morning they departed in a body. She herself would willingly have accompanied them, but her grandfather refused to move. It was, he said, mere moonshine. It was only when the Irish army had marched northward, and there came the frequent and alarming reports of robbery and murder, that he was seized with an uncontrollable dread, and insisted on fleeing to Londonderry forthwith. The girl had no one to assist her in their hasty flight but a brave and trusty servant who had served with her father abroad, and who had been since taken into her grandfather's service. Together they had bundled the old man into the coach, and leaving the great house to its fate, had set out for the city of refuge. How they fared on their way thither we have already seen.

Gervase walked by Bayard's bridle, unmindful of all weariness and regardless of all dangers, seeking, after the manner of young men, to make the most of the sweet society into which chance had so strangely thrown him. He was indignant with himself that he was ashamed of his rags, though by way of making up for these, he began to talk of his life in Dublin and the gay doings of the capital.

At this Dorothy's sense of humour was touched, and much to his confusion she began to laugh aloud. "Your talk in such a figure, of the Castle and of Tyrconnell and of my Lady, is a most excellent remedy for lowness of spirits. I cannot set matters straight, and must become accustomed to your mode. And yet I think I could have told that you were a gentleman."

"That is something," said Gervase, a little mollified, "and how?"

"Because," she answered, with a naïve glance that disarmed his resentment, "your present garments fit you so ill. But I am very wrong to jest at such a time, and your friend does not seem to admire laughter. I think that I could have told anywhere that he was a soldier. You could not mistake his carriage."

"A better soldier and a truer friend there never was," Gervase answered warmly; "and that you will have cause to admit before your journey ends."

"I think," she said, "that you yourself fight not so badly. Oh! why was I not a man that I might strike for religion and liberty? it is a miserable thing to be a woman in times like these."

"I hope I am not a coward," Gervase answered, "but I have already seen enough of warfare to dislike my trade, and would never fight if it were possible to avoid it. But fight we must for our rights and liberties and," he added, after a pause, "in defence of those we love."

"And," she said, smiling, "is it for these last that you are fighting? But I have no right to ask you that, though I have been told that men say love is out of fashion. Indeed I think that it is no longer in vogue."

"I care not for fashion in these things, but I have begun to think that there might be such loving as would make life a royal thing to live. I mean not love that asks to be loved in return, though I should like that too, but a love that fills the heart with great and splendid thoughts, and raises it above contemptible and base designs; the love I mean is wholly pure and unselfish and lifts the lover above himself. I know not whether you know the lines of that sonnet—"

"I think," she said smiling, "we will change the subject. It seems to me that you are far too romantic to conduct a young and unprotected damsel on a dangerous journey like this. Your grim Captain Macpherson were a far fitter and more becoming companion—he would not breathe out his aspirations in rhyme, or relieve his love-laden soul in a ballad. Heigho! I shall never understand you men. But now tell me about your journey from Londonderry, and how it came about that you were wounded?"

And thereupon Gervase proceeded to relate the story of his ride by night and the skirmish on the road, passing lightly over such incidents as might be unfitting for a woman's ear to listen to.

But when he mentioned the name of De Laprade she stopped him. "And you have met my cousin Victor, for it can be no other? I had not heard that he had come to Ireland."

"I mean the Vicomte de Laprade. He is not much older than myself, with a slight lisp, and very fair for a Frenchman."

"Yes, that is he. You do not know that he is in some sort my cousin, my mother having been of his family. He was in London when I was a girl living with my aunt, and he would come to visit us whenever he could tear himself away from the cards and the festivities of Whitehall. Poor Victor! he was a sad rake in those days, and I fear he would never have come to Ireland had he not run through his fortune."

"He hinted, indeed, at something of that sort," said Gervase, "but he is a gallant fellow, and one cannot but like him. He hath done a great deal for me."

"It would be strange should we meet here, yet who can tell? For it is as likely we shall find ourselves within the Irish camp as within the walls of Londonderry. I wonder in what manner we should be treated there?"

"Camps are ever lawless places," Gervase answered, "and offer little entertainment for a lady. I trust that you will not be called upon to make the trial. But Macpherson is calling upon us to stop; we have already travelled too far in advance."

The road now ran through a wooded and undulating country, and they were coming close to the ford by which they hoped to cross. At times they had been able to catch a distant glimpse of the river bright with the fading sunset, but so far as Gervase was able to see, there was no sign of the enemy, and he had begun to hope that they might pass unmolested.

"It is time," said Macpherson, as he came up, "that we should determine on our plan of action, for we can go no further. The ford yonder is guarded. I caught the gleam of arms but a minute ago from the top of the hill, and there is part of a troop of horse in the little grove yonder to the right. I know the sound too well to mistake it. If it be possible to cross I shall soon know; though—and here I speak, not with any selfish or dishonourable intention, but as a man of honour and a soldier, it were, perhaps, best that this lady and her grandfather should place themselves of their free will in the hands of yonder gentry, and trust to their humanity for generous treatment. It is a perilous undertaking that we have in hand, and bullets may presently be flying. However, as Providence has in some measure placed you under our care, should it be your good pleasure, we will do as best we can."

"My grandfather is an old and defenceless man," answered Dorothy, with spirit, "and as you have seen, carries with him a great quantity of treasure, which I would that I had never seen. What treatment, think you, is he likely to receive at the hands of those who live on the fruit of robbery and murder?"

"Miss Carew is right, Captain Macpherson," said Gervase, "and whatever your design may be, I shall abide with her, and so far as my help goes, shall see that she and her grandfather pass unscathed."

"I well knew," answered Macpherson bitterly, "that you would do nothing less, though it may come to pass that you will both suffer for it hereafter. My design, as you phrase it, is even to go gently forward, and see in what manner yon loons have set their guard, and of what strength they may be. In the meantime, I should advise that you withdraw into that clump of oak trees where you may safely await my coming, which will be within the hour. I had looked for some sense from you,

Mr. Orme, but I find that you are no wiser than the rest of them. 'Fore God we are all fools together."

Before Gervase had time to reply he had disappeared within the undergrowth that grew densely by the roadside, and Gervase and the girl stood looking at one another in silence; the same grave suspicion had presented itself to both of them. "What think you of your friend?" she said, with indignation.

"For a moment I hardly knew what to think," Gervase answered, "but my faith in him is not a whit shaken. Believe me, we may trust him unreservedly, and in good time he will prove that I am right. He will do whatever a man may to bring you safely through, and will risk life and limb to serve you. And now let us follow his directions, for if the ford be indeed guarded, 'tis a wonder that we were not long since discovered."

Taking Colonel Carew's horse by the bridle, Gervase led him into the oak wood followed by Dorothy. Here there proved to be excellent shelter, for the underwood had grown thick and high, and discovery was impossible so long as the enemy kept to the road, which it was likely they would do unless their suspicions were aroused.

The old man was helped from his horse and seated himself upon a fallen tree, with his precious box clasped upon his knees, speaking no word, but looking straight before him, with a fixed unmeaning gaze. He appeared to be unconscious of what was taking place round him, and insensible of the dangers to which they were exposed. Dorothy knelt down beside him and placed her hands on his. He was muttering wild and incoherent words.

"Grandfather," she said, "do you know me?"

He looked at her with a frown. "Ay, girl, wherefore not?" he answered. "Talk no more, but fill up my glass till the red wine runs over. There is plenty where it came from—plenty, and gold that is better than wine, girl; and bars of silver and stones of price. We who sail under the *Jolly Roger* cannot afford to be scrupulous. You are sly, wench, damnably sly, but you will not overreach me. Nay, you shall have a doubloon or two for yourself and a bundle of silks from our next venture. I am grown stiff with this long lying ashore, and am well wearied for a breath of the Spanish Main.

"'For the guns are all ready and the decks are all clear
And the prize is awaiting the bold Buccaneer!'"

Dorothy rose and wrung her hands with a gesture of despair. Gervase could see that the wild words of the old man had touched her beyond description. It was not so much that they showed his mind had left him; they had revealed the terrible secret of his early life—a secret that till now she had never dreamed of. She had instinctively guessed the truth, and it had covered her with shame, as though the crime and the reproach were her own. Gervase out of regard for her feelings withdrew to a distance, and busied himself in getting ready a supper, which matter, necessary as it was, had quite escaped his thoughts. But Dorothy, though he pressed her strongly, refused to partake of it.

"I cannot taste of food," she said, "and you know the reason—you also have heard the dreadful words. That accursed money comes—Oh! I might have guessed it, but who would have thought?—and he is so old and so frail and—and I think he is going to die. Oh! it is very terrible. I was so proud of my name, and the honour of my house, and now——"

Gervase had no words with which to comfort her, and so the three—the two men and the girl—sat here in the thicket, speaking never a word. But for the young man, he could not take his eyes off the sweet, strong face that looked so lovely in its grief—the lips that trembled, and the eyes that were dimmed with unshed tears. Half an hour passed in silence; only the far-off murmur of the river came faintly through the twilight, and the whirr of a startled bird, or the hasty scamper of a rabbit or a rat, broke the stillness round them. As yet there was no appearance of Macpherson. And then Gervase began to wonder whether, after all, Dorothy might not have been right in her hasty surmise, and whether he might not have sought his own safety in flight, and left them to their fate. But he instantly dismissed the suggestion from his mind as ungenerous and unjust.

Then, at that moment, a shot rang out in the evening air, and another, and another. The sound came from the river, and as they stood and listened, they could hear the jinging of bridles and the clank of weapons, for the air was somewhat frosty and very still. They had risen to their feet and stood listening, only Gervase had drawn his sword, and instinctively stepped nearer to where the girl was standing. Soon they heard the sound of hasty footsteps and the crashing of branches, as someone made his way with impetuous haste through the underwood. Then Macpherson appeared bareheaded, with a smoking pistol in his hand.

"There is not a moment to lose," he cried. "Into the road and make what terms you can. They are regular troops and may not use you ill, but escape you cannot, and I may not tarry here. I have done for one of them, and, I think, another will never hear 'boots and saddle' sounded again. 'Tis your only hope."

"And what," cried Gervase, "do you purpose doing?"

"Saving my neck if it be possible. I cannot serve you, but would only make your case the worse. It goes against my heart to leave you, but for your sake and my own I can do naught else. Stay," he continued, "there is one thing more. For that box they would cut your throats, and they must not find it with you. Madam, can you trust me? I am rugged and I am rough, but I think I am honest."

Dorothy looked at him fairly a moment and their eyes met. "Yes," she said, in a clear, strong voice, "I can trust you wholly."

"Then, sir," he said, stepping forward to the old man, " By your leave and license I must, for your own good, relieve you of your toys." With a quick movement he took the box out of the hands of the old man who stared at him with a bewildered gaze, and then with a hurried farewell, he passed out of sight. Colonel Carew uttered a loud, shrill scream and fell forward on the grass. Dorothy ran forward and tried to turn him over, but she had not strength enough. Then Gervase knelt down to help her, but when he saw the white, frowning face, one glance was sufficient to show him how it was. The old adventurer, with all his sins fresh in his memory and his wicked life rekindled, as it were, out of the ashes of the past, had gone to his account.

The dragoons, who had hastily mounted on discovering Macpherson, and had been riding down the road, reined in their horses, and dismounting, plunged into the coppice. The old man's sudden and startling outcry had guided them to the fugitives' place of concealment. They set up a loud shout when they were discovered, and one fellow was about to pistol Gervase when another struck up his hand and restrained him.

"Time enough for that. We'll put a question or two first," said the sergeant who commanded the party. "Tie his hands behind his back, and bring him out into the road. The old man is dead as a nail," he continued, touching the lifeless body with his foot, "and the wench is no doubt his daughter. By my soul! she's a beauty: now look you, the first

8

man-Jack of you who lays his finger on her, I'll blow his brains out, so help me God! and you know I'm a man of my word. Don't fear, madam; they're rough but kindly."

As they led Gervase out into the road, one hope was uppermost in his mind, and that was that they might fall in with some officer of sufficient authority to whose care he might confide Dorothy, and to whose sense of honour he should not appeal in vain. There were still many gallant gentlemen in the Irish army in whose eyes a woman's reputation would be sacred.

The dragoons who guarded him followed the sergeant out into the open, and they halted under a great oak that threw its broad branches across the road. Dorothy had implored them to bring her grandfather's body with them, and on their refusing had seated herself beside it. But without using any great violence, they had insisted on her following the rest of the party. She had shed no tears, but her face was very white, and her breath came quickly in little, convulsive sobs. Gervase looked at her for a moment, and then turned away his head.

"Now," said the sergeant, "we'll see what stuff he's made of. How say you, sir? On what side are you? Are you for King James?"

"I am for law and order," answered Gervase. "This young lady and I were on a peaceful journey, wishing ill and intending hurt to no one, and I know not what right you have to hinder us."

"That is no answer to my question, sir; but I'll

answer for you—you're a Whig and in arms against the King, or would be. Where is your authority? And now another question and I have done with you: Where is the prickeared knave gone who pistolled poor Cornet White and sent another of ours to kingdom come? I'll take my oath he was of your party."

"I saw no pistolling," said Gervase; "is it like in such force as you see us, we should fall upon a troop of dragoons? Why, man, it was because we were afraid to venture near you that we hid ourselves in the tangle yonder."

"This jesting will not answer, Master Whig. I'll give you one chance of saving your neck and only one—what way went he?"

"Look you here, sergeant," said Gervase, seeing the desperate position in which he was placed, "I'm a gentleman, and it would profit you little to shoot or hang me. See this lady and myself safe through to Londonderry, and you will have twenty golden guineas for yourself and five for every man here in your company. I cannot say you fairer, and if not for my sake or the money's, then for the sake of this helpless lady."

"This lady will be well cared for, never fear, and for your guineas, I'm thinking by the time you got to Londonderry, they would be own brothers to the lads they are making in Dublin. Come, my man, you'll have sixty seconds to answer my question, and then Hurrah for the kingdom of glory." So saying he took a piece of rope from the hands of one of the men and began leisurely to measure it, a foot at a time, looking up occasionally from the operation to see how it affected the prisoner.

"My God! you would not hang me?"

"Ay, that I would, with a heart and a half and high as Haman, if the rope were long enough. The time is nearly up—How say you?"

"I say that I care not how you use me, if you see the lady safe. Hang me if you will."

"The time is up and you have not answered an honest question. Now, lads, we'll see if this heretic rogue can do anything but prate. It seems to me he looks a strolling player and may be one for all I know." So saying he deftly threw the rope round the thick branch that grew over the road, and placed his hand on the prisoner's shoulder.

Up to this time Dorothy could not believe that he meant to carry out his savage threat, but she saw now that this was no mere jest but a matter of life and death. The business was evidently to the taste of the troopers, and two of them laid aside their firelocks and placed their hands upon the rope. Then she sprang forward and caught the sergeant by the arm. "You do not mean what you say," she cried, "he has never wronged you, nor have I, and had it not been for me and the dead old man yonder, he had not been in your power now. For my sake, for God's sake, you will not injure him."

The man seemed touched for a minute, so wild was she, and so beautiful, in her despair, and then he shook her off roughly. "Women have nothing to do in these affairs. Two of you fellows take her away, and leave us to finish this business in peace. Now, make haste about the matter, and get this damnable job out of hand. We must look after the other fellow before night comes down."

Dorothy turned white and faint, and seemed like to have fallen on the road as Gervase held out his hand to her and said, with a lump in his throat,

"Good-bye, Miss Carew, I regret quitting life less than leaving you in this company, but my last prayer on earth is for your safety. Could my life have brought you help, I should have given it up without regret."

Then she broke down utterly, and they led her away, with her face buried in her hands. Suddenly, at that moment there was heard the sound of a horse coming rapidly along the road, and the men who were busied placing the noose round Gervase's neck, stopped short in their work. Dorothy heard the sound also, and looked up. An officer, apparently of distinguished rank, accompanied by a couple of dragoons, was advancing at a rapid trot.

His military cloak, richly embroidered, was thrown open, and showed a burnished cuirass underneath. His broad-brimmed hat adorned with a single white feather, nearly concealed his face. As he approached, Dorothy struggled in the hands of the man who held her and freeing herself, ran swiftly down the road to meet him. As he came up he reined in his black charger.

"Thank God!" she cried, "you have come in

time. You, at least, are a gentleman, and you will save him."

"I hope, madam, I am a gentleman," he said, with a high, courteous manner and in a voice that was at once strong and musical. "I shall examine into this matter, and if I can in duty and in honour render you this service, you may rely upon me."

Then hurriedly, and almost incoherently, she told him her story, or as much as she thought necessary for her purpose; and when she had finished he called out to one of the mounted troopers to take his horse.

"Now, Miss Carew," he said, dismounting, and raising his hat with a stately courtesy, "having heard your story, I am rejoiced that I have arrived in time. These lambs of mine are hasty in their work and, I fear, have not always warrant for what they do. Believe me, I am sorry for your case and will do what I can to aid you. And now let us see how the gentleman has borne himself, who has so fair an advocate to plead his cause."

With these words, taking her hand he led her up to the group which stood under the tree awaiting his approach. Gervase had given himself up for lost, and had commended his soul to his Maker, for the rope had already been adjusted round his neck, and willing hands were only waiting for the word of command from the sergeant to turn him off. But as the mounted officer rode up and the fellows suspended their work, he felt instinctively that he had been saved. The look of baffled hate on the sergeant's face showed that. The officer came up leading Dorothy by the hand, and the dragoons saluted him silently. He gave Gervase one quick searching look, a look that flashed with keen intelligence and seemed to take in every detail in a moment, and then said sternly, "Unbind the prisoner, and take down that rope." He stood quietly, speaking no word, but waited with his keen eyes fixed on Gervase, until the dragoons had unbound the prisoner's hands and removed the hempen cord from his neck. The work being completed, the men fell back a few paces.

"Now, sirrah!" he said, turning to the sergeant, "what does this mean? By whose orders or instructions were you about to hang this gentleman? Is it thus that you do your duty? While the fellow who shot down your officer has been making his escape, you have been preparing to murder an unoffending traveller whom it was your duty to protect. Had I been five minutes later, I do not doubt that I should have strung you up beside him. Good God! it is fellows like you who make me blush for my countrymen. Now, look you, the man who has made his escape must be brought in before nightfall. Should you fail to capture him you will see how I deal with men who forget that they are soldiers and act like caterans."

"This fellow, if it please your honour——" began the sergeant.

"Silence, sirrah! Take your men and search the wood. This man must not escape, and when you return, report yourself to me at the house by the ford. Take all the men with you; I shall return alone. Stay, there is one thing more." Here glancing hastily at Dorothy, he walked a short distance away, and in a low tone gave orders with regard to the remains of Colonel Carew, which he directed to be brought down to the post and await his instructions there. The man saluted, and giving the necessary orders with a sullen and crestfallen air, left his superior standing alone with the prisoner.

"Give me no thanks, sir," he said, interrupting Gervase. "For I have only done for you what an Irish gentleman is bound in honour to do. Our men will do these lawless deeds, but with the party to which you belong rests the blame, having made them what they are. Till now they have been slaves with all the vices of the slave; they cannot learn the moderation and restraint of freemen in a day. However," he continued, with a smile that lighted up his dark face, "this is no speech to address to a man who has just escaped the gallows. Miss Carew tells me you are now on your way to Londonderry seeking refuge and safety there. I do not propose to advise you, but within a fortnight the city will be in our hands, and meanwhile must undergo the dangers of a siege. We do not make war on women, and Miss Carew may rely on me to help her to a place of safety."

"My friends are there," said Dorothy; "I have not elsewhere to go."

"We have indeed proposed," said Gervase, "to take refuge in Londonderry, and since Miss Carew has lost—is alone, I know not where else she can betake herself. For myself I am indebted to you, sir, for my life, and you may dispose of me as you will; but for the lady, I would beg you to allow her to pass safely through your lines and join her friends in the city."

"That might easily be done, but surely Dublin were safer?"

"As I have said," answered Dorothy, "my friends are all in Londonderry, and I should prefer to share their danger."

"Well! we shall see how it may be, but in the meantime, I shall ask you to share my hospitality, such as it is, to-night, and to-morrow we will devise some plan for your security. Miss Carew may safely place herself in the hands of Patrick Sarsfield," and he raised his hat with the *bel air* that sat so easily upon him.

Gervase looked with curiosity on the great Irish leader, than whom no more notable figure and chivalrous gentleman fought in the Irish ranks, and lent lustre and honour to a somewhat tarnished cause. He was little, indeed, above the middle height. but his bold and gallant bearing gave him the appearance of being of more than the ordinary stature. His brow was frank and open, and his eyes had the clear and resolute gaze of a man accustomed to bold and perilous action—ardent, impetuous, and courageous. His speech came rapidly, and his utterance was of the clearest and most decisive. Accustomed to camps he had yet the air of a well-bred man of the world, and when he smiled his face lost the fixed and somewhat melancholy air it wore when in repose.

"And you are Colonel Sarsfield?" Dorothy inquired. "Then we are friends, for you were the friend of my aunt Lady Bellasis."

"Truly she was my very good friend, and her son Will—your cousin, I presume—was my dear crony and companion-in-arms. We served together during Monmouth's campaign, and I might almost say that he died in my arms at Taunton. You are then the Dorothy of whom I heard him speak. I think his death broke his mother's heart. It is strange that we should meet here, but life is made up of strange things; we should wonder at nothing. Now, Mr. Orme, I shall give the lady my arm, and we will see whether even here in the desert they cannot furnish us with a bottle of wine, that we may drink to peace and a settlement of differences. Only I should like to say this: I ask no questions, and look upon you only as Miss Carew's companion and protector; I expect that you will close your eyes to anything that you may see, and ever after be silent on the matter."

"I hope," answered Gervase, "I know better than to take advantage of your great kindness. I shall observe your instructions to the letter."

"'Tis very well. Come, Miss Carew," Sarsfield said, extending his hand, "this hath been a melancholy journey for you, and henceforth I wish you happier fortune. I have given orders regarding the interment of your kinsman, and will spare you all the pain I can."

Dorothy thanked him with a look, and was silent. Beside the river was a farm-house which was evidently used as a military station, for before the door a number of dragoons—perhaps a dozen—were gathered in small groups, and several horses were picketed in the enclosure which had formerly been used as a garden.

As they entered the house they were saluted by the strong odour of tobacco-smoke. A man was engaged in cooking at the open hearth, and another was seated on a chair hard by, watching the operation as he smoked his pipe in silence, and beat a tattoo with his heels upon the earthen floor. The latter was a remarkable-looking man in every way. He was dressed in a plain red coat, with a tangled weather-beaten wig hanging down at full length. He wore a faded beaver with a narrow brim, and had a dirty yellow-coloured cravat tied carelessly round his neck. His legs were very long, his face was full of freckles, and his nose was tilted up in what had been a good-humoured fashion but for the heavy and forbidding expression of his mouth. As they came in he did not rise but merely removed his pipe from his lips.

"How now?" he asked.

"My special mission hath already borne fruit, Colonel Luttrel," said Sarsfield stiffly. "This lady is the kinswoman of a late very dear friend of mine, and your dragoons have used her with the scantest courtesy."

"The young lady hath reason to be thankful 'tis no worse, for they cannot stand the sight of a petticoat, and they could not be expected to know of the relationship. We'll trust to the supper, which is nearly ready, to cure her wounded feelings."

"This lady is my friend, sir," said Sarsfield, with a frown.

"And Colonel Luttrel's also, I hope," said Dorothy, with a sweeping curtesy, which made the soldier open his eyes to their widest with wonder and admiration, and drew a smile to Sarsfield's lips. "I think, sir, you speak very sensibly and am glad to hear that supper is ready."

The Colonel rose from his chair, laid down his pipe, and held out his hand. "You are of the kind that pleases me," he said, "and I would, my dear, that I was thirty years younger for your sake. Fine airs never pleased me yet and, damme! you're a beauty." Again Dorothy curtesied with becoming gravity. "Now, sit you down," he went on, "and let me hear of what the Colonel yonder complains, for he and I," and here he lowered his voice, "strike it off but ill. If any man of mine but dared to lay his finger on you, I'll give him a round dozen for your sake."

"I'm sure you are very generous," Dorothy said, demurely enough, and thereafter she and the old soldier began to talk together with great ease and friendliness. Presently he was laughing loudly at her playful sallies, and before he was aware she drew the heart out of him till he was completely her servant.

I have seen the lady's portrait painted but a few years after the events here narrated, and I say in all soberness that I do not wonder at her power. Of her mere beauty I can give no just description, but to my mind her chief charm lay in her eyes, the expression of which the painter—a Fleming, whose name has escaped my memory—had caught with marvellous fidelity. Full of pride and stateliness, they were yet prone to light up with tenderness and playful humour, to which her lips gave just and fitting emphasis. Had I not already known something of her life I should yet have willingly taken her for a heroine. And yet the contemplation of that sweet face saddened me beyond expression. Hanging there among the portraits of forgotten statesmen, and old-world soldiers who fought at Ramillies and Oudenarde, the presentment of that young and smiling face, so full of tender light and gracious sweetness, looked out of the past with pathetic warning that all things have the same fate and must go the same inevitable way.

In this little comedy it must not be supposed she was altogether acting a part, or that in anything she said or did she was inspired by any other feeling than friendliness, and it may be the frolicsome humour, that was in her a characteristic trait. From time to time she looked up archly at Colonel Sarsfield who stood smiling by the window, and then resumed her conversation with increased sprightliness.

"I never understand women, my dear," Luttrel said.

"And you never will, sir, for we do not understand ourselves. I think you have never been married?"

"The Lord be praised for all His mercies, that blessing is still a long way before me. I mean, my dear young lady, no offence to you, but my brother Phil married and saved the rest of the family."

"With Colonel Luttrel's permission we will draw a veil over his family history."

"'Tis mighty well," said the other; "commissary-general to a ragged army of fifteen, and his wife still a rare recruiting sergeant."

So saying he took his place stiffly behind his chair, waiting till Dorothy was seated at the supper table. "And I hope," he growled, looking askance at Gervase, "that this person is of fit condition to sit at the table with people of quality."

"Of that matter, sir," said Sarsfield, "I am perhaps the best judge. Mr. Orme, will you do me the favour to take this chair beside me? I remember when I was of your age I did not require much invitation after a long day. You will tell Miss Carew that soldiers' fare is ever of the plainest. And as far as prudence and honour will permit, I should like to hear something of your journeying, which seems to have been of the strangest, or so this fair advocate would have me believe."

Gervase long remembered this strange evening spent in this curious company. He was wholly unable to resist the fascination of the great soldier's manner, and long after that fiery soul had passed away in the onset at Landen, would dwell upon his memory with admiration and regret. He treated Gervase with perfect friendliness, delicately avoiding all matters that might cause offence. He related many incident in his own career with perfect frankness and vivacity, and spoke with great shrewdness and insight of many famous men that he had met. Of Marlborough, whom he had known in Monmouth's campaign, he spoke with great enthusiasm in his character as a soldier, though he affected to despise him as a man; and Gervase remembered the conversation in after years, when the hero of Blenheim returned amid the plaudits of the nation and crowned with the laurels of victory.

Luttrel listened with a hard and solemn visage; it was abundantly clear that he was determined that he should not go to bed sober, and was already far advanced in his cups before Dorothy left the table. But he was entirely silent under Sarsfield's eye, and merely plied the bottle with great assiduity. Presently Dorothy quited the room. Sarsfield standing with his hands on the back of his chair, wished her a stately "good-night." When she had retired he turned to Gervase.

"I shall not see you again this evening, Mr. Orme," he said, "and I have not asked you for your parole. Nor is such my intention. On your word I know that I could rely, but I know that I have better security for your safe custody there," and he pointed towards Dorothy's room. "Good-night, gentlemen, and I trust that you will not quarrel," with which words he went out.

Luttrel put his arms on the table and looked at

Gervase with a drunken sneer. "The Colonel thinks that he is a mighty pretty fellow, and that no man knows the points of a woman but himself. And he flirts with the bottle like a quaker, which I have never taken to be the first sign of manhood. Indeed, you are a damnable drinker yourself. Come, sir, fill up your glass cheerfully, or I shall be compelled to think you have an objection to your company."

"I have no fault to find with my entertainment," Gervase answered good humouredly, unwilling to create any dissension, and making a show of replenishing his glass.

"Why, there, that's right! But I may tell you frankly, Mr. What's-your-name, that had this thing been left to me, you should not now have been sitting drinking of this excellent usquebaugh in the company of your betters. I speak in the way of friendship, for I ever like to be honest, and, mark you, I mean no offence in the world, but if I had my will, I should even string you up with a hempen cravat round your neck to show you what I think of your principles."

"Meaning thereby that you would hang me?" Gervase said with a smile.

"Ay, that I would, with the best intentions in the world, but since I cannot carry out my purpose, I will even drink with you or fight with you, as you will."

"I should stand no chance with you either way, I am afraid; but I am very tired and with your permission,"—and here Gervase offered to rise.

The other clapped his hand upon his sword, and rose to his feet with a drunken stagger. "Nay, that you shall not. I am a hospitable man, and none shall say that I did not give you an opportunity of going to bed like a gentleman."

Finding himself thus placed between two fires, Gervase unwillingly resumed his seat, and watched his truculent host growing more and more intoxicated, while he entered into a rambling disquisition on his own fortunes and the wrongs of his unhappy country. He did not doubt but that the time of deliverance had come. The Irish gentlemen were about to strike a great blow for freedom and for James Stuart, though they cared not a whit for the quarrel, but he served their purpose as well as another. For the pestilent heretics in Londonderry, they would be taught a wholesome lesson: they would be made a warning to all traitors. His father was a man in Cromwell's day. Then his talk grew more and more incoherent, and finally, with his head fallen upon his arms, and the contents of the overturned measure streaming over the table, he fell fast asleep. Gervase then rose and sought his own bed, glad that, after all, the night had passed so amicably.

CHAPTER VIII.

OF THE RETURN TO THE CITY.

COLONEL SARSFIELD more than fulfilled the promise he had made. Seeing that Dorothy had set her heart upon joining her friends in Londonderry, he had accompanied her part of the way himself, and had provided her with an escort for the remainder of her journey. To Gervase he had shown unaffected kindness. He had provided him with a horse and apparel befitting his condition, and at parting had wrung his hand with an appearance of great warmth and friendship.

"It is right, perhaps," he had said, "that we should be on different sides of this quarrel, but we can part with mutual good-will. I have but one hope and one thought—to see my country once more a nation, great and free. I would that all our people were of one mind, and were striking together for their fatherland. But it is still our curse to be divided—torn and rent by civil feuds. But believe me when I say that Patrick Sarsfield has only one desire on earth, and that is that his country should have her own laws and her own government, and freedom for the meanest. I think I shall meet my fate on the field of battle, but I hope not before I have seen that splendid day. Think well of us, Mr. Orme, and though you do your duty on your own side, remember that there are among us those whose cause is sacred in their eyes, and whose country is dearer to them than their lifeblood."

They never met again, but Gervase felt in after days that there was one man in Ireland who might have saved his cause, had he not been checked by narrow prejudices and the bitter envy of those who did not understand his proud and chivalrous nature. At Limerick that fiery spirit blazed out for a while in all its native strength, but his cause was already doomed.

When Gervase had reached Londonderry in safety, and had seen Dorothy placed under the protection of her aunt, he returned to his old lodgings over a linendraper's shop in a small house near the Bishop's-gate.

In the meantime, memorable events had transpired in his absence. The Irish army, breaking through the defences of the Bann, had pressed on toward Londonderry, and having crossed the Finn, had closed upon the city. Colonel Lundy, whether through vacillation and cowardice or from deliberate treachery, had made no effort to oppose their approach, and had done his best to secure the surrender of the city. At the very moment when he was about to carry out his designs, the citizens awakened to his intentions, and took the authority into their own hands. They seized the keys and took possession of the walls; a new government was established in the city; the garrison was divided into regiments, and preparations were made to stand a long and stubborn siege.

A great change had taken place in the city and in the spirit of the citizens since Gervase had ridden out of the gate, a fortnight before. The old look of dejection and irresolution had disappeared; one of unbounded enthusiasm and zeal had taken its place. Every able-bodied man carried arms and bore himself like a soldier. Swords clanked on the causeway; rusty muskets had been furbished up, and gentlemen and yeomen alike were filled with the same ardour, and wore the same determined air. Every regiment had its post. On the ramparts the guards were posted at regular intervals; little knots of armed and resolute men were gathered in the great square, and companies were being drilled from morning till night in the Bogside. A spirit of unyielding loyalty filled the air. The paving stones had been raised from the streets and were carried to the walls; blinds had been erected to screen the men on the ramparts. From the grey Cathedral tower two guns looked down on the Waterside, and on every bastion were others ready for use. At the Market house also cannon were planted to sweep the streets. At every gate there was a great gun.

The siege had indeed commenced. Yonder beyond the Foyle lay Lord Lumley's command, three thousand strong, the white tents catching the last gleam of the sunset as the evening mists crept up the river. At Brookhall and Pennyburn Mill was a strong force that shut off communication with Culmore. Away towards St. Johnston's and Carrigans was the main army of the enemy under Eustace and Ramsay. From the heights of Clooney one could see at long intervals a swift leap of flame, and hear the sullen roar of a great gun breaking on the evening air. All thought of compromise or capitulation was at an end; here the citizens must make their last stand, and show the world how dearly they held their faith and freedom.

At first sight resistance might have seemed a midsummer folly.

On both sides of the river the high ground looked down upon the city, and that within the range of cannon. The streets clomb up the gradual slope toward the square-towered Cathedral; the walls were low and might be easily breached. Still, there were seven thousand men of the imperial race within those walls, and while one stone stood upon another they had sworn to make good their defence.

Gervase was up betimes on the morning following his return. He had seen Colonel Murray the night before at the guard house, whither that gallant soldier had just returned after a hot encounter with the enemy, and had heard from his lips an account of their first skirmish that had taken place that very day. Murray had promised him a vacant cornetcy in his own regiment of horse, and the prospect of plenty of service.

Gervase buckled on his sword after a hasty

breakfast, his mind full of the hope that a high-spirited young-fellow naturally indulges in at such a time. His imagination had been touched and his heart had been stirred by the peril of the situation. He had caught the joyous enthusiasm of the time, and he whistled merrily a bar of Lillibullero as he went down the crooked stair, and came into the ill-lighted shop. The door was lying open, but the shutters had not been taken down. Trade was not of the briskest of late days, and the stock was somewhat meagre. The varied assortment of wares—linens, broadcloth, and laces—had nearly disappeared, and the little linen-draper, Simon Sproule, was seated with a rueful countenance at his desk, with his ledger spread open before him. So intent was he on the open page that he had not heard Gervase come clanking down the stairs, and it was only when the latter stepped forward and laid his hand on his shoulder, that he raised his head with a startled look. Then he jumped up and held out his hand.

"God bless my soul! I am glad to see you, Mr. Orme; I had never thought to have laid my eyes on you again. It was only on Thursday I was telling Elizabeth—and she'll bear me out in what I say—that 'twas likely your dust was mingled by this time with the clods of the valley, and we were both grieved to have lost you."

"I am sure I am much bound to both of you," Gervase answered, laughing, "but you can see that I look little like a dying man yet; just as much as you look like an honest tradesman."

The little man surveyed himself ruefully, and with such solemnity of visage that Gervase could not suppress a smile of amusement. His coat of claret-coloured cloth had given place to a buff jacket which had already seen considerable service on a man larger than himself, and he was encased to the thighs in a pair of jack-boots that gave his nether extremities a very striking appearance. On a stool hard by was a steel head-piece of an antiquated pattern, and leaning against the counter was a musket, the lock of which he had apparently recently been oiling. The bulging forehead with its overhanging tuft of red hair, the nose that providence had carefully tilted up, and the blue eyes that always met you with a look of mild wonder in them, harmonized but ill with his military equipment. He shook his head sadly.

"These are but ill times that we have fallen upon. 'Tis very well, sir, for a young man like yourself whose trade is fighting, to go swaggering up and down with a long sword by your side and a murderous weapon like that in your hand, but for a married man like myself with eight children to his own share, 'tis altogether another matter. But I'm a loyal man and a good Protestant, and I'll even try to do my duty, hard as it seems, with the best of you."

"Why, Simon, three weeks ago you were the boldest man in the city, and I remember you made a great speech that was mightily applauded!"

"Ay, but the enemy had not crossed the Bann

then, and it is a different thing, let me tell you, when the bullets begin to whistle about your head. I was out yesterday, Mr. Orme, and do you know"—here he looked round to see that there was no one within hearing—"I discovered that I was no better than a coward."

"But you stood your ground like a man?"

"Indeed I did no such thing. I dare not tell Elizabeth, but no sooner did I see those devils of Berwick come galloping up, than I even ran like a coward for the walls, and never thought of my duty till I was out of reach of their sword-blades. It was too late to turn back then, had I been so minded. God hath made us all after our own fashion, and he never made me for a soldier."

"All young soldiers feel like that in their first battle," said Gervase, with the air of a veteran. "A fortnight hence you will be as bold as a lion. Mistress Sproule will see that you do not flinch, for I think she could carry arms herself."

"You know my wife, Mr. Orme," said the little man sadly, "and that is one of my main troubles, for I dare not tell her what I have told you. She must needs know the whole story when I came back last night, and my invention would not serve me better than my yard stick yonder. Do you think, sir, that there will be a great deal of work of the same kind?"

"In faith, Simon, I can give you but little comfort," said Gervase, half in amusement, half pitying his evident distress; "these are troublous times we are living in, and hard knocks are in fashion. You must even pluck up courage and show a stout heart in that buff coat of yours. You'll come to like the smell of powder by and by, and instead of running you'll go out to meet them as blithely as the boldest."

"What I have said I have spoken in confidence, Mr. Orme, and should you have speech with my wife on the matter, I know you will say a word in my favour. But I wish with all my heart we could see the end of our troubles. My trade is even ruined, and there is a list of debts for you that will never return me the value of a penny. Colonel Lundy himself owes me eight pounds sterling, which I do not think he will ever return to discharge."

"Indeed I do not think he will, and if that were all he owed us the city would be well quit of him. Are you on duty to-day, Simon?"

"I must turn out at twelve o'clock on the Church bastion," he answered gravely, "and I know not what devil's work I may have to do before the day is over. But I will take what you have said to heart, sir, and hope for the time when I'll have a taste for fighting."

"I'll be there to see," said Gervase, smiling, "and should it give you courage, I'll even blow your brains out should you try to run away."

As Gervase passed up Bishop's-gate street, he could not help laughing aloud at the look of consternation depicted on the face of his little landlord, who had been among the loudest and most eloquent advocates of resistance while the enemy were at a distance.

The morning was bright and clear, with a warm breath of spring in the air that blew across the river. The streets were alive with men hurrying hither and thither; men who carried every imaginable description of musket and side-arms, and wore the most diverse kinds of defensive armour, but men who looked as if they had a work to do and meant to do it. Four companies of Parker's regiment of foot he met on their way to the Bogside, and he was struck by their soldierly bearing and the precision and regularity of their march. From the Royal Bastion a great gun was firing slowly, in reply to the cannon of the enemy that spoke iron-lipped from Strong's orchard on the other side of the river. But what struck him chiefly was that there were neither women nor children abroad; the city looked like a great barrack-yard under arms.

In the Diamond, before the guard-house, he met Colonel Murray in company with Captain Ashe, and Walker, the newly-made governor. Gervase knew the fighting parson of Donaghmore at a glance. The tall, burly figure and frank face full of boldness and resolution spoke of action rather than of study, and the sword that he carried at his side was little in keeping with his clerical calling. As Gervase came up he was engaged in an animated conversation, emphasizing his points with copious gestures and disregarding all interruptions.

"This is the young gentleman of whose adventures I have been telling you but now, Governor Walker," said Murray, placing his hand on his arm. as Gervase doffed his beaver.

"I am pleased to meet with you, sir," said Walker with a fine, pleasant smile. "I learn that your mission miscarried, as I doubt not it was intended it should by those who sent you, and that you alone of your party have returned in safety. We have now, I trust, cleared out the nest of traitors, and brave men can fight without fearing the treachery of their friends. You were of Mountjoy's regiment, I think?"

Gervase bowed in acquiescence.

"Then, sir, you must show that your Colonel was the only traitor in the regiment, and I do not doubt you will. Our men are eager, but they want discipline. I am no soldier myself, but I have set myself to learn, and we want you gentlemen of the sword to teach us. You were not here for the fight of yesterday?"

"I had not the good fortune."

"'Tis ever ill fortune, sir, to be in a fight, but being there, 'tis well to strike hard and stand to it. You would then have seen what it is our soldiers lack. Their zeal outran their discretion."

"And some of them outran the enemy," added Murray, with a shrug of his shoulders, "but I have no doubt Mr. Orme will do his duty. Have you yet heard anything of Captain Macpherson?"

"Not a word. I fear he has fallen into the hands of the enemy or we should have seen him ere now.

He is not a man to let the grass grow under his feet."

"We can ill spare him now, for a stouter soldier I never met, and one with knowledge gathered on half the battle-fields of Europe."

"Was his heart in the cause?—that is the main thing."

"You would not ask the question if you knew the man; Cromwell won Naseby with his fellows."

"H'm!" Walker said, turning away. "Captain Ashe, will you walk as far with me as the Town House? Good-morning, sir."

Murray stood for a moment looking after the tall retreating figure of the old parson, and then turned to Gervase with a smile. "That smacks too much of dissent for the Governor's nose, Mr. Orme. There's a great heart in yon cassock but half of him is only a parson, after all. He would have us drilled from the pulpit steps, and no man may march but to the tune of the prayer-book. A very good tune too, but every man can't step to the time. But I wonder how it has gone with your old captain—I wouldn't lose Macpherson for a regiment."

"I spent a fortnight in his company," said Gervase," and none can know his worth better than I do."

"He will need to make haste if he is alive. In a week not a mouse could creep into the city. Even now, you can see how the enemy's lines are drawn round us, and I can hardly hope he will get through. And they will draw them closer yet, for they will have to starve us out; storm us they cannot. Pray

God, they do not sleep in England. Now, Mr. Orme, your commission has been made out, as I promised, and I would have you carry a message to Colonel Crofton at Windmill Hill. We have much work to do to-day."

Gervase found his first day of garrison life full of interest and excitement. Apparently satisfied with the sharp skirmish of yesterday, the enemy had not attempted any further offensive operations, but lay sullenly in their quarters, or employed themselves in exercising their levies. Occasionally indeed, a great gun sent its iron missive into the city, but the artillery practice was very imperfect, and as yet did little injury.

At Windmill Hill Gervase found four companies under arms in the trenches, but the enemy never came within musket-range, and to Gervase it seemed that the royal army had very little advantage in discipline and order over the silent and determined men who sat in the trenches round him. Ill-armed and ill-clad, the royal troops were wanting in the fine spirit that inspired the defenders of the city. In his own mind Gervase came to the conclusion that whatever might be the issue the struggle would be a long and bitter one.

It was nearly six o'clock when he returned home. Mistress Sproule was standing in the doorway, like a colossal statue of domestic virtue, with two of her eight children clutching at her gown. That something had disturbed her equanimity was evident, for her lips refused to relax in their severity, as Gervase came up with his customary salutation.

"'Tis a pity you had not come an hour ago, Mr. Orme; your supper is gone, and your friend is hardly satisfied. One would think he had not broken bread for a week."

"I had bidden no one to supper," Gervase answered in surprise.

"Then he hath bidden himself and overlooked your invitation. Had Simon been at home, I should have known more about him, but he stopped me short and told me to mind my own business. He hath very ill manners, and says that no man should reason with a woman."

In a moment Gervase surmised that Macpherson had returned. Leaving the exasperated matron at the door in her growing indignation, he rushed up the staircase, and burst into the room. Macpherson was still seated at the table, the empty dishes ranged before him. His long jaws were leaner than ever, and his clothes were torn and covered with dirt. His head was bound up with a handkerchief which was deeply stained with blood.

He rose up, holding out both his hands. "I met with a stout resistance, but nevertheless I have taken possession and wasted your commissariat," he said, with a smile on his brown face. "You have a stout guard below stairs, but an old soldier does not fear the rattle of an empty musket."

"You are a thousand times welcome," Gervase said, pushing him back into his seat, "and all the more as you seem to have fared but ill. We thought you had fallen into the enemy's hands."

"I have been fighting with the wild beasts at Ephesus these two days past, and since we parted I have not tasted food till now. Have you brought the lady safely back?"

"Ay, safe and sound."

"I'm glad of that, I'm glad of that. The thought of her hath weighed on my mind like lead. I could not but think she fancied I was playing the poltroon, and deserting my company when it came to the push of sword. But I could see no other way to help you after I shot yon swaggering ruffian through the head, and that in lawful self-defence. They were a score too many to deal with openly. Right glad am I you brought her through."

"Having looked through a hempen collar by the way," said Gervase. "Let me tell you, Captain Macpherson, it needs cool courage to look the hangman in the face."

"And the rogues would have hanged you? I had not thought of that. But in truth I did not think of you at all. 'Twas the brave wench that I feared for; she that stood up before me in the oak wood, and with the look in her eyes that I never saw in a woman before—told me she trusted me. 'Twas like the handshake of a comrade before the battle. She hath a fearless spirit, and a heavy burden, I doubt not, with the doited old man on her hands, and I know not what trouble besides."

"That burden has been taken away," Gervase said soberly, "We buried him the next morning, hard by where you left him."

"You do not mean they murdered him?"

"No, not that; the loss of the treasure broke his heart, and hardly had you left him when he was dead."

Macpherson rose to his feet, his two hands resting on the back of his chair, and a look on his face as of one stricken by a great fear.

"You are jesting with me."

"In truth, it is no matter for jest. Hardly had you gone than he gave a great cry and fell dead. The loss of what he loved better than life was more than he could bear, and he never moved again after he fell. Then the troopers came up, and had it not been that a gallant gentleman proved my friend, I should not have been here to tell you the tale."

"I knew there was a curse on it," said Macpherson. "A curse on it in his hands, and a curse on it in mine. A day and a night I carried it with me and all the while I felt like one pursued by a legion of spirits clamouring for a man's soul. I could not rest; I could not sleep; and I felt that in the end it must drive me mad. As I lay through the night in the bramble by the river-side, as God is my witness, I could see through the lid the glint of the gold and the shimmer of the precious stones, and I, who never feared before, quaked like a schoolboy at the birch rod. I prayed for light, but I could find no comfort. Then I rose up with my load, for the girl had placed her trust in me, and come what might I was minded that she should find me faithful.

A while after, I had some fighting to do which raised my spirits a little and let out some unwholesome blood. But I have come in empty-handed after all, and have but a pitiful story to tell for one who boasted so bravely of his skill and discretion."

"And the treasure?"

"'Tis safely buried, I trust, where I left it. You see, it happened in this wise: As ill luck would have it I came on a sergeant and two of his company, of Gormanstown's regiment, I think, rifling a poor fellow who had but lately fallen, and catching sight of me through a tangle of briars that I had hoped would screen me, they called on me to stand. I could not do otherwise, for my load would not let me run. That was how I came by my knock—a shrewd one too; but for them, they will never answer to their names again till the muster roll is called at the Judgment. I must have lost my senses for a while, for when I came to reason there were we four lying stretched upon the road, but myself on the top with that devil's box at my feet. With my load under my arm I set off again, but what with the loss of blood, and the enemy gathered round me so closely that I could not see my way through, I even crept into the shelter of a hedge and began to consider what I should do. Then it came into my mind that it were best buried out of sight for the present, and I even dug a hole for it where I sat with my sword blade; and marking the spot with what care I might—indeed, I have the record here—I went on blithely, with a great weight off my mind. That is the complete history of the venture, and I would that it had a different end."

"It was better fortune after all than I had hoped for; but how came you to get in?"

"Oh! that was no great matter. Putting on a bold face, as though no man had a right to question me, I even saluted all that I met, inquiring what way lay Butler's command, as one having urgent business there. It passed very well till a meddlesome captain of horse must needs take me under his protection, and know more of my business than I had a mind he should. I lied boldly and vehemently, which is a matter permissible by the laws of war, and having brought me hard by our lines at the Windmill, I even knocked him down with my fist, and ran for it as fast as my legs would carry me. They might have brought me down with their muskets had they taken time to aim, but though I heard the bullets singing about my ears, never a one touched me, and here I am in no very ill condition, after eating your supper and thanking Heaven for a merciful deliverance. And now let me hear how things fell out with you."

Gervase told his story with little circumlocution, but dwelling, unconsciously, more than seemed necessary in a plain statement of facts, on the courage and devotion of Dorothy Carew, a thing which brought a twinkle into Macpherson's eyes and a grave smile to his lips. Indeed, from the beginning to the end the adventure was hers, and the young soldier was only the companion who had shared her fortune in a humble way. He told how she had won the heart of Sarsfield; how she had broken down the boorish ill-will of Luttrel; and how she had carried herself throughout with a patience and fortitude that a man might envy; and all the while Macpherson watched him under his half-closed eyelids with the same grave smile upon his face. It was evident he was no less interested in the speaker than in the narrative, and when it was done he rose up and placed his hand on Gervase's shoulder, and bade him forget that he had spoken a word in her disparagement. "God hath made few women like her, my lad," he went on, "and had I met such another in my youth, I might not now have been the homeless vagrant that I am. Loyal she is and true, if the face and the eye have any meaning, and her voice hath a tender ring in it that might well touch a man's heart, even if he be an old fool like myself—which indeed I think I am growing. I have come to think of you, Gervase Orme, as a son, I who never had wife or child of my own, and I think here is a woman who might make your life happier than mine has ever been."

"Your conversion is of the suddenest," Gervase said smiling, but the praise of Dorothy brought a warm flush of pleasure to his cheek. His love was a thing so new and so incomprehensible to himself, that he preferred to dwell upon it in secret; and besides, he felt that she was so lifted above him that he dared not trust himself to speak of her. It did not come to him with surprise that Macpherson, whose cynicism he regarded as a matter of course, should have been captivated by her grace and spirit. It was the most natural thing in the world. But when he came to think of himself as her lover, the thought of his own unworthiness grew so great that it seemed to raise a barrier between them that it was a vain presumption to attempt to surmount.

So he passed lightly over Macpherson's suggestion, and assured him that he had not forgotten the warning that he had given him before the journey began. Then, with some solicitude, he insisted on his having his wound looked to, and making use of his own wardrobe as far as it would supply his wants.

The old soldier in his careless camaraderie, was at no time loath either to lend or to borrow, and after his wound (which, he said, proved the thickness of his skull) had been dressed, arrayed himself in a clean shirt and stockings, and then lighted a pipe of fragrant Virginia, to which he had been for some time a stranger.

Gervase in the meantime had with some difficulty prevailed on Mistress Sproule to furnish him with a second supper, and as she placed it on the table she cast a look of indignation on the unconscious Macpherson. She watched him with lowering brows, blowing a cloud of smoke in his placid contentment; then her pent-up feelings broke out. "Marry," she said, "there are some folk who care not what trouble they make in the world. To break into your house, and eat up your meat without even a 'by your leave', may be manners in some parts, but here we call it by a harder name."

"In some parts where I have been," said Macpherson grimly, "they have a bridle for the mouth of the shrew, and lead her down to the Market-place, where she stands for a warning to her neighbours. Your husband would be a happier man did the custom hold here."

Long accustomed to an easy conquest in the domestic battle-field, she was staggered for a moment at this bold attack, but when her surprise was over, the storm broke out with renewed violence, and while Macpherson placed his fingers in his ears, Gervase intervened as a peacemaker with little success. It was only when her passion had completely exhausted itself, that she flung out of the room with a tragic stride.

"The tow's in the fire," said Macpherson. "Man, that's a terrible woman. Have you often to meet a charge like that?"

Gervase laughed good-humouredly at Macpherson's serious countenance. "We have none of us the courage to cross her. Poor Simon fears her more than he fears the bullets of the enemy, and I think I am somewhat in terror of her myself. But she hath her virtues, and I will not hear her wronged."

"I will avoid her for the future like the pestilence. Now finish your supper, or so much as I have left you. I would have you accompany me to Miss Carew, and I think you will be willing enough, for I must give her an account of my stewardship before

I sleep, through how I shall bring myself to tell her what I have done after all my boasting, I do not know. When one has a man to deal with, he can take him by the hand or by the throat, but one cannot use plain speech with a woman."

CHAPTER IX.

OF HOW CAPTAIN MACPHERSON FULFILLED HIS TRUST.

LADY HESTER RAWDON'S house stood not far from the Cathedral, something larger and uglier than its neighbours, with a stone staircase running along the outside, and the lower windows heavily grated with iron bars. Gervase and his companion were shown into a long, low-ceiled room on the ground floor, wainscoted in black oak and looking out on a small garden.

In a corner of the room stood a harpsichord; a piece of fine embroidery lay on the table. On a chair by the window lay an open book with the pages turned downwards. Some spring flowers in a vase gave out a perfume which, somehow, Gervase came to associate with Dorothy, and brought her vividly before him.

Presently she came in herself, clad in a simple black gown without any touch of colour. To Gervase she gave her hand without a word, but with a quiet smile of welcome on her lips, and then she turned to Macpherson, who stood drawn up to his full height, with his hat under his left arm and his hand resting on his sword hilt. "I am very glad to see you," she said. "We talked much of you, Mr. Orme and myself, and I never doubted that we should meet again. But," and she looked at him with inquiring sympathy, "you have been wounded?"

"A mere scratch," he answered hastily. "And before I go further, you will let a rough old soldier say a word, Miss Carew?—though he cannot speak fairly, and in set terms such as please a woman. When we first met I spoke harshly and in anger, for which speech I am sorry now. In my rough journeys I have had knocks that somewhat hardened me, but I ask your pardon if I have in anywise offended you. I can do no more."

"I would not have you speak of that," she answered; "I only remember your service."

"The which I did not render you." Then he went on in evident perturbation: "You see before you one who played the coward and betrayed the trust he compelled you to place in his hands. Had I to go through with it again, it may be I should have done otherwise, but I acted for the best and followed the light I had. I know you will listen to me patiently."

"Surely I will listen to you, but I am certain you have broken no trust of mine."

Gervase retired to the window, while Macpherson went through his narrative without interruption and with an air of self-deprecation that he seldom showed. When he had done, he drew a piece of parchment from his breast and laid it on the table. On one side was written the message that Colonel Lundy had commissioned him to deliver at Enniskillen, on the other a number of lines and points were traced apparently in red ink.

"Now," he said, "that is the whole story, and here is the plan on which is marked, with what skill I could command, the bearings by which the spot may be found. I could indeed walk blindfold thither, but I shall not be here when the time comes. Perhaps Mr. Orme will follow me as I point out to you the meaning of this scratch."

Gervase came up to the table, and Dorothy and he together looked down on the red lines on which the old soldier had placed his forefinger. Then she looked up hastily: "With what have you done this?" she cried.

"Even with the first ink that came to my hand; 'tis none the less plain for that. Now," he continued, "here is the way from the city, and here are the cross-roads which you cannot miss. Fifty paces further from that point bring you to a sycamore. Ten steps due west is the hedge, traced thus. And there at the foot of the wild apple-tree you will find the hole I digged. 'Tis covered with a flat stone and concealed by bracken, but by those who know the sign cannot be missed."

"And I hope," said Dorothy calmly, looking up in Macpherson's face, "that it will never be found. Let it lie buried there for ever. Never let me look on it again. I would give the world that I had never seen it."

Macpherson looked at her in wonder.

"You do not understand me I know, but Mr. Orme does, and I know my secret is safe with him. Truly," she added bitterly, and with a certain wildness, "your chart was well written with blood."

"'Twas the best I could do: I am sorry that it does not please you."

"You mistake Miss Carew's meaning," said Gervase. "She finds no fault with what you have done, and I think you have acted discreetly. But others are concerned in this, and she must not act without consideration."

"However I may act," said Dorothy, "you will promise to say nothing of this till you have my permission; neither to my aunt nor to my brother. They must know nothing of it now. And, Mr. Orme, I know the favour that I ask is great, but I cannot bear the sight of this now; will you keep it till I ask it from you?"

Gervase consented with some misgiving, but had she ordered him at that moment to go in search of the treasure single handed, 'tis likely that he would have done her bidding cheerfully, and gone without a word.

Having no clue to Dorothy's meaning, Macpherson looked upon it as a piece of the whimsical extravagance one always found in a woman, and was content that he had delivered his message, however abruptly, and rid himself of his responsibility. For himself, he had no desire to meddle with family secrets, and a young fellow like Gervase Orme was a far fitter companion to share the confidence of a girl, than a rugged and plain-spoken soldier like himself. It might be there was more than her grandfather's death in the matter, but whatever it was, he would avoid other people's business for the future, and keep the beaten road, where he saw plain ground for his feet.

"Of my own motion," he said, "I will not speak of this thing, and though 'tis a pity to have the bonny stones and brave pieces lying in a ditch side, I would not for their worth have carried them a day longer. I even felt like Judas with the forty pieces—the price of the blood, hanging about his neck."

Dorothy shuddered, and hid her face in her hands.

"All is done now," said Gervase, seeing her distress, "and words will not mend it. Captain Macpherson and myself must even make for the walls presently, where he will find work in plenty to his taste. The guns have been speaking loudly for an hour."

"Nay," said Dorothy rising, "you will not go till you have seen my aunt; she hath been most anxious to thank you for the service you did me. She is seldom able to see strangers, but she is something better to-day, and bade me call her before you left."

Macpherson demurred stoutly and insisted on making his immediate departure, for he felt by no means at home as it was, and foresaw with a feeling akin to dismay, an interchange of meaningless civilities with a silly old woman of rank. But Dorothy would take no refusal; Lady Hester would not forgive her if she permitted them to leave without seeing her, and she was gone before Macpherson had finished his protest.

"This is what comes of dealing with a woman, Gervase, my son," he said, in a mournful tone, apparently still meditating retreat. "I had rather face a clump of pikes than come under the artillery of a woman's tattle. One is bound up hand and foot, and feels his manhood oozing out through the pores of his skin, while he beats his brains for a civil speech and looks in vain for a way of escape. They can talk of nothing I have knowledge of, and I am too old for quips and gallant speeches. But she is a brave lass, and I think I wronged her, so that I must suffer for it now with patience. But for this Lady Hester, a rough old war-horse like myself hath other business in the world than to stand like a page in a lady's chamber and hearken to her gossip. For young fellows like yourself it may answer, but were I out of this——"

His resolution, whatever it may have been, remained unspoken, for at this moment Lady Hester Rawdon came in, leaning on her nephew's arm—a frail old lady much broken with illness, who received Gervase with a show of homely kindness, and strongly expressed her sense of the good-will he had shown toward her niece. Motioning to him to sit down beside her on the couch, she drew from him the story of his recent adventure, and Gervase seeing the interest and pleasure she took in the narrative, entered at some length into the particulars of his journey. Regarding the Vicomte de Laprade she made many inquiries—the Vicomte's mother being her half sister—and regretted the unhappy state of the country that prevented her seeing a lad she was very fond of in his youth. No doubt he was a Catholic, which was to be deplored, but religion should not weaken the ties of kinship. He was of the same age with her nephew Jasper, and a fine lad when she saw him last. That was at Meudon, a great many years ago. There were many changes since then, and she supposed that she would not know him now. These were dreadful times and the roaring of the guns frightened her beyond measure, but there would soon be peace.

So the poor lady rambled on. All the while her nephew stood near without taking any part in the conversation. He was considerably older than Dorothy and very like her in appearance, but without the expression and vivacity which was the great charm of his sister. Gervase thought there was a look of unfriendliness in his eyes, and resented with some inward heat, the supercilious air with which he treated him. Macpherson had stood for some time preserving an awkward silence, until Dorothy withdrew him to the window, and by slow degrees broke down his silence, till he suddenly found himself talking with great ease and friendliness.

It was many years since he had looked so nearly in the face of youth and beauty and listened to the tones of a girlish voice, and who can tell what secret springs of memory had suddenly been unlocked? Certain it is that when Gervase and he made their way to the walls half an hour afterwards, there was an undertone in his voice and a softened look in his eyes that Orme had never heard or seen before.

"There are hard times," he said, "before yon sweet lass, harder than she dreams of, but you and I must help to make them easier if we can. That rambling old woman and that gay spark of a brother will be a poor help to her in the day of her trial. I like not yon lad; his eyes shift too much, and they are ever counting the buttons on your coat while you are trying to find what is the thought in his mind. I'm thinking he would be glad to be out of this, could he carry the old woman's fortune with him. But the lass herself hath a great heart, and if God sees good will make a fit mother to a noble race of bairns."

But Gervase paid very little attention to his speech. The presence of Dorothy and the look she had given him at parting, so rapid but at the same time so complete in perfect confidence, had filled him with happiness, and given him food for contemplation. The old stories that he had read of wandering knights and heroic paladins had come to be fulfilled for him; he had found a cause in which to use his sword, and a lady who was worthy of his devotion; and so a golden vista of great deeds opened out before him, and he saw glory and love at the end of it. We will not quarrel with the young fellow's idle fancies, but leave him with the girl's last words——"You have proved yourself my friend," keeping him awake that night and mingling with the substance of his dreams.

CHAPTER. X.

OF THE STAND IN THE TRENCHES.

"What is the hour?"

"Somewhat after three. The bell in the Cathedral struck the hour as we left the gate. 'Tis very dark."

"And colder than frost. . The wind blows from the river like a stepmother's breath, and dries the very marrow in your bones. On my word, Orme, I thought the relief would never come. Here have I been since the last night, getting what warmth I could from the shelter of the rampart, and keeping these fellows from sleeping on guard, while my own eyes rebelled against this sentry duty and closed in spite of me. I'm sleepy, and hungry, and tired, and am going to take a lesson in swearing from wicked Will Talbot:

"Oh, roll me down the brae and walk me up the hill,
And all the while you carry me, I'm only standing still."

"'Tis well to have a merry heart, Jack."

"And, prithee, why should I not be merry if I choose? Who could be sad with six hours of guard in the twenty-four; a measurable quantity of meat and French butter, with a qualified modicum of very thin beer, and a chance of getting knocked on the head every hour in the day. Is not that enough for one man, my dear Ajax, or will nothing satisfy you? Here we have been for a fortnight at this work, and only twice have we measured swords with the red-coated ruffians yonder, who prefer to bowl us over with their long guns and bury us in the mortar yonder. This soldiering is but dull work."

"We are like to find it brisk enough if all that I hear is true. There is talk in the camp yonder of a general onset on our position here at the Windmill, and when I left, Baker was sending a reinforcement to strengthen the guard. Have you heard aught in front?"

"Not a mouse stirring. Did I think it true, I should even snatch what sleep I could in the earth-works here, and be ready to stand by you when the knocks were going. But following the voice of wisdom for once, I'll even go home to bed and leave you to enjoy that frosty wind by yourself. Should the attack come you'll find me among the first."

Giving a brief word of command to his company, the young fellow went away whistling, and left Gervase Orme to his solitary meditations as he paced up and down the rampart, peering out into the darkness, and devoutly longing for the first streak of sunrise. Windmill Hill was a post of great importance and in some measure the key of the position. The highest point of the river to the south of the city, it entirely commanded the town; and only a fortnight before the enemy had made a bold effort to drive in the guard, and entrench themselves upon it. In this they had failed after a stubborn resistance, and since then the position had been strengthened by throwing up a rampart that ran across the summit of the hill almost to the river. The guards had been greatly strengthened, for the recollection of the first attack had taught the garrison a salutary lesson which they could not afford to throw away. It had become a thing of vital importance that the hill should not fall into the hands of the enemy, and from some source—it was scarcely known what— they had learned that the Irish intended to attack the position in force, and make a bold push once for all, to secure it.

Six weeks of hardship had had their effect on Gervase Orme. He had grown accustomed to danger, and had come to look upon death as an event that happened every day, and might be his own lot to-morrow. It had come to seem natural now that he should waken up in the morning to find his sword at his pillow, and listen all day to the thunder of the guns in the batteries on Creggan and the Waterside. Successful resistance had awakened in him as in others, an intense enthusiasm he was far from feeling the first day he had stood on the walls and watched the white tents stretching out on every side. At that time resistance had seemed almost hopeless; it was their duty to fight for a cause they looked on as sacred; but now they had measured their strength with the foe, and they had proved the valour of the fighting-men who manned the walls and lined the ramparts, and if relief came while there was a barrel of meal in the magazine they would make good their defence.

It was a fine thing to see the alacrity and courage with which the rough yeomen and citizens went into the fight, and the spirit with which they handled their muskets. Grumble at times they would, for horse flesh is but poor meat to the Anglo-Saxon mind; and French butter (only a cheerful pseudonym for tallow) and meal were somewhat apt to turn upon the stomach of a morning. But even the grumblers did their duty, and the cordial of religion was dealt out in plentiful doses in the Cathedral twice a day. It was a sight to see Walker, his duty as a stout Colonel of foot being laid aside for the nonce, mounting the pulpit with his martial air, and drilling his flock in the duty of resistance. When the sermon was over, and they came crowding through the door—men, women, and children—there was a look in their eyes and a catching of their breath, that spoke volumes for the powers of the homely orator and the earnestness of his appeal. There was indeed nothing wanting to inflame their zeal and strengthen their pride. The Celt was in their eyes an inferior and a servile race, and his religion the superstition of the scarlet woman. On them hung the fate of the kingdom, and if Londonderry fell, Enniskillen must also surrender, and Ireland would go with James from the Cove of Cork to Bloody Foreland. Their brethren in England—so they said—would not let them die of want; William of Nassau was a soldier trained in arms who knew the importance of the place they held, and he was not one to let the grass grow under his feet. Any morning they might rise to see a friendly fleet in the river; and they fought on from day to day with the roofs crashing over their heads, and the first pinch of want warning them of what might be in store.

We left Gervase Orme pacing the ramparts with his heavy cloak gathered closely round him, looking anxiously towards the enemy's lines. There was not a sound to be heard; only a light glanced here and there for a moment and then vanished into the darkness. The men lay in the trenches, screening themselves from the sharp wind, for though it was now early in June the nights were cold. It was weary work, this waiting for the morning, for a light that would never break, and an attack that would never come.

Then Gervase seated himself on an empty cask, with his face toward the bitter east wind, and fell to thinking of Dorothy Carew. It was a habit that had grown on him of late, for it was wonderful how it shortened the hours, and relieved the tedium of his guard. He had seen her frequently during the last six weeks, and though no word of love had ever been spoken between them, he had striven to show her that he looked on her as something more than a friend, and he thought that, though with maidenly reserve, she returned his affection. He was seldom able to see her alone, for Lady Hester was always anxious to see the young soldier fresh from duty with his news of how the siege was going; and though Gervase often longed for a tender *tête-à-tête* he seldom managed to secure it. How he had come to evoke the ill-will of Jasper Carew he did not know, but the latter took little pains to conceal his enmity and on more than one occasion, only the presence of his sister prevented Gervase from coming to an open breach with him. He took no part in the defence, and openly laughed at his sister's zeal. And yet Gervase knew that he was no coward, for he had come through several affairs of honour, and pinked his man very creditably. But however much Gervase might have desired his friendship, he saw no other way to peace than to avoid him so far as he could, and let his gibes pass unnoticed when they met. He could see that Dorothy was anxious to atone for her brother's coldness, and that was in itself compensation enough. And as Gervase sat on his cask, and drew his cloak closer about him, he saw again the tender smile in her eyes and felt the pressure of her hand. What mattered this dreary guard and the long watching and the hardship of his life, if she loved him?

So wrapped up was he in his meditations that the sky was all flecked with gray and barred with red, and the morning wind was blowing round him, before he awakened from his dream. The men of his company were walking in twos and threes below him, or were still lying crouched under the shelter of the ramparts. He himself was numb and stiff with cold, and as he rose to stretch his limbs his eye caught sight of the grey tents in the valley below him.

THE STAND IN THE TRENCHES.

The clear note of a solitary bugle was sounding fitfully. The camp was already astir, and away to the left several companies of horse were moving rapidly toward the strand. In a moment his dreams were dissipated and he was keenly on the alert. It seemed to him that a great body of men were being massed in the hollow. Already, as it grew clearer, he could see them gathering round the standards, and the grey glint of steel came fitfully through the morning mists. There was not a moment to lose, for he did not doubt that the attack was about to be made in force, and if they were to hold their ground, it would need every available fighting man the garrison could send out to defend the whole line of the rampart. He could not be mistaken; the attack they had been looking for so long, was about to come at last.

Leaping hastily into the trench, he collected the men of his command. He spoke to them briefly and to the point. "Now," he said, throwing off his cloak and drawing his sword, "Sinclair, you will make for the City with what haste you can. Tell Baker we must stand a general attack, and that the horse are gone toward the river. I think the grenadiers are upon the left moving toward the bog. You, Bowden, will pass the alarm along the line, and I myself will even go forward to reconnoitre, and see more clearly what their meaning is. Now, my lads, see that your priming is fresh, for we must stand to it this day like men."

The note of alarm spread rapidly down the

ramparts, and wherever the little companies were gathered the excitement grew deep and strong, and preparations were made for the coming struggle. There was now no longer any reason to doubt that the enemy were preparing to make a general advance. In the grey dawn they could see dark masses in motion to the right and to the left, and hear the drums beating their lively call, and the note of the bugle ringing out clear and loud.

Dropping from the rampart Gervase crept down the hillside, taking advantage of the straggling line of defence that ran zig-zag down the hill in the direction of the enemy. As he drew nearer and bent his ear to the ground, he could hear the measured tread of marching feet and the ring of iron hoofs. The dawn had come up with a leap; the light was now broad and clear, and lying screened by the shelter of the fence, he could see the different regiments rapidly taking up their position with as much order as the irregularities of the ground would permit. What their strength was he could not rightly estimate, but the regiment before him was Butler's foot, and on the left were Nugent's grenadiers. He could hear the hoarse word of command shouted down the ranks and the rattle of the firelocks as the men shouldered their guns. Already they were in motion. There was not a moment to be lost if the rampart was to be kept that day. With the speed of a deer he made his way back to the lines, calling out as he came up, and took the deep trench at a bound.

"They are coming," he said, clambering up the breastwork; "they are coming, and will be up in a quarter of an hour. We must give them a warm welcome here. Bring out the powder, and remember to fire low; we are not shooting snipe to-day, and must not waste a shot."

He looked anxiously toward the city for the support that had been promised, for he knew the little body of men who surrounded him could not stand for a moment against the force in front of them. But the city was all astir. The Cathedral bell was pealing out its warning summons, and already a stream of men was pouring from the Bishop's-gate without order or formation. And they were not a moment too soon, for the enemy came pouring up the hillside, a dark, crimson wave that seemed to undulate, swaying with a slow uncertain motion, as it advanced.

The men stood within the shelter of the ramparts clutching their muskets and watching far below them the enemy advancing slowly to the assault.

"I'm thinking I could put a brace of slugs into yon young cockerel with the feathers in his bonnet," said a tall, raw-boned man of Down, glancing along the barrel of the fowling piece he carried, and turning to Gervase with an inquiring look. "It were a pity not to let them have a foretaste of what they'll get by and by."

"You must not draw a trigger till they are close up; then you may bring him down if you will. God be praised! here come the reinforcements. I'm glad to see you, Colonel Baker, with all my heart. They would scarce have waited for you had you tarried."

"'Tis very well done, Mr. Orme. You deserve no small praise for your watchfulness. This had been a serious business had they caught us napping, but there is not a man in the camp yonder who is worth a pinch of powder, and they come on like so many drunken drabs. Now we will show the rogues what they may expect when they call on honest men at home."

Rapidly and with a joyful alacrity he drew up the men into three ranks, rank behind rank, and bade them look carefully to the loading of their pieces, and not to waste their shot. Then he directed the first rank that they should wait till the enemy came within forty paces of the rampart, and when he gave the word they should fire their volley steadily and all together; that having fired the second rank should take their place, and that they in turn should give way to the third. The simple measure was easily understood, and the men smiled in silence as they handled their muskets and waited for the word.

"The women are coming to see how you have done, my sons," Baker said, "but I think you will not want their help to-day. Yonder fellows are but three to one; you could spare them greater odds than that and beat them still. I would wager a golden guinea never a man of them will touch the rampart."

The enemy had advanced to within a hundred yards of the ramparts and then halted to complete their formation, which had been broken by the straggling fences of which we have already spoken. The silence behind the earthworks had been so complete that they looked for an easy victory over the guards on duty there. It was now broad day, and the defenders could see all along the line their enemies hastening to the attack. With a loud cheer the latter advanced at the double, and were close upon the ramparts when they were met by a sudden spurt of fire that ran simultaneously along the line, and by a shower of bullets that brought them to a stand. But the check was only momentary. Believing that they had now to deal with empty barrels, they sprang forward with redoubled ardour, and were within a few paces of that fatal rampart when a second time the leaden hail smote them with withering effect. They halted in confusion and fired wildly into the smoke-covered curtain. Above the clamour and din rang out the voice of Baker—

"Steadily, my children, they are nearly satisfied. Advance! Fire!"

And the men of Londonderry with sublime faith in their captain and with the steadiness of men on the parade ground, took their place and gave another volley. Then the foe broke up into confusion and lost all semblance of formation. Many of them threw away their muskets and made what speed they could for the rear; while others encouraged by the shouts of their officers and still full of fight, made for the ramparts, and leaping into the trench climbed up the curtain with muskets clubbed. But they had little chance of success. All along the line they were met by an enemy flushed with the first success and having the advantage of a superior position. In some places, indeed, they succeeded in topping the line, and a hand to hand fight took place, but they could not keep their hold on the ground they had won. They were driven back into the trench with their assailants on the top of them. But for the most part the garrison stood stoutly by the ramparts, meeting their enemy with the muzzles of their guns and a steady fire.

Then Baker turned to Gervase with his face all aglow. "Should you live a thousand years you will never see a prettier fight than that. 'Tis over now, for we have taken the heart out of them and they will not form again. I pray God we have done as well elsewhere, but I fear the horse have pressed us harder by the Waterside. You must not tarry here. Away thither like the wind, and tell Gladstanes that I can spare him a half dozen companies if he need their help."

However reluctant to leave till he had seen the end, Gervase obeyed and made what haste he could down the line of the ramparts towards the strand. All along the earthworks the men were standing steadily to their guns, but down by the river the fight was going hard.

Two hundred horse, gentlemen, for the most

part, of high spirit and rank, had taken a solemn oath, as the chroniclers say, to top the line or perish in the attempt. Gervase came up as they were about to make the charge and delivered his message to the stout soldier who commanded there. "Not another man do I want," was the answer; "we have enough for glory. Now, my lads, here they come, and let them have it!"

Carrying faggots before them with which to fill up the trench, the horse came on at a gallop, the steel swords and scarlet coats making a gallant show. Dashing up within thirty yards of the ramparts, they suddenly wheeled to the right, and made for the open space between the rampart and the river, intending to take the enemy on the flank. As they came on they were met by a storm of bullets that seemed without effect, for barely a man went down. Then Gervase heard a familiar voice call out—the deep trumpet tone of Macpherson: "They carry armour under their gay clothes. Aim at the horses and we'll take the riders afterwards."

But the order had come too late. Already they had passed the line of defence and gained the open ground within. Hastily clambering out of the trench, the defenders rushed to meet them with pikes and muskets, in a compact and stubborn body.

Gervase was looking about him for some more serviceable weapon than the small sword he carried, when he saw Simon Sproule making prodigious efforts to lift himself out of the trench under the weight of his heavy firelock. The face of the little linen-draper was ghastly pale, the perspiration was running in streams down his face, and his eyes were like those of a startled hare. Reaching him his hand, Gervase helped him to his feet.

"Now," he said, "steady yourself and play the man. If you attempt to flee, which I verily think you do, I'll even run you through the body, and tell your wife why I did it."

"Never fear for me, Mr. Orme; I'll stand by you like a man; but this is a fearful trade for a citizen. D—do you think they'll run?"

"We'll do our best to make them," answered Gervase, picking up a pike; "follow me, and do the best you can."

"Never fear for me."

The horsemen came on gallantly, but could make no impression on the iron wall that met them at every point. The horses went down in dozens, but the riders leaping to their feet still strove to make good the vow they had taken, and fought with a stubborn spirit. On every side they were surrounded by that cruel wall of pikes and scythes, and a spirit as stubborn as their own. Then they were broken up into little knots, and it became a hand to hand fight in which the advantage was altogether on the side of the garrison.

Gervase had lost sight of Simon Sproule in the melée, and, indeed, had altogether ceased to think of him, having business enough of his own to attend to at present. As yet the fortune of the fight hung in the balance. Back to back, and shoulder to shoulder, stood the men of the garrison, handling their muskets and pikes with the steadiness and precision of veterans. Never since the siege began and the first shot had been fired, had there been a fight like this. It was dry work and warm work, and Gervase felt his throat baked like a kiln. He heard some of the men crying round him for water and saw them go staggering, faint and exhausted, to the rear. And though Gervase did not see it there was help for them there. The women of the city, who had been watching with anxious hearts from the walls, could bear the suspense no longer, and regardless of the bullets and cannon shot from across the river, had come down to their aid with food and drink. It was even said, and the chroniclers record it with a touch of pride, that they took their share in the conflict, and fought with stones with as bold a heart as the stoutest among the men. Certain it is that they put new life into the weary fellows who were tired of hacking at the steel breastplates and head-pieces, and who for the most part had not tasted food since the evening before. It seemed to Gervase that the slaughter of horses and brave men would never cease. No sooner was one down than another had taken his place, hewing for his life at those pikes that would not bear back an inch.

"Stand close and strike home," a voice would cry, and a little knot of horsemen went rolling to the ground. There was now no hope of escape for them. A dense phalanx of pikemen and musketeers had drawn between them and the entrance to the lines. Back to back each man fought only for his life. No quarter was given or asked, but each man went down where he stood.

For nearly two hours by the sun the battle had been raging, and the end was now at hand. Gervase had been carried in the melée down toward the river, and was making his way back toward the ramparts among the slaughtered horses and dead and wounded men, when he saw half a dozen pikemen surrounding a dismounted horseman, who was making gallant play with his sword. Anxious to save his life Gervase was about to interfere, when he heard the sound of his voice raised in disdain of his assailants; "Five to one! *ventre de Dieu*, I care not for you all. A gentleman of France has never learned to yield."

It was the voice of his friend De Laprade. Gervase was just in time; another minute and he would have been too late. Pushing his way into their midst, he warded off a blow that was aimed at the Vicomte, and loudly commanded his assailants to forbear. Covered as he was with blood and grime, De Laprade did not at first recognize him, but still stood on the defensive.

"This gentleman is my friend," cried Gervase, placing himself before him and guarding him with the pike he still carried. "I will not have him touched."

Then as the men fell back willingly enough, the

Vicomte recognized his deliverer, and flinging away his sword, held out his hand. "There is no need for this now," he said, "and I could not surrender it even to you. This is the second time, Mr. Orme, I have to thank you for my life. I grow weary of your kindness."

"I am very troublesome without doubt," Gervase answered with a smile. "I hope you have not been touched."

"Not the prick of a pin point, but these men of yours fight like devils and against all the rules of war."

"They are learning their trade," Gervase answered, "and you cannot expect beginners to be perfect. But they have made a complete rout of your horse, and left but few of them to carry back the story to the camp. They have got Butler yonder, and are carrying him to the town."

"Whither, I suppose, I must bear him company? I am weary of the camp and would prefer to visit your city for a change. You do not eat your prisoners?"

"It has not come to that yet, but I think it may. Now, Vicomte, if I can do aught to lighten your captivity be assured I will do my best to that end. But in the meantime, I must send you in with the guard as my work is not yet finished."

"Put yourself to no inconvenience for me," said the Vicomte cheerfully, "I am quite content."

Placing De Laprade in custody of the guard which had already secured the other prisoners, and telling them that he was under obligations to the gentleman, whom, he hoped, they would treat with consideration, Gervase went to assist in looking after the wounded.

Only three or four of the horsemen had succeeded in cutting their way back to the camp, and it was a matter of congratulation that so complete a victory had been won with so little loss. A great victory, won in the open field against the very flower of the enemy's cavalry and with no great superiority of numbers, was a thing of which they might be fairly proud. The women were looking after those who had fallen, many of whom had crawled back to the trench and were waiting there to be carried to the city. A crowd of soldiers were gathered round their colonel, who was reading them a striking homily on the lessons of the day.

Gervase did what he could for the brave fellows who were lying round him, and was about to make his way back to the city, when he came upon Mistress Sproule looking the picture of despair.

"Oh! Mr. Orme, for the love of God, have you seen Simon anywhere? I'm told he was here among you in the very front of the fighting, but I cannot find him yonder, and I cannot find him here."

Then Gervase remembered having helped the little citizen out of the trench, and though he did not think there was much liklihood of his being very forward in the melée, he was concerned to hear that he had not made his appearance to receive his wife's congratulations on their successful stand, as he probably would have done had he been in the land of the living.

"I saw him," he answered, "when we were going into the fight, but I have not seen him since. Never fear for Simon; you will find him safe and sound, I have no doubt. He will have gone back to the city."

"That he hath not—he's killed, I tell you. Had he been alive he would have been yonder where the Colonel is preaching his sermon. He was ever fond of preaching."

Gervase was heartily sorry to think the little man should have been knocked on the head, and did all he could to comfort his inconsolable spouse. "Come with me," he said, "and I'll show you where I left him. We'll make inquiries by the way, and you'll find him, I warrant, safe and sound, as I say."

But no one had seen Simon either in the fight or afterwards, nor could anyone tell what had become of him, though he was well known for a courageous and eloquent little man, ever forward with bold counsels. Then they came to the trench where Gervase had lifted him up with his musket on his shoulder, and as they stood there looking up and down, Gervase caught sight of a figure lying half hidden under the shelter of the rampart. Leaping into the trench he ran down and bent over the prostrate body. The face was lying buried in the arms, and the feet were drawn up almost to the chin. Beside him lay his musket. There was no doubt of his identity; it was Simon Sproule. Gervase was almost afraid to touch him; then he bent down and turned him slightly over.

The little man raised his face with the fearful look in his eyes that Gervase had seen before. "Don't hurt me," he cried, "I surrender peacefully. Why, God bless me! Mr. Orme, is it you? Is it all over, sir? and have we held our own? It hath been a dreadful day. I do not think I shall ever walk again."

"Your wife is here to look for you, Simon," Gervase said, with a gravity he found it hard to maintain; "she will look after your wound; where is it?"

"Oh! it is even all over—from the crown of the head to the sole of the foot. This hath been a terrible time for me. Thank God! Elizabeth, you have come to see the last of me."

Raising himself upon his elbow, he looked at his wife with so forlorn and piteous an expression that Gervase imagined for a moment that he was wronging him by his suspicions, and that the little man had in reality been wounded. It never for a moment occurred to the mind of his wife that he had crept under the parapet to be out of the way of evil, and it was with grief and consternation that she began to investigate his injuries. With the aid of Gervase he was lifted out of the trench, and though no wound could be found on his person that would account for his condition, his wife continued to ply him with questions which he as resolutely refused to answer.

"I think," he said, after a while, "I shall try to stand. I thought my back was broken, but the feeling hath come back into my extremities, and I may yet recover the use of my faculties. Thank God for our merciful deliverance!"

"Had you been killed, Simon," said his wife, "I should have grieved sorely, but it would have been my consolation that you fell in the way of your duty."

"Truly that is the case," her husband answered in the same tone, "but I have, I hope and trust, been mercifully spared to you and the children. I think, though, I have got this day what will shorten my arm for the future. I even fear I have seen my last fight."

"I am thinking," said his wife, whose strong common sense was gradually overcoming her alarm, "that you are more frightened than hurt. I would just like to know how it came that we found you in the trench with never a scratch on your body?"

"And you'll know that," said Simon, plucking up heart and sending his imagination on an airy flight, a course his mind would seldom take.

"You will remember, Mr. Orme, how you and I were even plunged in the thick of it, with those swearing devils swinging their long swords and cracking their pistols about our ears. I saw you borne forward and like to come to evil, but I could not help you, strive as I might. I had work enough of my own to save my head, and I and some others—who they were I know not—were borne back here. We made a stout defence, but I was struck or pushed from behind and only remember falling back heels over head into the trench thinking I should never see wife or children again. And now, God be thanked! we have gained a great victory, and that let none gainsay."

"The day is hardly over," said Gervase, who could not restrain his amusement; "they are still pushing us hard in the ramparts down by the Bogside, and I heard a whisper that our men had been driven in there. If you feel able we might go thither and see if we cannot strike a brave blow together."

"The Lord forbid—I mean—that is—I have had my share of this day's fight, and so look you, Mr. Orme, I say with all courage, I think I'll even turn my steps homeward, if my wife will lend me her arm, and will not keep you waiting here. You are young and lusty, and hot blood must have hot blood."

Mistress Sproule who was herself so courageous, that she was unable to suspect cowardice in others, still imagined that Simon had sustained some internal injury, and with great tenderness and solicitude took him under her arm and led him to the city.

This was a memorable day in the annals of the siege. The men of the garrison had fought with heroic courage, and only in the intrenchment by the Bog had there for a moment been any doubt as to the result. There, indeed, the defenders had been taken by surprise, and the grenadiers had gained possession of the trenches, but only to hold them for an hour. That night the bell in the Cathedral rang out a joyous peal, and hearts that were beginning to despond took fresh courage.

Starvation and disease were now the only enemies they feared, but as they gathered on the walls that night and shook one another by the hand in joyful congratulation, they were unable to foresee the horror and despair that lay before them and the suffering they had yet to undergo.

Gervase had supped early and was about to retire to bed, when, with a humble knock, Simon Sproule opened the door and came into the room. "Elizabeth thinks I am safe in bed," he said apologetically, "but I could not go to sleep till I had seen you. I would not ask you to strain your conscience, but I will take it as a favour if you will tell her that I have done my best, which is but the plain and simple truth."

"But how can I do that, Simon?"

"With a full heart, sir. I did my best though I'm free to admit, it was far from well. I can march with the bravest and carry my musket like a man, but when the bullets begin to fly, and I catch sight of those murdering sword-blades, the Lord knows my knees are loosened under me and my heart dies in my breast. And all the while I would, if I might, be up and playing the hero, but I cannot. 'Tis a fearful position for an honest man to be placed in; my wife who is as bold as a lion itself thinks there is not a braver man in the city, and the neighbours that I have lived among all my life, cry out 'There goes the gallant Sproule,' and all the while I'm but a pitiful coward. I declare to God this life will kill me, Mr. Orme, and I want your aid and counsel——"

"Make a clean breast of the matter, Simon, and tell them how you feel."

"No, that I cannot do now. I have boasted like the Philistine and talked loudly like a man of war and how can I, who am an elder in my church and an honest burgher that may sometime be an alderman, confess that I am but a liar and a braggart. I could never hold up my head again among my neighbours; and for my wife—no, Mr. Orme, I cannot do it."

"Then I am afraid I cannot help you. You know", and Gervase smiled significantly, "you have been wounded, and such wounds are ever long in healing."

"A month?" Simon asked doubtfully.

"I trust to heaven less than that, but even a month if need be."

"You have struck the mark for me and saved my credit," cried Simon joyfully. "'Twill be hard work but there is no help for it. And you will lend me your countenance as far as your conscience will let you?"

"Nay," said Gervase, "I cannot be a partner in your fraud, but no man will know from me that you are not as stout as Murray himself, and that you have not got a wound as deep as the well of

St. Colomb. I can go no further than that. Now, Simon, away to bed, for Mistress Sproule must not find the wounded knight keeping his vigil here."

"Remember, Mr. Orme, I rely on your discretion," cried Simon, halting for a moment at the door; "and I think with your help I shall be able to save my reputation."

CHAPTER XI.

OF A SERIOUS COMMUNICATION.

The prisoners who had been taken by the garrison had been for the most part confined in Newgate, but several gentlemen of rank had been permitted on giving their parole to dwell at large with private persons in the city.

Among the latter was the Vicomte de Laprade. No sooner had Lady Hester Rawdon learned that her nephew was a prisoner than she insisted on his being brought to her house, and De Laprade willingly exchanged the confinement of his prison for the society of his cousin and the comparative freedom of her house. With his ready power to adapt himself to his circumstances he was soon at home, and his gay songs and cheerful wit enlivened for a time the gloom that was gradually settling down on the household in common with the rest of the city. But even the lively humour of the Vicomte was unable to withstand the horror and distress that surrounded them on every side and deepened day by day. The pressure of famine, as silent as it was terrible, began to make itself sorely felt. Pestilence that had been lurking in the byways of the city, spread on every side, and all through the month of June the shells were crashing through the roofs and ploughing up the streets. The hope of relief that had burned steadily for a while was now growing fainter and fainter. Early in June three ships had come up the river as far as Culmore, but finding the fort in possession of the enemy, had not attempted to dispute the passage. And again, a little later, the garrison had seen from the Cathedral tower the friendly fleet far down the Lough, and had watched them with anxious hearts, till they saw them riding of Three Trees in the western glow of that summer evening. In the morning the sails were gone, and now the enemy had thrown a boom across the river which shut out the passage to the sea. But still the men of the garrison stood by the walls and manned the great guns and handled their muskets with a cheerful courage. There were traitors, no doubt, who deserted to the enemy, and traitors who murmured and plotted secretly; but for the most part the citizens stood loyally by their leaders.

Gervase Orme had suffered with the rest. He had seen poor Simon Sproule bury two of his children, and all the humour out of it, had listened to the heart-broken little man declare that God had visited him for his cowardice. The wasted faces and hollow cheeks that he met began to haunt his dreams; it became his only relief to lose himself in action and forget the horrors he had seen. His visits to the Rawdon household lightened the gloom a little. Dorothy bore her troubles with a quiet strength that put his manhood to shame, and alone in the household declared that the garrison should keep their guard while one stone stood upon another. Since De Laprade's coming, Gervase's visits had not been so frequent, for it was now impossible for him to find Dorothy alone during the day. The light badinage of the Vicomte jarred on his nerves, and it might be without knowing it he had become jealous of his presence. For the Vicomte's admiration of the girl was open and declared and though he treated her with a quiet deference, it was plain he would willingly have surrendered his cousinship for a closer relation still. Dorothy appeared unconscious of his advances and turned away his flattery with a quiet smile.

Gervase had not called for several days, and had not seen any member of the household during that time. He was surprised to receive a note in Dorothy's hand, asking him to call upon her during the evening, if his duties permitted him. It was the first letter he had ever received from her, and though he could not surmise its cause, his heart beat somewhat faster in his breast, as he pressed it to his lips in the quiet of his room. Yes, it was Dorothy's hand, like herself, very strong and free, yet full of grace; and the words. "Yours in confidence, Dorothy Carew," sent him forthwith into a pleasant reverie full of tender hopes.

All day he went about his work with a light and buoyant heart, with the precious missive out of which he had read so much carefully buttoned up in his breast, and did his duty none the worse for thinking of the girl who wrote it. When he called he was shown into the room by Jasper's servant Swartz, and Dorothy was waiting to receive him.

"I hope, Miss Carew," said Gervase, "there is nothing wrong—that Lady Hester is not worse?"

"My aunt is very well," Dorothy answered, "but a little nervous and excited. This is a trying time for her, but she bears up wonderfully. I did not think she could have endured so much with so great patience."

"And the Vicomte?"

"Nay, he is well. My brother has lately kept much to his own room, and Victor has grown tired of our society and joins him often there. How they spend their hours I hardly know, but I think they both are fond of play, and give themselves to cards. Your hours are spent otherwise, Mr. Orme."

"Yes," Gervase answered, "but you see I am a soldier and have my work to look to."

"And why should all men not be soldiers?" said the girl excitedly. "If a woman might carry arms—but this is wild talk, and you know I do not mean it. What news is there to-day?"

"Nothing of much importance: the enemy have hardly fired a shot, but I hear there is talk of an expedition to-night, I know not whither. As for the ships, they have not been seen since Thursday, but the wind is from the north and they may be here to-morrow."

"If Colonel Kirke should be another traitor?" Dorothy said; "one hardly knows whom to trust."

"I hope," Gervase answered, "you will never find me false."

"I do not think I shall, and that is why I sent for you to day. Will you come with me into the garden, for we may be interrupted here."

Gervase followed her out through the open window and down the path, wondering what confidence she was about to impose in him that required to be so carefully guarded. They came to a little, open space of smooth lawn where she stopped short and looked round her cautiously.

"I have thought much of this," she said, "and I know no one but yourself to whom I can look for advice. I thought, indeed, of Captain Macpherson, but I did not know how he might act, and was afraid to trust him. What I am going to say I speak to yourself alone, and must be whispered to no other till you have my permission. Will you promise that?"

Gervase consented, hardly knowing what he promised, but seeing only the look of entreaty in her eyes.

"No matter what you feel to be your duty?"

"If it does not touch my honour nor the safety of the city."

"Then I cannot tell you, for I do not know. Surely," she went on pleadingly, "you can trust me, Gervase Orme? I stand alone and have none to counsel me, and—and I thought you were my friend. Surely you can trust me?"

"Every drop of blood in my veins is at your

"SHE STOPPED SHORT AND LOOKED ROUND HER CAUTIOUSLY"

service, and though it may be weak and wrong and we may both regret it, I promise."

She smiled a little sadly, and said with a touch of her old humour, "I had rather you had not promised, but you cannot go back on your word now. Do you think," she said, putting her hand to her breast and looking round her, "do you think there are traitors in the city?"

"Indeed I think there are," Gervase answered, "but we watch them narrowly and they do little harm. They would stir up rebellion if they might, but the Town-Major keeps them well in hand."

"But I mean more than that. Do you think there are any in the city who hold communication with the enemy?"

"It may be there are, but I hardly see how they could carry out their treachery. The walls are strictly guarded, and the men on the outposts are faithful and true; it were a bold thing to attempt it."

"Then tell me what you think of this."

Putting her hand into her bosom, she drew out a small scroll of paper and placed it in his hands. Gervase looked at her in amazement.

"Read it, and tell me what you think of it."

Gervase took the paper, and his astonishment deepened as he read:

"*'June 9. Pass the bearer through the lines. He is doing faithful service. Given under our hand. Hamilton.*'

"Miss Carew, where did you get this? If the man who held this paper be in the city, he is a traitor and a spy, and we should not lose a moment in discovering his villainy."

"I knew you would use words like these. But there is something more. Three days ago, Mr. Orme, I found this paper on the staircase. Now you know my secret and why I sent for you."

"Perhaps the Vicomte——" Gervase began.

"Nay, nay, you see the date, and my cousin Victor is still a man of honour. He has given his parole, nor would he break it for the world. It almost breaks my heart to say it, but I feel that this is my brother; I saw him searching for it where I found it, and he would have questioned me about it had he dared. And now I know why he left his room at night and seldom returned before the morning. What is to be done?"

Gervase knit his brow and stood thinking. If Dorothy was right, her brother was a traitor and in the habit of supplying the enemy with information. It was clearly his duty to report the matter to the authorities. But on the other hand he had given his word, however rashly and inconsiderately, from which he could not withdraw, and stood pledged to silence. He could not use the woman he loved as a witness against her brother and destroy him by her hands; he shrank in pain at the thought of such a course. Had it not been for the mysterious midnight rambles, the passport might perhaps have been explained. Hamilton had been in the habit of giving passes to persons in the city who had interest at head-quarters, but this was of another sort. If Jasper

Carew was the bearer, and that seemed evident, then he must be a traitor in active communication with the enemy.

"It is hard," Gervase said, "to know what to do, but I think you may let me deal with this. There is no need at present that any other person should know what has come to your knowledge, but meanwhile keep the paper safely, and tell me if your brother leaves the house at night. I will try to save him in his own despite, and for your sake and his own, because he is your brother, will watch him closely. Remember that you only suspect his guilt, and it may be you judge him wrongly."

"This is more than suspicion," said Dorothy holding up the passport. "Shall I tell him I have found it?"

"There is no need for that; we cannot undo what has been done, but we can prevent him doing harm in the future. Do not let this grieve or distress you. Your brother sees things in a different light from you and me, and while circumstances have kept him here, his heart is still with the enemy. He makes no secret of it."

But he could not drive Dorothy from the simple fact. "But to play the spy! To steal out by night, and to lie hidden through the day while brave men were fighting, and a great cause is being lost or won! He is no brother of mine. Say no more or I shall think——"

"Only this, Miss Carew, that as long as I live I shall not forget the confidence you have placed in me, and I shall do what I can to show that I am not wholly unworthy of it. This is no time or place to say more than that. If it were in my power to save you any pain——"

"I am sure," she said frankly, "you would do me a service; I know you are my friend."

As he took her hand and led her into the house, she turned to him and said, "You must not ask too great a price for all you have done for me when I come to pay you the debt I owe you."

"One word will repay it all," Gervase answered, about to forget the moderation he had promised himself to observe, when she suddenly withdrew her hand and entered the room before him. There was a certain restraint in her manner now that was foreign to her native frankness, and she kept Gervase strictly to his budget of news, and prevented him from again entering on any personal topic. Presently they heard De Laprade's voice in the hall, and he came in followed by Jasper Carew.

"Ah! ma belle cousin, we tire of one another and come to you to bring us peace. M. Orme, you do not often come to visit—what do you call it, my cousin?—valour in tribulation."

"Vice in bonds," growled Jasper, looking moodily at his sister.

"The Vicomte thinks his visit is growing tedious, Mr. Orme," said Dorothy, "and would be back among his friends. He has now exhausted all the gaieties of Londonderry."

"If every prison had so fair a jailor," answered

the Vicomte, "I should prefer captivity to freedom, but my jailor prefers to leave me to the society of her kinsman, whose virtues are exalted and whose graces are—what you see."

Jasper turned his back and walked over to the window where he stood beating with his fingers upon the panes. In a few minutes Orme walked over and joined him.

"There is a matter, Mr. Carew," he said in a low tone, "on which I would speak with you in private."

Carew lifted his eyes furtively, and looked at him with a questioning air. He was about to speak but hesitated as if in doubt, and then motioning to Gervase to precede him, followed him into the garden.

"Now, sir," he said, turning round, "what is the matter of mystery that cannot be spoken before my sister and kinsman? I think you take too much upon you."

"I shall pass by your discourtesy, for I have come to you in all kindness, as one anxious for your welfare. What I wished to say to you is this, and I will put it briefly. The night airs are dangerous to the health, Mr. Carew, and should be avoided for the future."

Carew turned pale for a moment, but the moody composure that was natural to him remained. Gervase could see from his eyes that he would have been dangerous had there been a fitting opportunity, but the window was open near them, and De Laprade was watching them where they stood.

"I do not apprehend your meaning, sir; or is this a further instance of your damned impertinence?"

"I have no wish to be offensive, but I will put the matter in another form, and if you fail to take my meaning, you must yourself take the consequences. It has been said," Gervase went on calmly, "that there are certain persons in the city, even gentlemen of rank, who are in correspondence with the enemy. Rumour is ever full of exaggeration, but the name of one at least is known," here he paused, "and others may be suspected. Perhaps you had not heard of this. But remember, sir, we will not quarrel, for I make no charge against you. And again I tell you that they who are not on duty should not walk of nights."

"We cannot quarrel here, or by heaven! I would even kill you where you stand."

"Neither here nor elsewhere," Gervase answered imperturbably. "I have given you a friend's advice, with all a friend's sincerity, and wish you well. Your prudence will direct you in your future conduct."

Gervase left him as he was about to speak and re-entered the house, where he shortly after took his leave and returned to his duty at the outposts.

CHAPTER XII.

OF A WARM MORNING'S WORK.

THE next morning Gervase was lying longer abed than usual, having had a double share of duty the night before. when he was awakened by the sound of Mistress Sproule's voice raised high in expostulation and anger. Of late she had lost much of her alacrity and it was only on great occasions and against those to whom her antipathy was strong, that the old fighting spirit manifested itself.

"The poor lad shall not be awakened, I tell you. He does the work of three, and you can see that he is even wearing himself to death, if you can see anything. When he first came to live in my house he had a cheek like a rose, and now he goes about like an old man as crossgrained as yourself. This blessed morning he will have his rest, if Elizabeth Sproule can keep you out."

Then Gervase heard the low tones of a man's voice endeavouring to reason with her. But the honest woman was not to be driven from her position. "Not for all the colonels or governors who ever wore sword or sash. He has neither wife nor mother to look after his welfare, and though he is a gentleman I love him nearly like one of my own.

For a week you have kept the poor lad marching and watching, and you are one of the worst of them, Captain Macpherson."

Gervase smiled where he lay, for he dearly loved a battle royal between the two, in which the victory usually lay with the weaker. Macpherson had gone grimly to the attack, but he had ended by falling nearly as much under her power as her husband himself.

"You are very right, Mistress Sproule," Gervase heard the voice of the old soldier say, "and though it is an urgent matter, he will have half an hour more. You are right to be careful for him, and I like you none the worse for your watchfulness. It may be you will let me sit down within till he wakens?"

"That I will not. And you may even go whither you came from and tell them that."

But Gervase, who had been greatly amused at his friend's conciliatory tone, thought it time to interfere, and called out that he was awake and would see him.

"You see how well I am guarded," he said, as Macpherson came into the room, "and I think you did not dispute the passage very warmly. The enemy was too sharp for you."

"I have been learning my own weakness," answered Macpherson, sitting down on the bed. "Now, my dear lad, how is the world going with you? I would that I did not see those deep lines on your young face, and the youth dragged out of you before your manhood has well begun. Did I not tell you what it was to stand behind stone walls, and hope against hope for the relief that would never come, and see the tender women and children stricken down without help or pity?"

"Nay, Macpherson, you are ill or you would not talk thus."

"Indeed, I think I am, and I am growing old and childish. But I have been mad or worse for a week. With the deep water to the quays, and the good ships yonder with brave hearts on board of them, to think of what might be done and is not! 'Twas all very well," he went on bitterly, "for Kirke, the lying rogue, to dragoon the poor ploughmen who stood gallantly by Monmouth, but 'tis hard to think that for want of a little courage we should die here like dogs. Better throw open the gates and let them murder us where we stand, than fight for those who will not help us."

"This is but wild talk," said Gervase.

"Truly, I know that, and I would be apt to shoot another through the head did he prate as I have done, but twelve hours' want of food and rest have somewhat weakened me."

Gervase sprang from his bed, and hastily dressing himself set out his scanty breakfast, for meat and meal had become precious, and he could not afford to waste them. "There is enough for both of us," he said, "and there is still tobacco for your pipe. The guns are going merrily yonder, and we'll set ourselves to work as merrily here. We march to the tune of 'No Surrender.'"

Macpherson smiled at the young man's simulated gaiety, and set himself down beside him to their frugal meal. When he had finished, he lighted his pipe and took a more hopeful tone. "I have not yet told you," he said, "why I came here this morning, but the day is young and we have two good hours before us yet. We had a brave night of it."

"A raid on the fish-house?" Gervase inquired. "I heard an expedition was forward, but I did not know that you were out. Have you succeeded?"

"In truth," Macpherson answered, "we came off better than I hoped. But the fish had never been caught that we hoped to catch, and we shot our nets in vain. Having given up hope of Kirke and his ships, the Fourteen thought we might open up communication with Enniskillen, and Walker found a lad who thought he knew the way, and had the heart to make the journey. So having first set the story going that we purposed making a push for the fish-house, we waited until dark, and then pushed off up the river with the purpose of landing the lad outside the enemy's lines. So there we were in the dark, Murray and myself and some fifteen others of the die-hard sort, holding by the gunwhale, and listening to the Irish mounting their guard and singing their idle songs. It passed very well till we got as far as Evan's Wood, and then by ill luck the moon must come out and ruin us wholly. They caught sight of us there in the boat pulling hard in mid-stream, and then a great gun sent the shot driving past our ears like ducks in winter. They kept up the fire from the shore, but the night was, as you know, dark and stormy, and the moon that had given us so ill a start, went down behind the clouds again. I was strong for turning back, for I saw the lad had lost his spirit, but they must needs hold on as far as Dunnalong, and so we got so far and proposed to land our messenger. But we might as well have been abed, for the great gun had taken away his appetite for the venture, and he would not set a foot on shore. There was nothing for it but to go back the way we came, and put the best face we could on our bootless errand. So we came pulling down stream, never knowing the minute when a round shot would send us to the bottom, when we saw two boats making for us in the gray of the dawn that was now something too clear for safety. They were our old friends the dragoons, and soon the bullets began to fly. and we returned their fire with so much fervour that they kept their distance, like the careful lads they are. Then says Murray, who likes nothing better than a melée, 'Lay us alongside the rascals, and we'll treat them to a morning dram;' and though they would have sheered off when they saw us resolute to close, we even ran up under their stern, and had clambered on board in a twinkling. We made short work of them and threw them overboard with a will. Some of them went to the bottom, and some of them got ashore, but for their boat we brought it with us, and it is even now lying by the quay."

"And what became of the other?"

"Oh! they did not like our entertainment and begged to be excused; so they stole off and left us with our prize."

"It is good news," said Gervase; "the best we have had for many a day. I would have ventured something to have been of your company."

"I thought of you, my lad, as we clambered over the gunwhale and gave them the ends of our muskets. But there is still fun in the fair, and I have come for you this morning to join in it. With the boats we purpose paying them a visit yonder by the orchard, and drawing the teeth of the great guns that have been barking somewhat vehemently of late. Baker himself hath asked for you, which is to your credit in a garrison where brave men are not few. I think myself, you have come to handle your sword in a pretty fashion."

"There is no lack of opportunity to learn," said Gervase laughing, "but you must not spoil me with praise before I have deserved it."

The old soldier looked at him with a friendly glance, as he bent down to examine the lock of his pistol. Most men were drawn towards Gervase Orme. His frankness, his courage, and his ready sympathy had no touch of affectation, while his handsome face and stalwart presence had made him many friends; but Macpherson, who had been on terms of intimacy with few for years, had come to look upon him as a father looks on a son. Gervase had found his way to a heart that had long been closed to human sympathy, and without knowing it, had brought light to a mind warped and darkened by a narrow and visionary creed. It was not that Macpherson's character had undergone a change, but during the fortnight he had spent in the farmhouse, a part of his nature had awakened to life which he had been sedulously trying to stifle, and which he had not been able to reconcile with the hard and narrow creed he had adopted.

"Lay down your weapon," he said, as Gervase with some eagerness was making his preparations to set out, "lay down your weapon, and listen to me. We have a good hour still; a man should never hurry to put his head in danger. Have you made it up yet with the sweet lass—you know whom I mean."

"I saw Miss Carew last night," said Gervase with some confusion.

"Tut, man, you will not put me off the scent like a young puppy that hath not yet found its nose. She is a wench in ten thousand—the good woman of the preacher, and was made to nurse a brave man's bairns. You must not let your gay spark of a Frenchman cut out the prize before your eyes, as he means to do, if I have an eye to read his purpose. You know not how to woo, my lad. Women are not to be taken like a town, with the slow approach of parallels and trenches; they ever love to be carried with a rush. The bold wooer is twice a man. You must go blithely about it and tell her what you mean."

"It is true that I love Miss Carew," said Gervase, "but this is no time to make love, and I will not distress her with any importunity of mine."

"Listen to the lad!" cried Macpherson, with a gesture of impatience; "importunity of his, quoth he! Our troubles will not last for ever, and a woman will not find her trouble the harder to bear because a brave man tells her he would have her to be his wife."

"You do not know Dorothy Carew," said Gervase good-humouredly. "I think she would not love a man the better for thinking of himself when other work is to be done."

"Being a woman, I think she would love him none the worse; but you are an obstinate lad and will take your own course. Her brother favours you but little, and the Frenchman is not much burdened with tender scruples. You will see what you will see. But I have spoken my word of warning, and will start when you please."

Gervase could see that Macpherson was dissatisfied, but he thought it useless to prolong the argument and prepared to accompany his friend.

The boats were lying at the quay, and the adventurers were already embarking when Macpherson and Gervase arrived. The expedition was full of danger. Every man who took part in it knew that he was taking his life in his hand; but there was glory to be gained, for the eyes of the whole city were upon them. On the other side of the river, encircled by its green hedge, lay the orchard with its battery of guns that seldom were silent for a day together. Only one company lay in the farmhouse hard by to protect the gunners, and it was hoped that by a bold and rapid push, the garrison might cross the river and spike the guns before a stronger force had time to interfere. But they must first face the fire of the guns, and having landed, must take their chance of finding the enemy prepared to give them a warm reception.

It was a fine thing to see the gay courage with which the men of the garrison took their seats, and examined the priming of their muskets. It seemed, from their bearing, rather a work of pleasure than one of life and death they were engaged upon.

Gervase took his seat in the stern of the smaller and lighter boat—the only one the garrison possessed before they took their prize that morning. Colonel Murray, who had inspired the venture, sat in the stern sheets, holding the tiller in his hand. A saturnine man, with the reserve and silent energy of his race, his face was lighted with the glow of excitement, and his voice was loud and deep, as he bade them push off into the stream.

"Now, my lads," he said, "this is a race for glory—we must be first across, and first we shall be. Keep low in the boat, and do not fire a single shot till we meet them on the bank; then we shall treat them to a taste of our cold steel."

The boat swung out into the stream, and the rowers bent to their work with a will. The other boat was heavier, and soon they had out-distanced it considerably. Murray had been watching the gunners in the orchard, who had already wakened up to the fact that they were threatened with an attack.

"What do you make of that, Orme? your eyes are younger than mine, but if I do not mistake they are about to carry off the guns."

"You are right," said Gervase. "One they have already carried past the farmhouse, and are preparing to do the same with the other. And the foot are coming down in force to their support."

"Let them come. We are still in time, and will not turn for twenty regiments. Now, my sons, bend to it with a will."

Already they were met with a dropping musket fire which sent the bullets singing about their ears and splashed up the water round them, but they held on stoutly and redoubled their efforts. The enemy had been taken by surprise. They had not dreamt that so small a force, in the light of open day, would have ventured to make so hazardous an attempt. But they were now undeceived, and made their preparations to receive their visitors. They were dragging off the guns to a place of safety, and three companies of foot were lining the hedge that ran parallel with the bank. Then the bow of the boat grated on the beach, and the men of the garrison leaped into the water, holding their muskets above their heads.

Without waiting for their comrades who were straining every nerve to come up to their support,

A WARM MORNING'S WORK.

they clambered up the bank, and rushed at the hedge where the red-coats showed through the green foliage. As they came up they fired a volley, and clubbing their muskets, came crashing through the thorns with the spirit of men who would not be denied. The fight was short but stubborn. Foot by foot the defenders of the hedge were driven back, and then as the men of the second boat came up, they broke and fled. The guns were now being hurried down the road, and every moment the chance of overtaking them grew less. The delay caused by that bold stand was fatal. But still the assailants kept pressing on, hoping that they would be in time to reach the guns before they were intercepted.

As they came up the gunners abandoned the pieces, but it was too late now to wait to spike them. Already a strong force was drawing between them and the boats, and it was with a bitter sense of failure that they turned their faces towards the river, and prepared to cut their way back again. The odds were four to one against them. It seemed as if they had been caught in a trap of their own making. From every clump of bushes flashed the blaze of the muskets, and here one and there another went down in his tracks.

"This will not do," rang out the voice of their leader. "We must 'try them hand to hand. After me, my lads!" Leaping the orchard fence they met the enemy hand to hand, but still pushing forward to where the boats were lying in the river.

The trees that grew closer here and were covered with their summer foliage, protected them from the fire of the foot who lay on the other side. Then Gervase saw Macpherson in front of him stumble and fall, and he feared it was all over with the brave old soldier. But he was on his feet before Gervase could reach him.

"Don't tarry for me," he said, as Gervase seeing him stagger forward, took him by the arm. "Make what haste you can and do not mind for me. This trifle will not stop me."

"We'll find our way together then. Hold on a little longer and we'll reach the boats in spite of them. Ah! that is bravely done."

From tree to tree and from hedge to hedge the men of the garrison cut their way, presenting a front, that though ragged and broken, sent the enemy to right and left. Then they reached the open space by the river, and restraining the impulse that would have driven them to rush to the boats, fell back slowly and steadily. The wounded whom they carried with them were first helped on board, and then they rapidly embarked; the last man to leave the bank being Murray, who with his sword held in his teeth pushed off the boat into the deep water. How they lived through the storm of bullets that were rained upon them Gervase hardly knew, but barely a man was touched, and they sent back a ringing cheer of defiance as they passed rapidly beyond reach of the muskets.

It was a glorious, if fruitless and foolhardy

deed—one which only brave men would have undertaken in a spirit of despair, but one that they might look back on in after years with pride for the glory of it. The deed was done in sight of all the city. Their friends had watched the charge from the walls, and seen the stubborn fight for safety, and now they poured out to meet them as they came through Ship Quay Gate, and welcomed them back as if they had come in triumph. From want of the sacred poet their names have grown dim through the gathered years, but they did not fight for renown—only simple men who sought to do their homely duty.

Macpherson's wound had proved a trifling one after all, and with the help of Gervase he was able to make his way home on foot. A spent bullet had struck him on the knee, and the wound though painful, was not likely to incapacitate him for service. He thought, on the whole, they had had a pleasant morning's work, and declared that with such stirring entertainment he would need but half his rations.

CHAPTER XIII.

OF A STRATAGEM OF WAR.

DAY by day the time crept on toward the end of June, and brought no change to the garrison. There were fewer mouths, it is true, to feed now, for disease and battle had laid them under heavy contribution, but the store of provisions was rapidly becoming exhausted. A fortnight more, so they believed and said, would bring them face to face with actual starvation, and the city must fall from want of men to line the walls and man the guns. For surrender they would not. "First the prisoners and then each other," was their grim jest that had an edge of earnest with it. No man now dared to whisper the prudence of surrender, for the spirit of resistance, which had been strong before, now burned with a wild and splendid flame as they felt the end was coming. The enthusiasm of the Ulster man does not find its outlet in boisterous speech— as his excitement increases his silence deepens, and he is, unlike his Celtic countryman, ever readier with his hand than with his tongue. And now, though hope was growing fainter as the days dragged on, their pride—the stern pride of religion and of race— inspired them with an obstinacy that had something sublime in it. Yet all the while the ships lay in the Lough and made no effort to come to their relief. Day by day they signalled in vain from the Cathedral tower and the great guns rang out, but Kirke would make no move. So close was the investment now, every loophole guarded with the extremest vigilance, that communication was impossible. One brave man had indeed made his way from the fleet to the city after passing through perils innumerable; but though he made the attempt, he found himself unable to return. Another messenger had bravely volunteered to carry out their message of despair, but he never reached the ships. A day or two after, the enemy erected a gallows on the bastion across the river, and there in the sight of the city the gallant fellow met his fate.

Dorothy Carew never looked back on this time without a shudder. She suffered more than many, for to the hardships she endured she added a private and peculiar sorrow of her own. The first she bore cheerfully and uncomplainingly, but her brother's secret, so base and so contemptible, oppressed her with a terrible feeling of shame and distress. After her first outburst of confidence to Gervase Orme, which she sometimes half regretted, she watched her brother jealously, and lay night after night listening for his footsteps.

But whether the warning he had received had taught him caution, or whether he had fulfilled his mission, his midnight excursions were now abandoned and he kept closely to the house. Still, to her keen and high sense of honour it was intolerable that her brother—the head of the house—should be a traitor whose guilt might be discovered at any time, and among so many brave men should act the coward and the spy. Had he gone over boldly to the enemy and thrown in his lot with them, she could have loved him. But now her love had been crushed out of her heart, and only comtempt and shame were left. Physical suffering seemed a light thing in comparison, and she envied the women who sent their husbands out to fight, and prayed for their safety when they were absent. But still she bore up with uncomplaining fortitude, and no one guessed the secret grief that was preying on her mind. Lady Hester, who had suffered agonies of fear while the bombs were raining on the city, she had encouraged with a simulated cheerfulness, and ordered her little household as she might have done in times of peace. The pinch of famine had hardly affected them yet—that was to come—but even that she looked forward to without any fear for herself.

But besides all this, she had another source of future trouble in her cousin. She could not long remain blind to the fact that his admiration for her was undisguised, and that beneath his cynical and flippant manner there had grown up a regard that was more than cousinly. It is true that he did not annoy her with his attentions, for Jasper and himself spent much of their time together. But he had shown clearly on more than one occasion that he was only waiting for a fitting opportunity to declare himself her lover. That opportunity she was anxious should not present itself. It was not, she reasoned with herself, that she loved another better, but she did not love De Laprade, and she did not wish to wound him. She did not wholly understand him, and could not tell whether he was ever in earnest or felt sincerely about anything. Then she thought of Gervase Orme, with his frank laughter and quiet speech, who treated her with a distant reverence and that was all. It was a pleasant thing to have him as a friend, full of quiet strength and honest as the day. But these were no times to think of such things, and so she put away the thought and went about her simple duties, hoping that Gervase would call to see her soon.

That evening she was seated by the open window, for the day had been close and sultry and the night was warm, a volume of Quarles' Emblems spread open on her knees. Her brother and the Vicomte had been closeted together during the day, and Lady Hester, fatigued and desponding, had retired for the night. She was very busy with her own thoughts, and had not heard De Laprade enter the room. He came softly up and took a chair beside her.

"Of what is my cousin Dorothy so full of thought?" he said.

She looked up with a blush, for just at that moment she was wondering what a certain fair-haired, long-limbed young giant was doing in the outposts or elsewhere, and the voice recalled her to herself with a feeling of self-reproach.

"I am afraid," she answered, "my thoughts would have little interest for you. A woman's head is ever full of idle thoughts."

"Not the wise head of my cousin; it is only the men of her family who give themselves to folly."

"The Vicomte de Laprade for example?"

"Truly he is a chief offender, but he is growing wise and sober and hardly knows himself. He has not smiled for a week, and thinks he never will be able to smile again. Even his cousin Jasper has ceased to amuse him."

"You are greatly to be pitied," she said with a smile. "But it is not duller than you would have found Vincennes. There too you would have grown wiser."

"Nay, I think not. A long time ago—it seems like years, I grow so old—I was for six months a prisoner in the Bastille, and when His Majesty relented and I returned to court I was no wiser than before. My folly only took another turn. But then I had not found a friend to warn, nor a counsellor like my fair cousin to teach me better things."

"I dare say you deserved your punishment. Now tell me something of your offence."

"Indeed, I hardly know myself, but I think it was — yes, I think it was a lady. By accident I trod on her train in a minuet and she refused to accept my apology. I could only smile and do penance for my clumsiness, for one may not lightly offend a great lady like Madame de——"

"Madame de——?"

"I have forgotten her name, but it does not matter now. She has forgotten Victor de Laprade, as he has forgotten her."

"I do not believe that, my cousin Victor."

"That I have forgotten the circumstances? Ah, well! it is possible that I might recall them to memory, but I would rather let them die, as I would all that belongs to the past. If my cousin Dorothy would but give me leave I would begin a new life to-day with new thoughts, new feelings, and a new heart. She smiles, and thinks it is not possible that I, who have wasted my youth, should try to save my manhood."

"Indeed you have my leave, but your reformation is too sudden, and you know you are not serious."

"I have been serious all my life; my cousin does not know her kinsman. Because I followed the fashion of my time, and fought and drank and played, wasting my youth like many another reckless fellow, therefore I was merry and had no thought or care. Because I am a gentleman, and not a solemn citizen who looks with a grim frown on all the devil's works, therefore my heart knows no sadness. It is thus the world has judged me, and so it may. But it is because I am sad and weary that I would have my cousin judge me differently."

For the first time since Dorothy had known him, he had lost his light and cynical manner and spoke with simple earnestness. He had made no display of emotion, but though he was calm and self-restrained, it was yet evident he spoke with abundant feeling. If he was not sincere, his humility and contrition were well assumed.

"I have been looking all my life," he went on, looking at her steadily as she kept her eyes bent on the book that still lay open on her knees; "I have been seeking all my life for a quiet heart—I, the libertine, the gambler who have squandered my patrimony and wasted my heritage. It was not to be found where I sought it, and my search was in vain. But now I know the secret that I was too blind to see before. Do you know, my cousin, what it is? Nay, you will not rise, for you must hear me out. It is love—the love a man may feel for what is purer and better than himself, the love that fills him with fresh hopes and new desires, the love that raises him to the pure heights of her he worships."

Then he suddenly stopped. Hardly knowing what answer to make, Dorothy rose from her seat and the Vicomte stooped down to pick up the book that had fallen to the floor. He said gravely as he reached it to her, "That is all my secret, my cousin, and does not sound so terrible when all is said. I trust you will remember it, for some day I may tell you how I came to make the great discovery."

"Lady Hester would have made a better confidante or, perhaps, my brother Jasper. And that reminds me, Victor," she continued, with a too evident anxiety to change the subject of this conversation, "I have often longed to ask what Jasper and yourself find to talk about during the long hours you spend together in his chamber."

"Jasper is learning a very useful lesson," answered De Laprade resuming his old manner, "which I teach him out of my experience. But now his education is nearly finished and we shall see whether he will profit by it."

"I suppose like all who learn their lesson in that school," said Dorothy soberly enough, "he will pay for it?"

De Laprade looked at her gravely, and then took her hand in both of his. "It would be an idle affectation in me to pretend that I am ignorant of your meaning, but I think you are wronging me with an unjust thought. I am a gambler, it is true, and love the music of the dice, but your brother, heedless as he is, will not suffer at my hands. Were he not my kinsman who has given me shelter, he is the brother of Dorothy Carew."

"I know you will forgive me," said Dorothy contritely. "But if I know Jasper he will look to you for payment of your losses. And he is rich while you——"

"Am standing in my kingdom," laughed De Laprade. "Do not trouble your mind about our play—'tis all for love."

While this conversation had been going on, a little knot of officers were gathered on the bastion near Butcher's Gate. Hard by was Alexander Poke, the gunner, loading a great gun carefully with Gervase Orme seated near watching the operation. The siege had already placed its mark on all of them: the daily horrors were not passing over them without leaving their traces. Anxious and depressed in mind and wasted in body, they were like men who had passed through a long vigil without hope. Their clothes hung loosely about them and were torn and frayed; and it was clear they had long since ceased to regard appearances and only looked to what was serviceable. They moved slowly and without enthusiasm, but on the faces of all of them was to be read the same hard and stubborn look, as of men who knowing the worst were determined to endure to the end. A month ago they might have listened to liberal terms of compromise; now they were determined there should be no surrender while a man remained alive.

Walker, with his snow-white head and stately presence, bore up under his anxiety with a higher spirit than many of the younger men, and as he stood in the centre of the little group, appeared to have suffered less than any other among them.

"I know not, gentlemen," he had been saying, "what this missive means with which this barbarous soldier has favoured us, but this I know, that they cannot frighten us with a cartel of paper when they have failed to do so with their guns. For the threat of putting us to the sword and refusing quarter even to the women, that they may do when they have it in their power, but for the other—I think 'tis mere bravado spun out of the Frenchman's brain. What say you, Colonel Mitchelburn?"

"I have served with De Rosen," said Mitchelburn, "and know that he hath the heart to do this and more, and while it seems to us an act too base and cowardly for words, for him 'tis but an ordinary stratagem of war. To drive a few hundred wretched women and children under the walls to starve there, will not trouble the man who has seen the sack of fifty cities. But there are gallant gentlemen yonder, men of spirit and honour, who will never suffer this savage Russian to carry out his threat."

"I know not that—I know not that. They will believe we cannot help but take them in, and how in Heaven's name, can we do otherwise? We cannot stand here and see them starved before our eyes. It is not well to meet sorrow half way but at most there is not more than a fortnight's food in the magazine and then "——

"No, Colonel Walker, though it break our hearts to see it, there is nothing must drive us from our purpose, and though my wife and children stood yonder they should not enter by my will."

"Then let us pray God that He may harden our hearts, a prayer I never hoped to pray. But I take this letter, such as it is, for an omen of good. They are growing weary of the stand we make and fearful that relief is coming, though whence we cannot tell, and so would hurry us by threats. Is Kirke about to make a push at last, think you?"

"When they have strung the bully up to the yard-arm and put a stout heart in his place, we may look to see the vessels at the quay, but not till then. And if we had another month's supplies I do not think we should need their help, for they have their own troubles in the camp yonder, and have lost nearly as many men as we. The prisoners say the sickness is increasing."

"And the supplies are failing fast."

"Nay, they say more than that. One fellow declared roundly that there are still traitors among us who supply the enemy with information. I saw him myself and questioned him roundly, but he did not know the names or kept the secret to himself."

"The traitors, if there are such, can harm us little now unless they are strong enough to hold the gates and drive us from the walls, and that could hardly be without its coming to our knowledge. You may have a quiet mind on that head; treachery has done its worst, and we have all our foes in front now. And now I think we may quietly disperse, for De Rosen has not kept his promise, or more humane counsels have turned him from his purpose. Had he meant to fulfil his threat, we had seen his victims under the walls before this."

Half an hour afterwards the alarm bell rang out calling the citizens to their posts, and word went round that the enemy was about to make an attack in full force. In the grey evening they could see them from the walls advancing over the hill opposite Butcher's Gate, and coming down steadily towards the lines. The citizens hurrying from their houses, came thronging to the walls, buckling on their weapons as they came. And the great gun was turned upon the force that came steadily down the hill in silence. Once the great gun flashed and only once, for as they came nearer the men upon the walls listened and held their breath, and then set up a great cry. The army that came down the hill came without purpose of offence; not the regiments of Slane or Gormanstown, but a crowd of tender women and fearful children and old men whose day of labour and strife was over. On they came with the sound of weeping and of sorrow, that to hear once was to hear for ever, for the memory of it would never pass away.

The savage marshal had fulfilled his promise. Torn from their homes and hurried to the front with expectation of a sudden and violent death, they had been collected in a body and driven to the walls. Pregnant women and women carrying their babies in their arms; old men who could hardly totter forward; the weak, the infirm, all who had not the power to escape; were gathered together for his purpose, and driven forward without remorse. And there in sight of their friends, of sons and brothers, of fathers and lovers, they stood between the famine-stricken city on the one side and on the other an enemy who showed no pity.

The first impulse of the garrison, an impulse that could hardly be restrained, was to throw open the gates and bring them within the shelter of the walls. But an instant's consideration checked their generous instincts. It was to this end that they were collected here; and once admitted, they might as well throw open the gates and throw down their arms. There was no food for so many mouths—nay, there was no food for themselves.

No greater trial, no trial half so great, had overtaken them since the siege began, or brought them so much suffering. They were not given to emotion, but there was not a dry eye among them on the walls that night, as they hardened their hearts and swore a deep oath of vengeance.

Then Walker and others went out to have speech with the wretched crowd of outcasts, and in a little while after came back, filled with admiration and wonder. Far from desiring shelter with their friends, they refused to enter the city, and were content to die where they stood rather than that the safety of the city should be put in peril. So they made their way toward the lines by the Windmill Hill, and spent the night huddled together under the open sky, while the enemy looked on in wonder, and their friends turned away, as if the sight was more than they could bear.

But a gallows was hastily erected on the Double Bastion in full sight of the camp, and it was resolved to hang all the prisoners if De Rosen persisted in his savage purpose. Hitherto they had been treated with consideration, but now those who were at large were collected and placed in Newgate, and Gervase Orme who was answerable for the safe custody of De Laprade, went late in the evening, with a sorrowful heart, to carry his friend thither.

CHAPTER XIV.

OF A GAME OF CHANCE.

Jasper Carew appeared but seldom in public, and then with a moody brow and a preoccupied air. For the most part he kept to his own chamber, attended only by Swartz, who was as silent and reserved as his master. In the daily incidents of the siege he appeared to take no interest whatever, seeming regardless of his own safety and wholly careless of the safety of his friends. He seldom saw his sister, and then only in the most casual way. It was in vain that she endeavoured to break through the icy barrier that had grown up between them. He repelled her efforts and frequently left her in tears. It is true he had seldom troubled himself with any display of affection, but latterly his entire character seemed to have undergone a change. Between himself and De Laprade a close intimacy had sprung up. They were closeted together for hours, and it not unfrequently happened that their evening sitting was prolonged far into the morning following.

Sitting in her lonely room when the household had retired for the night, Dorothy would hear the gay laugh of the Vicomte breaking at times on the quiet of the house, the rattling of the dice box, and the muttered oaths of her brother as fortune went against him. To her high spirit the shame of it was intolerable; she did not dare to speak and she could not be silent. With De Laprade she knew that she had much influence, but she had now reasons of her own for declining to make him her confidant—with her brother she was long since aware that entreaties would prove unavailing. But the fact could not be denied. A fatal passion for play had seized upon his heart; it had completely absorbed and overmastered him; he was entirely its slave. Night after night and day after day, the two—De Laprade and himself—were closeted together, and the cloud upon her brother's brow grew blacker and his speech harsher and more abrupt. In De Laprade there had been no change perceptible. He carried himself with an easy *insouciance* and treated her with tender deference.

On the day in which De Rosen had executed his barbarous threat they had spent many hours together in the little chamber in the basement. The roar of the cannon that had been sounding all day, the marching of men, and the tumult of the crowded street, had been hushed to a still and almost unnatural quiet. Swartz had carried away the remains of the supper that had been served to them here, and had lighted the candles in the tall silver candlesticks that stood upon the table. They had both already drunk more than enough, but this was perceptibly the case with Jasper. His face was flushed, his eyes were bloodshot, and his hands shook upon the dice-box: he had loosened his lace cravat from his throat and it lay on the floor beside him. He frowned heavily and flung down the dice-box with an oath.

"Seven's the main," said the Vicomte, gaily rattling the box. "We who woo fortune should court her lovingly. Ah, *grace de Dieu!* I told you so!"

Carew pushing back his chair and walking to the window, threw it wide open. The cool air blowing freshly through the lattice, caused the candles to flicker where they stood. The night was cold and the sky was full of stars. All the while the Vicomte sat watching him with a faint smile on his face and balancing the dice in his hand. The other after a moment turned round and looked at him. His face was now deadly pale. Neither spoke a word. Only the distant challenging of the sentinels broke the silence of the chamber.

The Vicomte pushed back his chair and gently snuffed the candles. His face displayed no emotion. Then after a while he said, "That completes the play. Your revenge has been a costly one, my friend."

"My revenge has been a costly one," answered Carew; "there remains but one thing more."

"And that?"

"To send my life after my houses and lands. There is nothing more left."

"Bah! you are but a fool; I have gone the same way myself. With a light heart I have lost more in a night than would buy your barren acres three times over. I, who was already a pauper, have staked my mistress, my buckles, my rings, nay, my very peruke itself and lost them too. And I did not complain. I had my sword and my honour, and could wait on fortune with a cheerful mind. I laughed at misfortune."

"Oh! 'tis very well for you to talk thus," cried Carew moodily, "with the first estate in the country in your pocket—a rare exchange for your castles in Spain."

"Monsieur Carew will remember that I did not press him to play. He who tempts the fortunes of the hazard should learn to bear his loss with equanimity. One should bear misfortune like a gentleman."

"I will have no sermons, my lord; 'tis enough that you should have stripped me of every rood of my land and every doit that I could raise, without presuming to lecture me on deportment. I would have you know that I will follow my own manner. I find no fault with you—'tis my own accursed folly that has made my heirship of the briefest, and left me a beggar before I had entered on my inheritance."

"Play is an admirable moralist," said De Laprade, altering the position of the candlesticks, "and preaches excellent homilies. You have had three weeks in the society of the coyest mistress in the world, and now you grudge the tavern charges.

> 'Je crois Jeanneton,
> Aussi douce que belle;
> Je crois Jeanneton
> Plus douce qu'un—mouton.'"

"You are mocking me, my lord."

"In good faith I do not think I am. Sit down, Carew, and let us look the matter in the face as sensible men should. I have no wish to put your money in my pocket or act the country squire on your beggarly paternal fields, but my ears are for ever itching for the pleasant rattle of the dice-board, and I thirst for the sight of a royal hand at cards. Fortune, which hath hitherto treated me so scurvily, hath taken a turn at last, and I am richer by some thousands than when I landed in your island with nothing in the world but a sword and two portmanteaux. For that, I am wholly indifferent, and will stake my new possessions as readily as I threw away my old. I am sorry for you, but I do not think you would take back what you have lost as a gift, even if I offered it now."

"Would I not?" said Carew, with a hoarse laugh, throwing up his hand.

"I do not think you would," answered the Vicomte gravely, but with a certain elevation of his eyebrows. "Your sense of honour would forbid. But there is a matter for which I have some concern—how will this affect your sister?"

"Leave my sister out of the question. I am her protector and allow no man to question me on that head."

The two looked at one another steadily—the one frowning, the other coldly impassive, but there was that look in De Laprade's eyes that made Carew shift his gaze. To carry off his confusion, he poured himself out a full glass and drank it at a breath.

"There need be no secrets between us, my good cousin. I have never doubted that you have already staked your sister's fortune and that it has gone after the rest into my pocket. I have known even honourable men tempted to do such things, but for my own part, I do not care to lend myself to aid them. The question still remains—how does this affect your sister?"

"In the name of God, do you purpose driving me mad?" cried Carew, flinging his empty glass into the fireplace, and leaping to his feet in the access of ungoverned passion. "You have stripped me bare as a bone and brought me to shame and dishonour; now you sit laughing at your handiwork."

"Your own, sir," said the Vicomte sternly. "These heroics will not serve their purpose; the question still remains unanswered. I would not willingly take on my shoulders any portion of your disgrace, though indeed I think you would not be loath to let me bear it all. In fine, what do you purpose doing?"

"Oh! you are a rare moralist."

"There is not a better in the world. From the pulpit of my own transgressions I shall read you an excellent sermon. But, again, this is not to the purpose. I would have you know, my excellent cousin, I love your sister and would willingly make her my wife."

"Before that I will see you——"

"You may spare yourself the trouble. Were the lady willing, I think not that I should ask your favour. But she is not willing. I fear she loves a better man who deserves her better—for which I do not find fault with her taste."

"You appear to have studied my family affairs to some purpose, sir."

"Mr. Orme is a better man than I, nor would I willingly do him an injury," continued De Laprade softly, "but all things are fair in love, and I think I must ask your help."

"What hath Mr. Orme to do with the matter? You put more, sir, on me than I can bear, and by heaven, I will put up with your gibes no longer. I am not a schoolboy to be lectured by a bully."

"I have told you that we will not quarrel. I ask not your friendship but your help, and it may be also much to your own advantage. Therefore listen to me with all the patience you can command. I am mad enough to love Miss Carew—I, the prodigal, the spendthrift, whose career was run before I was a man, but so it is! She is much under your influence—the wise and prudent elder brother. Lend me your assistance, not to coerce her affections or thwart her will, for by heaven, I would not wrong her tender heart! but to bring her with all kindness to think favourably of her poor kinsman, and in the end it may be to return his passion. Hear me to the conclusion. I would not buy your help—you would not sell your aid. We both love the rattle of the dice-box. On the one side I place my gains, the rich lands, the fair demesnes, the ancestral house, the broad pieces—and on the other you will stake your persuasive speeches and fraternal affection. Let chance decide the fate: I would not do dishonour to your sister even by a thought. I do not think the stakes unequal; why should you?"

Carew stared at the speaker, unable to gather his meaning, and said never a word.

"Why, my friend, there is your chance of redemption," said the Vicomte, taking up the box and rattling it gaily, "three is the number of the Graces; three throws for fortune and love; three throws for honour, riches, and reputation. Ah! there is a royal stake, and heaven send me favour."

"This is but a piece of midsummer fooling; you do not mean this?"

"Truly I am in a sad and serious vein. Your barren acres grow heavy on my back and I would be rid of them."

"Then have with you," cried the other eagerly.

But hardly had he spoken than the sound of footsteps was heard on the stone passage, and an importunate knocking upon the door. Carew rose to his feet, pushing back his chair with an oath. The Vicomte did not stir.

"It is best to see your impatient visitor," he said. "Do not hurry fortune."

Carew went to the door and threw it open.

"Well, sir, what is your errand at this unseasonable hour?" he said, peering out into the darkness which screened the intruder.

"My errand is with Vicomte de Laprade," said a voice, "and is of the most urgent. I must see him immediately."

"Ah! that is the true Israelite, Mr. Orme," said the Vicomte, in his usual nonchalant tone, without turning in his chair. "You are arrived most opportunely. This is the Temple of Fortune and here are her worshippers."

"This is no time for jesting, my lord," said Gervase, gravely. "I have come to carry you to the guardhouse, where I can promise you no favourable reception. Our hearts have been sadly stirred; your life even is in danger."

"So much the more reason that we should decide this matter now. Look you, Mr. Orme, my friend and I have a difference, the nature of which I cannot now make clear to you, though it may also concern you nearly, and we have agreed to leave it to the arbitrament of chance. A few minutes more or less will not imperil the safety of the city. Pray be seated, and see how fortune deals her favours."

"Oh! this is past a jest," cried Gervase, "I tell you, my lord, you are in deadly peril."

"And I tell you, sir, this is a matter of more importance. Nay, my good friend"—and here he held out his hand, "my mind is set on this, and I pray you to indulge me."

Though his eyes and lips laughed, there was a

serious undertone in his voice, and after hesitating for a moment, Gervase finally said, " Ten minutes you may have, my lord, but with your pardon, I shall wait without. My mind is full of care and my heart is heavy as a stone. I can take no part in this. I have seen this day that which I shall not forget did I live a thousand years. Good night, Mr. Carew. My lord, you will not keep me waiting."

His steps rang along the stone pavement; then there was the sound of an opening door and the whispering of voices in the basement hall.

" 'Jacob was a plain man and dwelt in tents,'" murmured De Laprade. " Come, Carew, we who tempt the fickle goddess must not sleep. Jacob yonder would filch my birthright, and I will not lose the lovely Rachel."

Carew, who had been as one bewildered and suddenly awakened out of a dream with the terror of it still upon him, drew a chair to the table and caught up the dice-box with a trembling hand. As his fingers closed upon the box, his face grew deadly pale; his heart stood still in his breast in an overmastering agony of fear and hope and hate. To him this meant everything in the world. The man opposite to him had stripped him naked—the man whose smile stabbed him like a knife, and whom he hated with a bitterness of hatred that he had no language to measure. Should he retrieve his fortune, and on how little that depended, not all the powers on earth would again tempt him to such unspeakable folly. A mere gull who had flung away his inheritance before he had possessed it! The happy chance of redemption had come to him unexpectedly. What had moved De Laprade too make this strange and curious proposal, he did not stop to ask, he did not care to know. It was enough for him that it had been made. He knew that he could exert no influence on his sister's mind; that his intercession would rather injure than advance the cause he advocated. That was the Vicomte's business. He was a gambler and accustomed to take the chances, and it was he who had proposed the stakes. He passed his hand across his eyes to clear away the mists; the room seemed full of moving haze through which the candles burned with a feeble and uncertain light. He drew a deep breath.

The first throw Carew won; the second fell to the Vicomte. Then there happened a curious thing—when Carew was about to throw for the third time, the Vicomte stooped down to lift his handkerchief from the floor where it had fallen a moment before. While he did this somewhat clumsily for one in general so dexterous, the dice rattled on the table. Making a slight motion with his fingers Carew, hardly pausing, cried "Sixes."

The Vicomte slowly raised his head. "Your play improves, sir," he said drily; "that was a lucky throw. Come, sir, you are not yet out of the wood, and perhaps I shall yet see you through." Then he threw himself. "By all the saints, the

Venus! This grows interesting. We must have one more cast for fortune."

"The devil's in them," cries Carew, his eyes fairly aglow and his lips twitching like one in a fit.

This time the Vicomte won. "I knew how it would be," he said, with an air of pensive sadness; "I have no luck, I can do no more."

Carew laughed loudly, almost as if this last stroke had touched his brain. "Luck, what more would you have? Here have I been sitting for three weeks while you plucked me like a hen feather by feather, with a smile on your face, and I know not what devil's craft in your fingers."

"These are foolish words, sir, for which I will not ask you to account. To talk of craft comes but ill from one who himself——" Here he stopped and looked at Carew steadily. "God knows I am but a pitiful fellow myself, and yet I would I had never seen your face."

The words were spoken slowly, with an emphasis that carried home their hidden meaning; they struck home like a knife. Then without warning Carew reached suddenly across the table, and struck the Vicomte a blow with his closed nand fairly on the lips.

"You are a liar and a cheat," he said, "and I will kill you like a dog."

For a moment or more the Vicomte did not stir; apparently he was afraid to trust himself to speak; only with his handkerchief, which he all the time carried in his hand, he wiped the thin trickle of blood from his lips. Then he rose to his feet and going over to the door, turned the key in the lock. Thereafter he whipped out his sword and advanced into the middle of the room. There was a high colour in his cheeks and his eyes shone with a fine glow in them. Otherwise his manner was perfectly calm, and his voice came slowly and with distinct utterance. "Mr. Carew," he said, "no man living will dare to do what you have done to-night and live to tell it. I would have borne with much for your sister's sake; here not even she can save you. And yet it is almost a dishonour to cross swords with you and treat you as a gentleman—you, whom I have myself seen to cheat and cozen like a common tavern-brawler. And you have dared to use these opprobrious words to me—to me who did my best to return your losses without offending your nice sense of honour. Now, sir, draw your sword and say your prayers, for I think you are going to die."

Carew was not wanting in physical courage, nor backward at any time in a quarrel. But at this moment it was his own vehement and overmastering desire—a desire too deep for any mere speech—to find an outlet for his passion of hate and shame in a struggle with the man who held his fortune and good name in his hand. To hold him at his mercy was at this time his dearest wish on earth. He drew his sword, and taking his ground lowered the point sullenly as the Vicomte saluted with his weapon.

Then their blades were crossed. The light was faint and low, for the candles had nearly burnt themselves out, and as the spacious chamber rang with the clash of the sword blades, the deep shadows came and went with a grotesque and everchanging motion. Carew had the advantage in the length of reach and once he touched his opponent in the arm, but after a few passes he saw he had met his superior, and a feeling of great dread overtook him. How he hated the man with the cold, impassive face and disdainful smile! But for that bit of glittering steel that guarded him like a wall, how gladly he would have taken him by the throat and glutted himself with vengeance. And he saw that the Vicomte played with him as if unwilling to strike him down too soon, and that, too, added to his passion of fury and hate.

The Vicomte still stood on the defensive and parried his thrusts with the greatest ease in the world. Again and again he tried to enter upon his guard, but always with the same result. Then there came a violent knocking upon the door and the sound of voices raised in alarm and expostulation.

"We must end this," cries the Vicomte deliberately parrying a thrust in tierce, and almost at the same time Carew passaged rapidly, and catching the Vicomte's sword in his left hand, buried his own sword to the hilt in the Vicomte. The stricken man swung round, threw up his hands, and fell in a heap to the floor without uttering a sound.

Gervase had left the room with contempt and indignation strongly present in his mind. It had seemed incredible to him that men should become absorbed in these trifles, surrounded by the horrors that he daily witnessed, and lose themselves wholly in this degrading passion. No doubt it was none of his business—so he told himself—but his sense of fitness revolted at it. He had reached the outer door and his hand was on the lock to open it, when he heard a door open on the staircase above, and a voice calling in low tones, "Is that Mr. Orme?"

"It is I, Miss Carew," Gervase answered, feeling that the hope of this rencontre was the real reason why he had left the Vicomte to decide his matter of importance by himself.

Dorothy came down the stairs holding a taper in her hand—Gervase could see the traces of tears on her cheeks, and he was greatly struck by the change that the last week had made in her looks. Not that her beauty was in any way dimmed or diminished, but sorrow and care had set their seal upon it.

"Swartz has told me the news," she said, "and the horror of it gives me no rest. Will they not bring them into the City?"

"God knows it is what we all desire," Gervase answered, "but it is not possible. To bring them in would mean that we have fought and you have suffered for nothing; it would but make their fate ours. Londonderry must not fall."

He continued in a sad constrained tone, "I think I shall never forget till I die what I have seen to-day. There are children there, and babies at the breast, and tender women, and, Miss Carew, we must let them die. We dare not take them in. There is hardly food for a fortnight longer and then——"

"Then," said Dorothy, "we can die. I almost think I shall be glad to die."

"Nay," said Gervase taking her hand, "if all were as brave and strong as you are! Macpherson says that yours is the boldest heart in the city."

"He does not know me," Dorothy answered, withdrawing her hand with a faint gleam of her old humour kindling in her eyes; "he does not understand women. I am a poor coward. But why should I talk of myself? Will nothing be attempted to save the poor wretches who are now below the walls?"

"Ay," said Gervase pausing, "it is proposed to make use of the prisoners we have taken, and, indeed, that is the reason I am here to-night. The Vicomte must quit your house and take up his abode in the guard-house, but I trust not for long."

"They will not injure him?"

"I hope not, and I do not think you need fear for him. My lord Netterville hath writ to De Rosen, who is surely a devil, to tell him how it stands with himself and the other prisoners, and I do not doubt his letter will move him more than the voice of humanity, assisted as it is by the gallows we have now erected."

"There is nothing but horror on horror," said Dorothy. "It is just, but it is hard to bear. And I think I could bear it all but for the great trouble I told you of—but why should I thrust my own private griefs on a stranger?"

"Nay, no stranger; your troubles are all mine. You know that I love you better than my life."

A moment before he would not have ventured to make this speech, but something in her voice had for the first time awakened a wild hope in his breast. She looked at him with a frank and honest look. "Yes," she answered, "I think you love me better than I deserve, but this is no time to talk or think of such things."

"But, Dorothy—"

"Nay, I will not have a word. Listen! Oh God! what is that? They have quarrelled, and that is the sound of swords."

The clash of steel could be heard plainly, and the sound of feet moving rapidly.

"Remain where you are," said Gervase, hastening down the passage; "I shall prevent this."

Dorothy stood at the foot of the passage, her hands held tightly against her breast; the taper had fallen to the floor, and she was in darkness. Then she heard the voice of Gervase at the door.

"Out of my way or I will run you through; I must enter."

"By your leave you shall not. My master must fight this out; I've taught him to fence, and I'll see that he gets fair play."

It was the voice of Swartz. Gervase had found the man at the door listening to the sound of the strife within.

"Out of my way," said Gervase, losing his temper.

"Damn you! I tell you I shall not stir. The Frenchman hath robbed my master and he'll pay dearly for it to-night. No man in Londonderry will pass the door till he hath settled with that thief."

Gervase was in no humour for temporizing at this moment. He caught the old servant by the throat and with a quick movement hurled him to the other side of the passage. Then placing his shoulder against the door and exerting all his strength, the strong framework fell in with a crash. The room was in complete darkness and he stood to listen. There was not a sound. Then Dorothy came down the passage with a light.

"You must not come any further, Miss Carew," said Gervase, advancing to meet her, with a white face. "I am sure something has happened." He took the light from her and entered the room, Swartz who had picked himself up muttering a malediction, following close on his heels. Lying in the middle of the room in a dark pool of blood was De Laprade, while Jasper Carew stood over the body, with the point of his rapier on the ground and his hands resting on the handle.

"I killed him in fair fight," he said as Gervase came into the room, and running over, knelt down by the fallen man. Gervase opened the Vicomte's coat and placed his hand on his heart; it was still beating feebly.

"He is not dead yet. For God's sake run for the surgeon; he may yet be saved," he cried, turning to Swartz who stood behind him.

"I'll not stir a step to save his life," the old man answered doggedly.

"Do as you are bidden, sir," said Jasper, without moving, "and make what haste you can." Then he went over and sat down by the table, looking on coldly as the man went out and Gervase tried to stop the bleeding with his handkerchief. Dorothy had crept into the room, pale and frightened, and knelt down beside Gervase.

"Is he dead?" she said with a gasp.

"No, he still lives. I can hear his heart beating."

"I would give my own life a hundred times over to save his. He must not die; I say, he must not die."

"It is as God wills," answered Gervase gravely. "I think he is coming round."

The Vicomte opened his eyes and smiled a faint smile of recognition as his eyes fell on Dorothy; she lifted his hand and pressed it within her own; then she shuddered at the touch—it was clammy with blood. No one spoke or stirred—only the feeble tide of life appeared to be slowly returning. The minutes seemed to drag themselves into hours while they waited for the coming of the surgeon. Dorothy had placed her hand under De Laprade's head, and anxiously watched the deathlike pallor disappearing from his cheeks. Her heart leapt joyfully as she saw him attempting to speak.

"'Twas a fair fight but—but," and he spoke as if communing with himself, "he should not have caught my sword."

Gervase looked suddenly up at Carew where he sat by the table looking on sullenly, and he was filled with horror at the awful likeness that he bore to the old man, his grandfather, whose frowning face he had seen in its death agony. It was the same face, the same dark passionate look, transformed from age to youth. He had never noticed the likeness before and he wondered at it now.

Jasper rose and coming over looked down at the Vicomte with a look of bitter hate. "The man is a liar," he said; "a liar while he lived and a liar now that he is dying, for I hope that I have killed him. I fought him fairly, and I should have stabbed him where he sat. I shall answer the world for what I have done."

He turned on his heel and left the room, as Swartz and the surgeon entered it. The latter, a tall, gaunt Scotchman with an exasperating precision and judicial slowness of manner, began to examine his patient carefully; it seemed as if he never would have done. Then he turned to Gervase and spoke almost for the first time since he had entered the room.

"Wherefore did you drive the puir laddie sae hard? less would have done. You young callants have no sense."

"Will he die?" said Gervase eagerly.

"How can I tell you that? I'm no' a prophet, but I'm thinking his vitals have not been touched. These small swords make clean work; they're no' effectual like the pike or the broad sword—and he was a likely lad. I think we may even bring him round yet, but he must not be stirred. Have ye not unco' guid sport outside that ye must begin to throttle ither within?"

"God knows that is true, but you do not understand."

"Nae doubt, nae doubt," answered the other drily, "but I understand the lad has gotten a whinger through his body, and that is a fact anybody can understand. Howsoever the care of the body is my concern, and my two hands are full enough. I'm tell't you're mighty quick with your weapon, Mr. Orme."

"This is none of my work," said Gervase. "I would have given my right hand to prevent it."

The surgeon looked doubtfully at Swartz who stood near with his hands behind his back. "Why! that body there—but it is none of my business. We'll even make him comfortable now and we can talk more about it in the morn, for I'm thinking they must hear of this work outside. This bonny lassie will be my care next," he continued, turning to Dorothy. "This is no place for you, my dear," he said, laying his large hand with a rough sympathy on her shoulder.

"Indeed I could rest nowhere else in the world. Do you think he will live?"

"I'm sure he'll no' die if your sweet heart will save him. He's a gay, likely lad and he'll give a deal of trouble in the world yet before he leaves it, if he keeps clear of small swords in the future."

"Thank God for that!" cried Dorothy, bursting into tears for the first time.

Saunderson looked at her with a grim smile on his homely features.

"Women sometimes thank God for unco' little. But he'll do for the now, and I'll be back in an hour. Come, Mr. Orme, you'll see me to the door, for I have some directions to give you and my time is precious."

Gervase went out with him to the door and they stood on the great stone steps together. Then the surgeon laid his two broad hands on Gervase's shoulders and looked at him steadily. "Look ye here," he said, "I learnt the practice of medicine in the University of Glasgow, but there's ane thing I learnt since. I'm no sure I've got to the bottom of this devildum, but I'm sure o' this, that if yon chiel dies, the lassie will even break her bonnie heart and the same small sword will have killed them both. Swartz says the deed was yours, but he's a fause loon to look at, and I ken now it's a lee. I ken you love her too well—I've learnt that too—to do her scaith, and I leave him in your hands till the morning. When a woman's in love she's no' to be trusted. I'll send you a draught and ye'll see to it that he gets it."

He left Gervase hardly understanding the speech

he had heard. Then its full meaning dawned on him. Till now it had not occurred to him that Dorothy had cared for De Laprade, but the mere suggestion awoke a thousand trivial recollections that lent colour to the thought. He had believed that her great distress was only due to the fact that her guest and kinsman had fallen by her brother's hand. But if it was otherwise—if she loved De Laprade and looked on himself only as a friend—it took the strength out of his heart to think of it. This great passion, the first that he had known, had transformed his life and inspired him in the midst of all the dangers and privations he was passing through. And now it seemed to him that his hopes had fallen like a house of cards. He was a fool to think that she should care for him—and yet who could tell? So with hope that was not altogether dead, and doubt, and a touch of jealousy, as has been since love came first into the world, he went back to help his stricken rival.

CHAPTER XV.

OF HOW THE VICOMTE WAS BROUGHT BACK TO LIFE.

For several days De Laprade hovered between life and death, apparently conscious and that was all. Dorothy hardly left his bedside night or day, attending upon him with sedulous care and devotion. Seeing that she was about to give way under the strain, Saunderson took affairs into his own hands and forbade her the room altogether. While she had been in the sick chamber De Laprade had used to follow her with his eyes—eyes in which there was little sign of intelligence—but now that she came no more, he sank into a deep and deathlike lethargy from which he seldom awakened. Whether for Dorothy's sake or from the nature of the case, Saunderson gave up much of his time to the wounded Viscount, and invariably reported his patient's progress to the anxious girl who was awaiting his departure from the sick chamber. So far from adopting the physician's usual diplomacy, he had endeavoured to keep up her spirits from the beginning, assuring her that with skill and care, ill as he seemed, he would yet dance at her wedding.

"You will see," he had said, with rough kindliness "there are twa bodies tha'll no die lichtly—he that's gain to be married and he that's gain to be hangit; and when this braw callant hath had both prospects before him he'll no leave us this gait. He should have been a corp three days syne by every rule of the faculty, but yon bit thing never touched his vitals after all. You'll no greet your bonnie een out, Miss Carew, but just tak your rest and leave him to Providence and me."

For Saunderson had come to the conclusion that the Vicomte was Dorothy's lover, and that in some way or other, that was the cause of the quarrel in which he had been wounded. He had at first believed that Gervase had been the assailant, but Dorothy had undeceived him on that head; but on the other she had remained entirely silent and made no effort to remove his misunderstanding. She had, however, seen, or thought she had seen, through the friendly deception of the surgeon, and when she had been closed out of the sick room she had believed the end was approaching. She had not understood, though she had guessed, the nature of the tragedy that had been enacted between her brother and her cousin; and though she was not aware of all the circumstances she had come to think she owed the Vicomte a great debt. She had remembered every word of their brief conversation an hour or two before the brawl, and knowing his high sense of honour, she had laid the blame entirely on her brother. All that was passing without seemed like a dream now—only the death chamber was real to her and this tragedy with its deep and indelible stain of guilt. She had felt that she was grieved for the wretches who had been driven to starve under the walls, and she felt rejoiced when she heard that De Rosen had relented, but she felt also that she had not realized the news. It seemed wholly remote. This domestic tragedy, so near and so terrible, entirely filled her mind with its abiding horror. She felt there was no sacrifice she would not willingly make to avert this calamity, and each day she waited with a suspense that was intolerable for the coming of the surgeon from the sick room. Even Jasper's treachery had passed into the background in the presence of this new and more appalling crime. Gervase Orme had called every day but she had refused to see him, for though she yearned for sympathy in her distress her pride compelled her to nurse her sorrow in secret. Jasper came and went with perfect *sang froid;* he seemed to be the only person in the household to whom the wounded man's condition was a matter of indifference.

So the days went past and there seemed to be little or no change in the Vicomte's condition. But at length he recovered perfect consciousness and asked eagerly for Dorothy. It was indeed his first question after he recovered speech. Saunderson was in the room and seated by his patient's side feeling his thin and languid pulse, when De Laprade suddenly looked at him with an eager and questioning gaze. The change was so sudden that the surgeon was startled. "I saw Dorothy—

Miss Carew—but now," said the Vicomte. "Where is she?"

"She'll no be long, my friend; just keep yourself cool and ye'll see her the now. That's a good laddie."

"I have little time to spare and I must see her before I die."

"Ye'll no die this time. Ye'll scratch grey hairs yet, if ye keep yersel' blate and dinna fash without reason."

"You're a good fellow," said De Laprade, with a faint smile on his thin, wasted face, "I think I have seen you here in the room with me for months, but I will not trouble you much longer. Now bring Miss Carew here and complete your kindness."

"Ye must not excite yoursel' in that fashion. Ye have been ower long in coming round, and we maun keep ye here when we hae you. Now drink this like a good laddie, and I'll even fetch her mysel.'"

He poured out a draught and held it to the Vicomte's lips, who drank it obediently. Saunderson believed that the crisis had come and though he hoped that he was wrong for Dorothy's sake, had come to the conclusion that this was the last feeble flicker of consciousness in his patient before the end. As he left the room De Laprade followed him with the same eager gaze. He found Dorothy in the corridor and told her what had happened. "And now," he said, "ye'll just keep him quiet and humour him like a baby. Let him gang his ain gait and say 'Ay' to all his clavers. I'd rather you were elsewhere, but he'll no bide till he has seen you."

It was with a heavy heart that Dorothy entered the sick room. There was something in the surgeon's manner that told her she must hope no longer; and as she saw De Laprade lying with the deathlike pallor on his wasted face and the eager famished look in his dark eyes she thought that he was dying. She went over noiselessly to the bed and sat down beside him, laying her hand on the coverlet. Neither of them spoke, and it was with an heroic effort that she restrained her tears. Then De Laprade took her hand in his and a look of contentment lighted up his dark face. She wondered to herself at the change that had taken place in so short a time. There was something almost boyish in the face that was turned toward her.

"I am starting on a long journey, my cousin," he said, "and I would see you before I go. You will not think unkindly of me when——"

She could make no answer but only bent over his hand to hide the tears that were welling to her eyes, though she strove to repress them.

"This is a fit end for me," he went on, "but, believe me, I tried to keep my promise toward your brother; he did not understand and——"

"You must say no more," said Dorothy; "I never doubted of your faith and honour. You will yet live to know that I trust you."

"Too late, too late!" he said, sorrowfully. "Why should I live? I have had my chance and wasted it. In all the world there is no one who will regret me but yourself, and you will forget me when — it is but right you should. Victor De Laprade — a stranger — that is all, and I deserve no better."

"I will never forget you," she said, touched beyond expression by the pathos of his speech; "you must not think such thoughts; you will yet live to smile at them."

"Why should I live for whom there is no room and no need? I have wasted my life. As I lay here I have lived it all again, and seen its folly. You have helped me to see what I never saw before, and I could not go before I told you. Nay, it is best for me to die. It is not hard to say farewell with your hand in mine. I had hoped some day to tell you what I am going to speak, some day when I had shown myself not altogether unworthy, but I cannot wait for that now, and must say it here if it is ever to be spoken."

She knew what he was about to say; full of pity she did not withdraw her hand, but continued to hold his in her own. At that moment she almost felt she loved the man who looked at her with such fervent longing in his eyes.

"I have come to love you, my cousin, with such love as I never felt or dreamed of before — a love that makes me ashamed of my life, and desire to forget the past and all its follies. That love has taken the terror away from death. I do not think

I should have made you happy. I had too much to forget. And you know you did not love me, Dorothy; as indeed why should you."

"Indeed, I think I do," she answered honestly, and lifted his hand to her lips with the tears in her eyes. "Oh! Victor, do not wrong yourself in speaking thus."

"I am but a poor fellow, Dorothy," he said slowly, "but if this is true I would not change my place with His Christian Majesty. In happier times you will remember me as one who loved you, and died content because he loved you."

"You will not die, but live to let me help you to forget the past. There is no sacrifice I would not make to bring you happiness."

"I would not let you sacrifice your life for me, my cousin."

"Nay, I did not mean that. I am but a weak and thoughtless girl and cannot say all that I would, but I love no other, and—and I think I love you dearly."

She could not have imagined before she came into the room that she would have spoken these words, but the pitiable sight of this wrecked and wasted life filled her with a great flood of compassion, and she spoke almost without thinking of the meaning of her words. Then she bent over and pressed her lips to his forehead. His pallid cheeks flushed a little; the act was so spontaneous and so foreign to her manner, that it carried to his heart the happiness of hope and love. For a time he did not speak.

"I do not know," he said, "whether this is a part of my dream; it seems too much to believe that this great happiness should have come to me at the end; but I shall believe it true, and carry your love with me whither I am going. It will be a light to the way. The good Saunderson would not let me die when I desired, and you make it hard to go. You see I thought you loved——"

She interrupted him hastily, "I have not thought of love till now. My foolish Victor, you must drive these idle fancies from your head; if I do not love you, I love no one."

"If this were not the shadow of a dream, the happiness is too great!

> "'Amis, le temps nous presse;
> Menageous les moments que le transport nous laisse!'

"Kiss me again, my sweet Dorothy, for the darkness is coming."

She thought that all was over and the end was come. He lay pale and exhausted, with his hand in hers and his breathing so low and faint that she could not catch the sound of it. There was the shadow of a smile on the open lips; a smile of contentment like that a child smiles while dreaming. She was afraid to move or withdraw her hand, and when Saunderson came into the room she made a gesture of warning.

He came over quietly beside her. "I think," he said, "ye have given him a more efficacious remedy than any in the pharmacopœia. He is sleeping finely, puir laddie! Ye may leave him now and ye'll see a change for the better when ye come again. I kenned ye would either kill or cure him, though I thocht ye would do him little harm if ye could help it."

"He is not dying?"

"Indeed, that he is not, but just making up his mind to live bravely. I would like to bottle up your specific and carry it about in a phial; it's what I have been wanting this many a day."

However it came about the surgeon's prediction was verified, and a sudden change for the better took place in the Vicomte's condition that evening; he had fallen into a refreshing slumber which lasted for some hours; and when he awakened, the fever had entirely disappeared, leaving him very weak indeed but on the high road toward convalescence. With the considerateness that was always natural to him, he had refused to allow Dorothy to remain in his room, and had asked to see Jasper, with whom he was anxious to make his peace. What passed between them no one ever knew, for De Laprade was silent on the subject, but Carew was heard whistling gaily as he returned to his own room.

Dorothy was for a long time unable to realize the events of the day. It filled her with happiness to think that De Laprade was likely to recover, and that the shadow of crime was to be removed; but when she began to think of the new relation that was springing up between herself and her cousin, an indefinable and restless feeling took possession of her. She knew that she had been carried away by pity and regret to speak without examining her own heart;—she had desired to bring a momentary happiness to the forlorn and wasted life that she thought was passing away before her, and she had spoken with deep feeling and entire sincerity. But when she came to think over it now that the danger had passed away and her mind had grown calm and reasonable, she felt that she had spoken rashly and without due premeditation. She feared that she had mistaken compassion for love. But if she did not love him now with a strong and devoted affection, it might grow and all might yet be well. She could not now tell him that she only pitied him. Then her thoughts went further afield, and with a start she wakened up wondering what Gervase Orme would say when he heard that she had plighted her troth to his friend. The idea filled her with pain; she shrank from it with a feeling akin to dismay. While Orme was nothing more to her than a friend, her thoughts had involuntarily dwelt much on him, and she had come to look to his strong and silent nature for help and consolation, sure of perfect sympathy and understanding. She knew, though she now strove to forget it, that he loved her. Had she been free to choose her own way, and had duty so plain and so self-evident not lain in her path—but no, she did not love him and must not allow her mind to dwell on these idle imaginings. There was only one

"JASPER BUCKLING HIS SWORD ABOUT HIM"

thing for her to do,—to be true to the words she had spoken and bring her wayward heart to respond to the promise she had made. There was no one to whom she could go for advice or help; she must rely upon herself alone, and happen what might, there was at least one Carew who would be found faithful to her word and jealous of her honour. The sin and wrongdoing of her house might be visited upon her, but she would bear it cheerfully.

She had visited Lady Hester at midnight and was about to retire to her own room, when she heard her brother's door open and someone passing down the corridor. Without waiting to think, she came down the stairs hurriedly, and found Jasper in the hall with his cloak and hat on, buckling his sword about him. He was evidently very angry at seeing her.

"These are no hours for a woman," he said; "you should have been abed hours ago."

"They are not hours for some men either," she said, looking at him earnestly. She knew from the look that he cast on her that he was certain she had learnt his guilty secret. She did not flinch but stood up before him, with a firm and steadfast look. He drew on his gloves slowly without raising his eyes to meet hers. Though there was neither sympathy nor love between them, and though she had striven devotedly to win his confidence without success, she longed to save him from this dishonour, and to hold him back from ruin, for that ruin and dishonour were impending she did not doubt.

"These are not hours for some men either. For your own sake and for mine, you must not leave the house to-night."

"And pray, madam, why not? It is not enough that I should be mewed up in this damned town with a couple of women and a mad Frenchman for my companions, but that I must have my actions spied upon and my coming and going brought in question. I have borne with you in patience, my good sister, but I will not let you spy upon me longer. There must be an end on 't."

"You can speak no words that will make me fear you," she said quietly. "I would have been your loyal and loving sister, but you know what I know, and if I can prevent it you shall not play the traitor longer. It is true that I have watched you, watched you day and night; and was there not need? Shall it be said that a Carew, for I know not what base reward, sold his honour and flung away his good name? Can Hamilton or Tyrconnell or James himself save you from this disgrace?"

"These are mad words," he said doggedly; "I know not what you mean."

"I am only a woman with a woman's weakness, and I cannot turn you from your purpose. But before I had carried such a paper as I have seen you carry, I would have died a thousand times. Jasper," she continued pleadingly, laying her hand on his arm, "It is not yet too late."

"I was right after all, and it was you who set yon slow-witted coxcomb to lecture me with his mysterious threats. Now listen to me, Miss Carew; you have shown a more than sisterly interest in my affairs; and you may as well know it all. I have followed my own course, and laid my plans that I will suffer no woman to wreck with her whims and fancies. These beggarly citizens and these foolish country gentlemen are nothing to me. I stand by my lawful king, and on that side is my service and my interest, I have taken no great pains to conceal my thoughts, and perhaps to-morrow——" here he checked himself.

"Then go over to your friends."

"It does not suit my purpose. Now I will give you a word of advice before I go. Make no more confidences for the future—they are dangerous for those who speak and for those who listen to them, and I will not have my acts questioned by you or others. For the paper you speak of, you may keep it now and it may prove useful hereafter, but for your friend I shall call him to a reckoning if I live. I think that hereafter you will keep my secret more closely, for it does not redound to the credit of the family that you should take the world into your confidence."

He opened the door and stood looking at her threateningly; then he went out, drawing it noiselessly after him.

Though he had borne himself with a high hand, she could see that he had felt her words keenly, and that he was already fearful for his own safety. What course she should take she did not know, for she shrank from making his treachery public and from bringing punishment by any act of her own on the offender. It was clear that no entreaty nor expostulation of hers would have any weight with him; she knew his headlong and obstinate nature too well to hope that it might.

She remained standing for a long time lost in thought, and then she crept to her own room, wondering whether, after all, Gervase Orme might not keep his word. They had not renewed their conversation since the day that she had placed the pass in his hands, but she felt certain that he had not relaxed in his vigilance. And then it struck her suddenly that by this act she might have imperilled his safety, for her brother had already threatened him, and she knew that in this, at least, he would keep his word, if he had the power or the opportunity to injure him. She regretted now that she had not taken the initiative earlier herself, but on this she was determined, that she and her brother should not remain under the same roof, even if she was compelled publicly to denounce his crime. But she was saved the pain, for she never saw her brother again.

CHAPTER XVI.

OF A DEED OF TREACHERY.

GERVASE had not forgotten the promise he had made to Dorothy, but in the intervals of his duty had watched the house narrowly, and so far as he was able to discover, Jasper had not attempted to repeat his visits to the enemy. He had begun to think that his thinly-veiled threat had had a salutary effect, and that Jasper knowing himself to have been discovered, would not again rashly put his safety in peril. The task was not one for which he had any great relish, but he had determined, however irksome and unpleasant it might prove, that he would save Dorothy from a public exposure and from the pain that such exposure must necessarily inflict upon her. Had it not been for her he would have taken a summary method with the traitor, but his long vigils were rendered light by the thought that they were undertaken for her sake. While he stood in the dark street in the shadow of the opposite doorway, his heart was stirred when he caught sight of her crossing the window of her chamber, and so long as her light burned there he felt that he was not altogether alone. For matter-of-fact as he was, his love had waked whatever of the pathetic and the heroic there was in his nature; and he felt that this service was a link that bound them more closely together. Macpherson who knew something of his solitary watching, had laughed in his own fashion, and told him that no woman could be won in such a fashion, for while one was sitting sad outside another was fiddling in the chamber. But Gervase had kept his post, though nothing came of it and though he had not spoken to Dorothy for days.

To-night he had been ordered with his company to the lines. The enemy who had been waiting in sullen patience for the famine-stricken garrison to surrender, had made some show of movement, and it was believed they meditated another night attack. The guards had therefore been doubled, and precautions were taken to prevent a surprise. Gervase went the more willingly since he believed his services in the city were no longer needed, as a fortnight had elapsed and Jasper had made no sign of renewing his intrigue; and it was a relief once more to find an outlet for his feelings in vigorous action. He felt that he had lost his youth and that he was growing old in witnessing the sights he saw every day—the gaunt hollow-eyed wretches who came tottering from their ruined houses in search of food; the men stricken down with hunger where they stood on duty at the walls; women who had lost their children; children motherless and fatherless, and left without a protector; the want, the sorrow, and the death that increased every day. If they might but have fought out the fight upon the open field, and in one brave struggle have decided their fate, how willingly he would have taken his part! But half the fighting men had fallen since they closed the gates, and of the other half many of them could hardly shoulder their muskets and drag themselves to the walls.

It was a relief to pass out of the gates, and the sight and sound of so much misery, into the quiet night with the cool air blowing about him and the new moon lifting itself slowly through the summer haze. In the distance he could see the gleam of the watch-fires of the enemy, but there was a great and unbroken silence round them, as the company made its way along the path that had been beaten into white dust with frequent marching. Macpherson was in command of the outpost that night, and Gervase found him seated by himself in the bastion on the carriage of a gun that had been brought up from the city. He was quietly communing with himself while he drew consolation from his favourite pipe. Of late days the old soldier had been foremost in attack and counsel. Hard work and scanty fare had had no effect upon him, but his spirits seemed to have risen the higher as their privations and hardships increased. In all expeditions of danger he was among the foremost to volunteer, and on more than one occasion his coolness and resource had been of immense service to the besieged. Walker's antipathy he had long since overcome, for though they had serious differences on points of doctrine, they had each come to recognize the excellent qualities of the other.

When Gervase had completed the arrangement of his company, he joined the old soldier in the bastion. He made the usual inquiries as to the movement in front, but Macpherson, apparently in a fit of abstraction, had answered his questions in monosyllables. There was in the face of the latter the hardness and solemnity that Gervase had seen early in their acquaintance, but which had disappeared of recent days. Then he rose up and laid his hand on the young fellow's shoulder.

"Let us walk down the rampart," he said, as if awaking from his reverie, "my legs have grown stiff, and there is something that I would say to you. Our lads are veterans in the service now and stand up unwinking without the need of a ramrod."

With his hand resting on Gervase's shoulder, they walked along the trench down the hill. There was no need for speech between them now, for Gervase had come to understand his friend's varying moods, and had long since ceased to resent the fits of silence into which the other was accustomed to fall. "Here is another day gone," he said, "and no move from the Tangier Butcher. Whether he come by Inch or by the river, he will come too late, if he come at all. I have been thinking that I might hurry him."

"You are not serious?"

"Faith! the man who drops into the river, and floats himself clear of the lines yonder till he reaches the ships by the good guidance of God, would need to have a serious mind. I have been thinking it all over, as I sat there to-night, and of the poor souls in their tribulation yonder. If I was a year or two younger I would try it blithely, and I think Kirke would listen to his old comrade. There were certain passages between us once—however, as I say, this might be done by one who took his life in his hand, and I think I am the man. Do you believe in omens, lad?"

"I know not." Gervase answered; "I think they are but an idle superstition."

"Then you may laugh at me if you will, but as surely as my name is Ninian I have been called this night to that work, and perhaps to more also."

"I had thought," said Gervase, "you had forgot these idle dreams and warnings."

"Though I am a man of prayer," he went on, disregarding the interruption, "I am not gifted with the vision, but twice before I have heard the same voice, and twice my life was put in grievous jeopardy. When I heard it before, it spoke as if in anger, but to-night it was sweet and soft like his voice that was my friend. You see I was sitting there on the bastion figuring out how I might reach the ships, and reproaching myself for my backwardness in desiring to make the venture, when I heard a voice as if a great way off coming from up the river yonder. I listened attentively but there was a deep silence, and I began to think that it was a mere trick of fancy. Then it came again, sounding nearer, till I heard the words of his voice."

"Whose voice?" said Gervase, wonderingly.

Macpherson turned towards him with a white face. "The voice of my old friend—him that I told you of. But, thank God, I know his spirit is at peace with mine, and I can die content. I could see him before me with my mortal eyes, as I heard that familiar voice that has not sounded in mine ears for twenty years. He has called me and I am going yonder."

There was no trace of excitement in his manner or in his speech, but he spoke with the calm deliberateness of a man who has fully made up his mind and cannot be shaken in his opinion. Gervase knew that it was useless to attempt to reason with him; and indeed, if the truth must be told, he himself was not a little impressed by the tale he had heard. The supernatural played a large part in the lives of the people among whom he lived, and it was not curious that his own mind should have been touched by the prevailing spirit. But to Macpherson it was a fact that required no explanation and hardly seemed to call for wonder.

"And were you not afraid to hear that disembodied voice?" Gervase asked, "if it be that it was not more than your fancy?"

"Wherefore should I be afraid? was it not the voice of my friend who spoke to me no longer in anger? I know that my sin is forgiven. Some day, my lad," he continued, with the kindly and almost caressing tone he had adopted towards Gervase, "some day you will understand what I mean, but not yet. Now forget what I have spoken and help me with your young and nimble wits."

"It is madness for you to dream of it," Gervase answered. "No man could reach the ships by the water alone, and to land would be certain death."

"When we were campaigning on the Danube I swam further than that and was none the worse for it, while the Janissaries were potting at us from their flat-bottomed boat a good part of the way. But this is an old story now."

"Ay! and you were a young man then. If any should undertake this task, why should not I? I am sick and weary to death of what I have seen yonder, and I had rather die once and for all than die by inches. Were there but a chance——"

"My lad, you must not think of it. You are young and there is still need for you in the world. The bonnie wench yonder could ill spare you; but there'll be none, but mayhap yourself, to wait for the home-coming of Ninian Macpherson; and the folk yonder are worth venturing a man's life for. I have been through many a siege, but I think since the beginning of time there hath been none like this."

"Truly there is a fat Cathedral yard," said Gervase bitterly, "and God knows when it will end. There are two more of Simon's sturdy lads dead yesterday, and I hardly think the little girl I told you of will hold out till the morning."

"Poor soul, poor soul!" he continued, "and to think that it should all be happening under that—" and he lifted up his hand. The night was clear and cloudless. The river lay before them reflecting the starlight in its calm unbroken waters, and the moon lifted its slender crescent through a mellow haze. They were about to retrace their steps along the lines when Macpherson, whose sight was marvellously keen, caught sight of a figure moving rapidly under the shelter of a sunken fence. He had seen it for a moment as it showed clear against the river, as it made its way swiftly in the shadow. He caught Gervase by the arm, pulling him under cover of the embankment.

"There is foul play here," he whispered. "Yon binkie travels too fast to have an honest errand. He will come this way, if he intend, as I verily think he does, to pass through to the camp yonder."

The man made his way toward them rapidly, without stopping for a moment. It was clear that he intended to pass the angle were they stood, and they would not have to stir to intercept him as he passed.

"There may be need of this," said Macpherson, drawing his sword, "but I think not; the traitor is nearly always a coward."

They could now hear the man breathing hard as he ran; he was preparing to leap into the trench, when Macpherson presented himself before him, with his drawn sword in his hand.

"Stand, and give me the word."

The man stopped short as if astonished at the unexpected rencontre, and then thrust his hand into his breast. But Macpherson divined his purpose. "If you move that hand I will run you through the body," and he held the point of the sword perilously near the man's throat.

Gervase had not moved forward but was still standing in the shadow. Something warned him that the traitor whom he had been watching so long had made his attempt to-night, and was discovered at last.

"Now, sir, what is your errand here to-night? if you do not answer me I shall call the guard."

"You need not call the guard, Captain Macpherson. I am here on no sinister business, but have come to seek for Mr. Gervase Orme, who, I am told, is in the lines to-night."

He lifted off his hat and stood bareheaded in the midnight. As he listened, Gervase knew that it was a lie, but did not move from his place of concealment.

"Good God," cried Macpherson, "'tis the brave wench's brother. I'm thinking, Mr. Carew, it was a strange way you took to find the gentleman you speak of. It looked like as if you thought to find him yonder."

"I am not familiar with your outworks, sir," answered Jasper, who had recovered his composure, and spoke with studied coolness, "and I thought you had another line of defence along the hill."

"There is no accounting for a man's thoughts,"

said Macpherson, "but the message must have been urgent that needed so much haste. In the future I would advise you to move more circumspectly when musket balls are plenty. Now, perhaps, as the gentleman is my friend, you will even give me your news and I will contrive that it reaches him."

"It can be delivered to none but himself. If you will tell me where I may find him, I have no doubt I can make my way thither myself."

"I have no doubt you could, but you see I cannot let you out of my sight. We must even see the gentleman together."

"You do not mean that you doubt my word?"

"Your word, sir, cannot interfere with my plain duty. I am one of those who strive to give no tongue to their loose thoughts. I would think well of you for your sister's sake; and I think we will hear, after all, what Mr. Orme has to say about the matter."

"I have no doubt," said Carew, changing his ground as he saw that Macpherson was inflexible, "that I have acted heedlessly in venturing hither, and it may be best for me to return to the city. If you should consider it well, I am ready to give any explanation that may be necessary in the morning."

Macpherson smiled grimly. "I have no doubt you would, but it is a pity that you should have come so far without fulfilling your errand, and I think Mr. Orme hath been waiting with some impatience to hear what you have to say to him."

Gervase stepped quickly forward.

"You can go no further with this deception, Mr. Carew," he said, "I gave you a friendly warning before which you have not followed, and you must suffer the consequences."

Carew stepped back with a look of hate on his face. "The curse of heaven light on you for an intermeddling rogue!" he cried. "Do what you will, I care not."

"You knew," Gervase continued, "that I had learned your secret, and I think though I may be deceived, you knew how I had learned it. I was anxious to spare you the humiliation of making a confession of your treachery, and for the sake of others would have averted the punishment. But you have not taken my counsel to heart, and for myself I bitterly regret it."

"I want neither your counsel nor your regret. Tell me what you mean to do and let us have an end of it. I cannot see why I should not leave the city if I would."

Macpherson had listened to this brief conversation in surprise. He had not imagined that Gervase had had any suspicion of Jasper's treachery, and for a moment it pained him to think that he had withheld his confidence. Then he said in a low tone, "Does his sister know of this?"

"There is no need for concealment," Gervase answered; "it was from her that I first learned it, and I have been watching for a fortnight that this did not happen. It will break her heart."

"That need not be: we will even take the law into our own hands, come of it what will. Now, sir," he said, turning round towards Jasper, "there is no need for further deception, for it cannot profit you a whit. I never doubted that you were a traitor from the moment that I caught sight of you by the dyke yonder. You know what is the punishment of a traitor? Hanging is not a very fit end for any man, and hanged you will be if we carry you back to the city. I cannot tell what is your intent in stooping to this dishonour, but I think in letting you pass I can do but little harm. They know how it stands with us, and you can bring them but little fresh news. Did I think of you alone, as God is my witness, I should string you up with my own hand without compunction, but for the sake of them that loved you, unworthy as you are, the way is open for you. You may go. You may tell them from Ninian Macpherson that never a man of them will put his foot inside the walls, and you have seen the last of the city yourself."

For a moment Jasper could not realize the good news, and appeared overcome by surprise. "I may be able to return your favour some day, sir," he said, "however poor a figure I may cut now."

"I would take no favour from your hands," answered Macpherson; "now go before my mind changes, for I doubt whether I do right in letting you pass thus easily."

Without a word Carew crossed the trench and clambered up the rampart. On the top he turned short, "I have to thank you for your kindness," he said, "and for the courteous speech you have made. You, sir, as I have said I will do my best to repay, but for you, Mr. Orme, you may take my favour now."

Quick as thought Gervase saw the barrel of a pistol flashing in the moonlight, presented straight at his breast. Macpherson saw it too, and sprang forward as if to leap the trench, when there came a blinding flash and a loud cry as Macpherson fell forward on his face.

Gervase followed his impulse, which was to secure the miscreant who had done this base and cowardly act, but when he had reached the summit of the rampart, he was rapidly disappearing in the darkness and it was impossible to overtake him. So with a bitter feeling in his heart and something that sounded like an imprecation on his lips, he turned back to his wounded friend.

The sound of the shot had attracted the attention of the men nearest to them in the trenches; they came hurrying up believing that the attack had begun, but when they saw Macpherson lying on the ground and Gervase kneeling by his side, their alarm was changed to suspicion and surprise. There was an unbroken silence in front under the quiet summer sky; not a blade of grass was stirring on the hillside. It was clear to them that this blow had not come from the enemy, and full of surprise and wonder, they watched Gervase as he bent over the fallen man and opened his vest to find the wound.

Macpherson was still conscious; the blood that was pouring from a wound in his breast had dyed his shirt deep red, and they noticed that he had not let go his hold upon the hilt of his sword. But there was that look in his face that every man in that company had seen too frequently for months to mistake—that look in the presence of which there is no hope, and which speaks inevitably of a speedy dissolution. It was clear to them all that the last sands of his life had nearly run out.

A sergeant of his regiment running up the lines had brought down a blazing brand of fir, by the light of which Gervase stanched the flowing blood as well as he was able. He felt his hand shaking as he bound up the wound, nor could he trust himself to make any answer to the eager questions that were poured upon him. It required no skill to tell that the wound was mortal; it was only a question of hours, perhaps of minutes; and the thought that pressed most strongly upon him was that it was to save his life that Macpherson had lost his own. Rugged and staunch and true, a loyal friend, a valiant soldier, he had hardly recognized his worth or the affection he had begun to bear toward him, until the time had come for them to part.

From the moment that he fell Macpherson had not spoken; he lay motionless with his face turned up and the light of the blazing torch falling on it. Only once he pressed the hand of Gervase with a gentle pressure; that was all the sign he gave of consciousness. A surgeon had been sent for but there seemed to be no probability of his arriving in time, and they hastily began to construct a hurdle on which to carry the old soldier home. Though he had been quick to punish any breach of discipline, he had always been forward with his praise, and they had long since learnt that he would not ask them to go where he was not ready to lead them. They had come to impose implicit confidence in his wisdom and courage, while they had seen in a thousand instances that a warm and kindly heart lay under his rugged manner and surly speech. They had been wont to say that Roaring Meg and the old Captain were children of the same mother; but there was many a moist eye in the trenches that night when they learned that the old fire-eater had come to his end.

While they were getting ready the hurdle on which to carry him to the city, Gervase had not moved but still knelt holding his head on his knees. The blow was so sudden and so unexpected that he had not had time to realize it. Notwithstanding the evidence of his senses, he could not believe that he was in the presence of death. He did not once think of his own miraculous escape nor of how this might affect the woman he loved, but stunned and bewildered, he endeavoured to make clear to his own mind that his friend was dying.

Macpherson's lips moved and Gervase bent down to catch the words, but for a time they were broken and inaudible. Then with an effort he lifted his hand and motioned to the men who were gathered round, to withdraw. He had still much difficulty in speaking but Gervase was able to catch the meaning of his words now.

"I'm going home, lad," he said, "going home. I was called, and—and—you will promise me."

Gervase did not speak but only pressed his hand.

"She must never know who has done this—never till the Judgment. She is proud, and it would break her heart. Only you and I—we know, and we will keep the secret. You will promise; you are a good lad, and my old heart was turned toward you."

Gervase was not ashamed of the tears that streamed down his face. He brushed them away with the back of his hand, and tried to speak as well as his feelings would permit him.

"I am glad you promised. Don't grieve for me; it was better that I should go than you. The campaign is over and I am going home."

They placed him on the stretcher and carried him back to the city.

Already as they passed through Bishops-Gate, the crimson light of the dawn had filled the sky, and the stars had failed, and the shadows had passed away in the rosy glow of the pleasant summer morning.

As the bearers of the hurdle halted with their burden on the stone steps of the house in which Macpherson lodged, he called out to them to stop.

"Let me look at it once more before I go. I'll never see it again."

And so they stood there in silence fronting the sunrise; he raised his head for a minute and then motioned to them to carry him in. They laid him in his own bed, and left Gervase and the surgeon to examine his wound.

But it was evident that nothing could be done for him. He was already past all mortal aid, and as he suffered from no pain they had only to wait for the end that would not be long in coming.

"He'll no' need my aid, Mr. Orme," said Saunderson, "for there's none of us could bring him round. 'Tis a pity there's no woman body to close his eyes; but I'm told he was a fine soldier, and I'll look in and see the last of him mysel'."

"No one shall touch him but myself," said Gervase, "I shall never have such a friend again, and God knows there is none will miss him as I will."

Gervase had never been in the room before, and as he sat down by the bed he looked round him with a saddened interest. On the table lay the leather-bound volume he remembered so well. Above the bed hung a broad sword with its hilt of silver richly chased, and he could see from where he sat, that there was a legend upon the blade. A pair of spurs, a silver-mounted pistol, and a long pipe of foreign make, lay on the mantelshelf. A couple of high-backed chairs, a few simple cooking utensils in the hearth, and an oak press, the doors of which lay open, were all the furniture in the room. It looked bare and comfortless, and it seemed to add to the pathos of the tragedy that a man with so much that was gallant and loveable, should die friendless and unregretted in a room like this.

Gervase had found a little wine in a bottle and with this he moistened Macpherson's lips from time to time. He lay motionless all day with his eyes half closed, but toward evening he seemed to Gervase to grow delirious, and began to talk in a rambling way, with a thick and broken utterance. His mind was busy with his old campaigning days, and his speech was full of foreign cities, and of battles and sieges and ambuscades, and of women he had loved in his wild free life. There was no coherence in the matter; only a meaningless confusion of unfamiliar names. Only once before had he raised the curtain that hung over his past life, but he had made no secret of the fact that his youth had been a riotous one and full of wayward passion; and he had seemed to have broken with it utterly. But now it had all come back again, and his mind was full of the tavern brawl and the low intrigue and the horrors of sack and siege. It was strange to hear the old man with the white head and haggard face that had grown so old looking in a day, babbling of the fierce delights of his youth as if he were living among them again. Gervase would willingly have closed his ears but he was in a manner fascinated by it.

"A thousand devils, here they come. Lord, what

a change! They ride as if Hell were loose after them. The pike men will never stand. Close down your ranks. There they go, rolling one after another. Pooh! a mere scratch. I'll pour out my own wine and drink it too; a woman's lips are sweeter after a draught like that. Open the windows; we want air—air and a song. Jack will——"

Then he gave a loud cry and started up as if in pain. "Oh, God! I have killed him—wipe it off, that is his blood upon my sword—wipe it off, I tell you. You see how his eyes will not shut; they stare at me as if he were still alive. You she-devil, I will kill you as I killed him. I cannot draw this blade from the scabbard. Listen, and I will tell you why: his blood hath glued it fast, and I can never draw it again—never. Pooh! you are a fool."

So he rambled on, while Gervase sat compelled to listen and put together the history of that stirring and eventful life. Then the paroxysm died away, and exhausted with his passion he lay quiet, only his lips moving and his spare brown hands catching at the coverlet. Once or twice Gervase thought he heard his own name, but it might have been mere fancy, for it was now impossible to catch the words his lips tried to frame.

According to his promise, Saunderson had looked in during the course of the evening, but as he said, rather to cheer the watcher than in the hope of assisting the patient. He had been amazed at the great hold he had upon life, for no ordinary man could have survived such a wound for an hour. He'll be away before the morn," he said; "you can see how he's trying to loose himsel'. Man, 'tis a strange thing this dying, and we a' take our ain gait about it. Some die hard like the auld man there, and some slip off easily, but licht or hard 'tis a' ane. I've seen a guid few lately. I'm afeard ye can't sit here this nicht, and I'll look up some stout body to tak' your place."

But Gervase would not hear of it. He had determined to see the last of his friend and was determined to spend the night at his bedside. He had seated himself in the chair by the window, and had taken up the little book which bore the owner's name on the title page and the words "Utrecht, 1664," and was worn and marked by repeated using. He read on till the sunset had died away and it became too dark to see the page. Then he closed the book and went downstairs in search of a light.

When he came back with the lighted candle in his hand, Macpherson was sitting up in the bed, with his eyes staring wide open and his hands stretched out. The wound had burst out afresh and the blood had stained the white counterpane.

"Listen, Gervase," he said, "listen, my son! Do you hear how he is calling me? I would know the sound of his voice among ten thousand—the sound of his voice that I loved. I would have waited for you, but I knew him first and loved him first, and I cannot tarry. Jack, dear Jack, good comrade, I am coming. Oh! the marvellous light—"

He struggled as if to leave the bed and Gervase was running forward to restrain him, when he fell back on the pillow, with his eyes and mouth wide open. At a glance Gervase saw that it was all over; his faithful friend was dead, and there was no need for watching now. As he stood for a long time looking at him, the hard and rugged face seemed to soften into a smile, and the lines that were cut deep in the forehead and the cheeks had disappeared, and he lay like one asleep. The fight was indeed over, and the reveille would awaken him from his rest no more.

They buried him the next day in the Cathedral yard, four men of his own regiment carrying the body on the stretcher on which they had brought him home. As Gervase saw him laid in the shallow grave, he felt that he had lost the best friend and the truest comrade he was ever likely to find. And there the ashes of the old soldier still lie mingled with those of many another who fell in the same quarrel and found a resting-place there from all their labours. In after days Gervase erected a tablet to his memory, with nothing more than the name and the date upon it and these words: "He laid down his life for his friend."

CHAPTER XVII.

OF A GREAT ADVENTURE.

MACPHERSON died toward the end of the second week in July, when the city had already begun to suffer the dire extremities of famine. The provisions in the magazines were almost exhausted; the meal and the tallow were doled out with a sparing hand. Already the citizens had begun to live upon food that at other times they would have turned from in disgust and loathing. Horse-flesh was almost becoming a luxury, dogs, rats, and cats were greedily devoured, and even of these the supply was beginning to fail. Putrid fevers had broken out which carried off multitudes; loathsome diseases of the skin grew common, and even the strongest began to find it hard to draw themselves to the walls or to help in repelling the frequent attacks on the outposts. Added to this, there was hardly a whole roof in the city, for during two months the iron hail had been continually pouring upon them. Many of them felt indeed that death would be a welcome relief, and they envied those who were already laid in the churchyard. But still they held out grimly, and with faces blackened with hunger, declared that they were ready to die rather than surrender. The spirit that may still be found here and there in the Imperial Province burned with an unabated flame—a pride which two centuries has not been able to remove, and strong almost to fanaticism. Yet it was not to be wondered at that discontent and suspicion should grow and spread. Some few proved insubordinate, others deserted to the enemy, but for the most part they stood loyally by their leaders.

Hamilton who was now in command of the royal troops, believing that the time had come when his overtures would be listened to, had sent a message containing liberal terms, but after some fruitless negotiations, they refused his offer and determined to hold out. A messenger had been able to find his way from the ships with a letter which had revived their hopes a little, but they had lost all faith in Kirke, and looked only with stubborn despair to the time when they could defend themselves no longer.

After the death of Macpherson, Gervase had gone about his duty as before, but he had greatly missed the wise and faithful counsellor whose friendly comfort had helped him to bear his trials. The blow that he had sustained had been very great, and he had felt unwilling to face Dorothy Carew while the wound was still fresh. He had determined to observe the old soldier's dying injunction that she should not know by whose hand he had fallen; and he himself would have desired even if the command had not been laid upon him that she should remain in ignorance of it. He knew that she had already suffered much, and he was desirous of sparing her further pain. Jasper had not appeared again in the city nor was it likely that he would, so that it could serve no purpose of any sort to denounce him as the murderer.

When he had summoned up courage and met Dorothy for the first time since Macpherson's death, she had displayed much emotion, but it had not occurred to her that she was connected in any way with the old soldier's end. She had told Gervase that her brother had disappeared, and that she had no doubt he had gone over to the enemy, but the subject was one on which she seemed naturally unwilling to dwell much, and he on his part did not press it. It struck him, however, as singular that she did not mention De Laprade; and it was only in answer to his inquiry that she told him that he was making rapid progress towards recovery. She herself was looking very ill and wretched—so ill that Gervase was alarmed at her appearance, and her eyes were red as if she had been weeping recently.

"I thought I was strong and able to bear anything," she said, "but my heart is breaking. Is there no hope for us anywhere?"

"There is always hope——"

"I see that you can give me no comfort. My aunt is dying slowly, and she bears it very patiently. In a day or two there will be no more food and then——"

"And then there will be plenty if God helps us,

Miss Carew," Gervase went on. "You have not despaired till now. You have shown us an example in patient courage we might all have profited by, and you must not let your heart fail you now. You may tell Lady Hester she will not have long to wait. In three days the ships will be at the quays and all will be well."

"I think you have always told me the truth," she said; "but how is this to happen?"

"When we meet again I shall tell you that and more; you must not ask me now, but I believe I speak sincerely and with truth."

"I have always trusted you."

"And always may; there is nothing I would not try to do for your sake. But I am growing a boaster, and I have done nothing and perhaps can do nothing. Only do not let your heart fail. When we meet again I trust the joybells will be ringing, and there will be bonfires on the ramparts; if not——"

"It is too good news. We have waited so long but it seems as far away as ever."

"I think it is coming now. Miss Carew, if we should never meet again, I want you to remember that I thought of you till the last, and that all I did was done—nay I should not say that. I feel that we shall meet again."

She looked at him with a look of awakened fear. "You are not going into any great peril?"

"We live among them, one and all of us."

"But you——"

"Would only carry your thoughts with me—Dorothy, my best beloved," he cried, taking her hand in his, "before I go I want you to say you love me as I love you."

She drew her hand away quickly.

"I cannot I cannot. I will tell you why hereafter. My God! I love you."

He caught her in his arms and kissed her again and again unresistingly. Then she tore herself from his embrace, and with a stifled cry rushed from the room. But he went away happy, with her last words ringing in his ears, and feeling himself ready to do the work he was about to undertake. For while he was talking to Dorothy he had hastily formed a resolution that was lying dormant in his mind for days. In his last conversation with Macpherson, the old soldier had declared his intention of reaching the ships, and Gervase had been dwelling on the project for the last ten days. He knew the task was full of deadly peril—it had already been twice attempted without success, and it seemed so hopeless that he had shrunk from undertaking it. But the sight of Dorothy's thin and wasted face had removed all his doubts, and he had determined to make one last effort to induce Kirke to undertake the relief. He himself believed that the undertaking was not nearly so formidable as it seemed, and if once a move was made he did not doubt that the boom would prove no very serious barrier. But the great problem was to reach the ships which were lying far down the river. On both sides of the bank the enemy were watching with a vigilance which it seemed impossible to escape. Even if he succeeded in eluding them, he could hardly hope to swim the long six miles in the condition he was in, and to land was almost certain death. But he made up his mind to make the attempt and to trust to the chapter of accidents to carry him safely through.

As he went to look for Walker from whom he desired to obtain his credentials, he felt strong enough for anything. Had not he heard from the sweetest lips in the world the sweetest words he had ever heard spoken. Had he not everything to move him to the attempt? If he lived he would show her that he was not unworthy of her love, for this deed was one that all men would not attempt, and few could carry safely through. There was glory in it and renown, though it was neither glory nor renown that he sought.

When he had told the old colonel of his intentions, the latter at first tried to dissuade him. He was only flinging his life away, he said, for nothing. Others had tried and failed; he could not hope to succeed. Even if he succeeded in reaching the ships, which he could not do, he could tell them nothing that they did not know there. Kirke was a coward or a traitor, and they could not hope for help from him. He could send them letters that meant nothing, but that was all. But Gervase was not to be dissuaded by any argument. He had set his heart upon making the attempt, and his resolution was so evident that at length Walker unwillingly consented, and with a homely piety commended him to the protection of Providence that, however it might frown, had not forsaken them.

"We will say nothing of this to any," he had said, "but will keep the matter closely to ourselves, for the folk yonder have long ears and can hear our whispers here. Some time before midnight we will even go down to the Waterside together, and as you are a brave man and a courageous, there is one old man who will pray for your safe keeping and deliverance. I shall have the epistle writ out, and I pray God Kirke may be the first to read it."

Gervase's preparations for his adventure were easily made. He had left a letter in which he had made a disposal of his effects, in case anything happened to him, and had written another which was addressed to Dorothy Carew. The only weapon he had provided himself with was a small hunting knife that had belonged to Macpherson, which he hoped he would not require to use but which might prove useful in an emergency. There had been some rain during the day, and the night promised to be dark and cloudy. So long as there was no moonlight there was a possibility of his making the attempt with a reasonable chance of success, but should the moon show herself he could hardly hope to remain undiscovered.

The time hung heavily on his hands while he waited

for the hour when he was to meet Walker, and then he found himself trembling with feverish impatience. Walker, however, insisted on his taking supper before he left, and it was weeks since Gervase had seen so plentiful a meal spread before him. The old colonel watched him with a serious admiration as he made huge inroads on the food, and when Gervase had finished, he went to a cupboard and produced a flask.

"You have had the last of the meat," he said, taking the cork out of the bottle, "and now you are going to have the last of the drink. There are two glasses left, and you shall have both of them. Whenever we meet again, if Heaven pleases, we will crack a bottle together. I love a brave lad, and if age had not taken the oil out of my joints, I should have liked nothing better than to bear you company. Now drink that off for it will keep you warm in the water."

Going down Ship Quay Street together, they passed through the gate and came out upon the quay. The night was very dark and a slight drizzling rain had begun to fall. On both sides of the river they could see many lights, some moving, some stationary, and could hear the sound of voices calling and answering from the other bank. But the river was flowing darkly at their feet, and a night better suited for his purpose Gervase could hardly have found. When he had divested himself of his boots coat and vest, he stuck the short knife in his belt, and fastened round his waist with a strip of canvas the piece of bladder in which the letter from Walker was rolled.

"God bless you, my lad, and send you safe back to us. I feel even like the patriarch when he would have offered up his son, but here too, it is my trust the Lord will not require a life."

"I feel that I shall come back, colonel," said Gervase; "never fear for me. Have the bonfires ready to give us a welcome."

The old man in the excess of his emotion, took him in his arms and kissed him on the forehead, and then Gervase wringing his hand, dropped noiselessly into the water and struck out into the stream. He knew that it was necessary for him to husband his strength for it would all be needed; so after he found himself well in the middle of the river, he began to swim slowly, and to let the current carry him down. If the night should continue dark it would be impossible that he could be discovered from the land; he himself could only dimly make out the banks, and trusted to the lights to help him to direct his course. But the rain had ceased and he feared that the clouds were beginning to break; in the moonlight they could hardly fail to see him.

Still, every yard he made was a yard nearer safety, and to some extent lessened the chances of discovery, for the further he descended the stream, the more lax in all likelihood would their vigilance become.

As he swam on steadily with a slow strong stroke, his thoughts were busy with many things.

He thought of Dorothy, who loved him and would repay him for his labour; of Macpherson, whose brave spirit was perhaps keeping him company on this perilous venture; and pardonably enough, of the honour he would gain for this deed. It never occurred to him that having reached the ships there would be any difficulty about the relief of the city. When once his story had been told, they must up with their anchors, if there was any manhood among them, and try the mettle of their guns. He imagined to himself with what joy Dorothy would welcome him back when he came among the first with the good news.

So he swam on for half an hour carried slowly down by the current, and then for the first time he began to feel that he had overestimated his strength, and that his extremities were growing numb and cold. He had long since passed the lights of Pennyburn; he must now be coming close to the boom where would be his first great danger, for the lights yonder on either side of the river must be the lights of the forts that guarded the barrier. The water seemed somehow to have grown colder and less buoyant, and worst of all, the moon was beginning to show through the masses of broken cloud. Three months ago he would have found little difficulty in swimming twice the distance, but now he dragged himself with difficulty through the water, and his shoulders were growing stiff and painful. What if he failed to reach the fleet after all! His mind was filled with despair at the thought, and he pulled himself together with an effort and swam on with an obstinate determination to keep himself afloat. With the wind blowing freshly, the waves came leaping past him with an icy shiver that seemed to take away his strength.

But there was gradually forcing itself upon his mind the conviction that, after all, he must land and make his way upon foot till he came opposite to where the ships were riding at anchor. It would be better to make for the shore at once while three hours of darkness still remained, for when the light came it would be impossible to travel. While he was making up his mind as to where it would be safest for him to land, the moon came out suddenly with a startling brilliance, lighting up the river and the banks on either side. He could now see Charles Fort distinctly, and he fancied that he could discern lying across the river the dark fabric of the boom, with the water leaping into white waves against it. It was out of the question to attempt to cross the barrier now; even where he was swimming his position was perilous in the extreme.

Then he saw, near the shore, a small hooker lying at anchor, and almost without knowing why he struck out towards it. There was little or no likelihood of there being anyone on board and if, as seemed to be the case, he should have to lie concealed the whole of the day, he might find some food on board the little craft. He swam cautiously round her, but he could hear no sound; then catching hold of the cable, he lifted himself up by the bowsprit and found himself on board. She was decked forward, and though he did not know for what purpose she was used, there was a large gun covered with a piece of canvas lying amidships. But though there was no one on board, a small lamp suspended from a beam was burning dimly in the forecastle. He felt that it would not be wise to tarry long, so diving hastily down the companion, he began to investigate the contents of the lockers. In one he found several louis which he left undisturbed, but in another to his joy he discovered some oat-cakes and a quantity of rum in a case bottle. The latter was particularly welcome, and after a dram he felt that he had got a new lease of strength and vigour.

The circulation was beginning to return to his hands and feet. He sat down on the edge of a bunk and chafed his limbs till the cramp that he had begun to experience, was entirely gone. He was beginning to think that it was time to take his departure, when he heard the sound of oars creaking in their rowlocks and voices almost alongside. Hastily extinguishing the light he drew out the knife with which he was armed, and creeping out of the forecastle dropped cautiously down close to the great gun, where he concealed himself under the canvas. Then as the bow of a boat grated against the side of the hooker, he could see from where he lay a man and a lad clambering on board, the latter with the painter in his hand. "Make fast," said the former, " and come and help me to get the mainsail up. They'll be aboard in an hour."

The man made his way into the forecastle growling and swearing at the lamp having gone out, while the boy clambered over the boom and made fast the painter to a ring in the stern-sheets. Gervase had hoped that the boy might have followed the man into the forecastle, and that he himself might then have dropped overboard unperceived. But in this he was disappointed, for the boy instead of going below began to unloose the earing by which the mainsail was fastened, whistling as he did so with a clear shrill note that Gervase remembered for years afterwards.

Presently the man came up from below swearing at the boy for the noise he was making, and began to take in a fathom or two of the cable by which the craft was moored. There seemed to Gervase no chance of escaping unperceived, and a better opportunity than this might not present itself. So while the man knelt with his back turned towards him, and the boy was fumbling with the halyards in the darkness, he rose from his place of concealment and leaped upon the bulwark.

The lad hearing the noise turned round with a look of terror on his face. "Holy Mother of God!" he cried, "it's a spirit;" and as the man turned round where he was kneeling at the cat-heads, he seemed for a moment to share his belief and participate in his alarm.

As Gervase dropped noiselessly into the water

they were both too bewildered to raise any alarm, and the river bed was already under his feet before he heard their outcry. Then they called out loudly to someone on the shore. Wading through the water toward the land, Gervase noticed for the first time a low fort built of sods and rough timber close to the bank. At the hubbub that was raised by the crew of the hooker, the door was opened and a man came down towards the water's edge in the uniform of a French sergeant.

Seeing Gervase come upon the bank and mistaking him for one of the crew he called out, "*Que le diable faites-vous ce bruit, coquin?*" But as he came down and saw the young fellow closer, clad only in his shirt and breeches, he immediately divined what was wrong and came running down the bank. Gervase waited till he came close up; then, and it was an old trick he had learned years before, he put out his foot and struck him a tremendous blow with his left hand. The man went headlong into the water, and without waiting to see what became of him, Gervase ran at full speed along the bank, and never halted to take breath till he found himself in the shelter of the wood, that at that time grew thick along the bank.

He knew that in a short time the pursuit would be hot after him and that there was not a moment to be lost. But to hasten was another matter; his feet were torn and bleeding, and so painful that he could hardly put them to the ground. While he sat down to rest his head swam like one in a vertigo. But if he was to carry out his mission he could not rest now. He tore off a piece of his shirt which he wrapped tightly round his wounded feet, and set off again. The only way in which he could make certain that he was travelling in the right direction was by keeping close to the river, which he caught sight of from time to time through the trees. But his motion was necessarily slow; it was terrible work picking his way over the fallen branches and rough stones that jarred his nerves whenever he set his feet upon them. But the fate of the city was on his shoulders and the hope of the woman he loved.

It seems strange to me, the writer, and may seem strange to you who read, but the last words of his sweetheart restored his drooping heart and renewed his failing strength whenever he thought of them through this adventurous journey.

The night was nearly over and the dawn was coming up, when he still found himself in the wood, dragging one foot slowly after another. How far he had gone he could not tell, but he knew that he must have travelled several miles, and could not be far from his destination. He feared to leave the shelter of the wood, but he knew that he could not spend the day here, for he was already becoming weary and was consumed by a raging thirst. After a while the wood broke and there was a stretch of fields before him, with farther on some growing timber and a ruined building.

But with awakened hope he could now see the

ships where they rode at anchor some two miles away. While it was yet a grey light he determined to take advantage of it, and gladly left the tangle of the wood for the soft, green turf that gave him some relief in walking. Then he came to a running water where he quenched his thirst and bathed his wounds. Following the course of the stream would bring him to the beach where there was standing a house, probably a fisherman's cottage, surrounded by a fence and a few fruit trees growing about it. It was yet probably too early for the inmates to be astir, and the hope dawned upon him that he might perhaps be able to find a boat upon the beach, for he knew that any thought of swimming was now out of the question. There was a further advantage in following the little stream, for the briars grew thick along its course and would afford him shelter, while the country was open beyond. He did not hesitate, but set off with as much speed as he could make. His destination was now in sight and his chance of escape had considerably increased. If he had only another half hour of twilight, he thought; but this was not to be, for it was rapidly growing lighter, and as he came down to the cottage it was already broad day.

He had just gained the fence that surrounded the cottage, when looking back he saw a body of dragoons beating the edge of the wood that he had left half an hour before. They had not caught sight of him for their attention was fixed on the fern and briars that skirted the wood, but he had not a moment to lose. He could not retrace his steps and so gain the friendly shelter of the little stream, nor could he now make for the beach as had been at first his intention. But crushing his way through the thorn hedge, he came into a little garden. The door of the house was lying open, and he saw what he had not noticed before, that the inmates must be already astir, for a thick smoke was rising into the morning air. He knew that his pursuers could not fail to find him in the garden, and he determined to take his chance, and to trust to the humanity of the people in the cottage to conceal him. This resolution he had taken not without some hope of finding friends, for there was a homeliness and air of comfort in the place that seemed to him little in keeping with the character of the Celt.

When he entered the door he found himself in a spacious kitchen. A woman was standing on the hearth cooking some fish that gave forth an appetizing smell. As she heard him coming in she dropped the frying pan, and running over to the corner of the dresser, seized an old musket that was lying against it.

"For God's sake, hear me," cried Gervase; "do not shoot."

"What do you want?" she said, still holding the weapon ready for use and looking at him with a doubtful air. Her speech at once assured him that he had found a friend.

"I have come from the city," he said; "I have

been travelling all night and am trying for the ships. The dragoons are after me now, and if you do not help me, I will be taken."

She dropped the musket, and running over took hold of him by both hands. "My poor lad, my poor lad," she cried, "you are but a woeful sight. If they haven't seen you coming in I think I can save you. My good man lay a day in the loft and they couldn't find him, though they searched high up and low down. He's in the city like yourself and now —but I would like to ask you a question or two. Where are they now?"

"Close by the edge of the wood and I think they are coming down this way."

"Then my questions will keep. You'll step softly after me, for the young folk are still asleep upstairs, and it would never do they should see you now. I was before Derry myself," she continued, as she led the way up the ladder to the loft above the kitchen, "but they are well-mannered enough and don't trouble me now."

In the loft above were two beds, in one of which three flaxen-headed boys were lying sound asleep, and as Gervase followed her the woman gave a warning gesture, and stopped for a moment to look at them. Then with Gervase's assistance she noiselessly pulled away the other bed, and disclosed a recess in the wall which was wide enough to admit him. "Get in there," she said, "and I'll call you when they are gone. If they haven't seen you they'll never think of looking there; if they have, God help me and the children—but I'll do more than that for the good cause."

When she had left him and had gone down the ladder after replacing the bed, Gervase began to regret that he had imperilled the safety of the kindly soul who had shown anxiety to assist him. But it was not his own safety that was at stake; it was that of the city and the lives of the citizens.

He lay listening for the sound of his pursuers, but the moments seemed to lengthen into hours and still they did not make their appearance. Meanwhile the good woman downstairs had gone on cooking the breakfast for herself and the children, and had set out the rough earthenware on the table by the window. When she saw the dragoons coming across the fields straight toward the house, she walked to the threshold and met them with an unconcerned smile on her face. "You are early astir this morning," she said. "Is there to be more trouble in these parts? I'm thinking, Captain Lambert, I've seen you before."

"Troth, that is very possible," was the answer, "and I don't think you have seen the last of me either. Now, look here, I want you to tell me the truth, a thing most women find hard enough to do, but the truth I must have or I'll know the reason. why. Have you seen anybody afoot this morning?"

She looked at him with an air of well-assumed astonishment.—"Why, 'tis barely five, and the children, bless their hearts, are still abed. My good man, you know, is away yonder, and the neighbours don't trouble me now."

"Come, my lads, we must search the house. We'll get nothing out of her, she's as close as perdition."

"If you'll tell me what you want," she said, "I would try and answer you. The boys are sleeping upstairs and there is nobody below but myself."

"A fellow from the city has come this way, and I'll take my oath he's here or hereabouts."

"God help him then, for I think he'll get little further."

"That's as may be, but we'll see if he's here at any rate. Now, my men, don't leave a mousehole that you don't go to the bottom of. I've a shrewd suspicion that he's not far off."

They searched the garden and lower part of the house without success, and then ascended the ladder into the loft. The boys were asleep when they came up, but the noise awakened them, and frightened at the red coats of whom they stood in deadly terror, they set up a great crying which highly amused the soldiers. It may also have somewhat diverted their attention, for they failed to find the hiding-place in which Gervase lay concealed. Returning downstairs they reported that it was impossible that the prisoner could have concealed himself above, at which the good woman who was entertaining the captain, expressed her unbounded surprise.

"I thought," she said, "you would have brought

him down with you. I'm sure my man would be glad to hear there was somebody in his wife's bedroom. But you have strange notions, you soldiers, and I'm sorry, Captain, I can't ask you to stay and share the breakfast with me."

The dragoon laughed good-humouredly and flung a couple of coins on the table. "We're not so black as we're painted," he said, "and there's for your trouble; but had we found him it would have been another story. Now, my men, to the right-about and let us make up the stream the way we came. He hasn't left the wood yet."

When they had quitted the house, the woman took her pail and followed them as far as the well, watching them till they had reached the wood and disappeared among the trees. Then she released Gervase from his hiding-place and he was now in no enviable condition either of mind or of body. He was so weak that he found it difficult to make his way down the ladder into the kitchen, and he could scarcely set his feet to the ground. The woman looked at him with a face on which compassion was plainly written; then she went over to a press and took out a coat that belonged to her husband, a coarse shirt, and a pair of worsted stockings. "Now," she said, "just step behind there, and make yourself cosy in these. If Sandy Graham was at home he would make you welcome to the best he has. Then you'll come and sit down and tell me about my good man and the city, and how they fare there while I make ready something to eat, for God knows you look as if you needed it."

Gervase gladly did as he was directed, and when he was dressed, as gladly fell to upon the fresh fish and coarse bread which seemed to him the sweetest meat he had ever partaken of in his life.

While he went on with his breakfast he answered the numerous inquiries as well as he was able, while the boys, who were now stirring, gathered round in admiration of the young giant for whom their father's ample coat was far too scanty. "I'm sorry you don't know Sandy," she said; "it would have been some comfort to know that you had seen him. I knew it was ill with you in the city, but I never thought it was as bad as that. They'll be thinking of ye now with an anxious heart."

"They know nothing about me," Gervase said; "only Colonel Walker and myself are in the secret. If I fail——"

"Tut, man, ye'll not fail now. I think," she went on, looking at him admiringly, "ye could find a way in anything. You just take a rest on the bed upstairs, and I'll watch that you're not disturbed. They're not bad bodies, the redcoats, and they haven't troubled me much since I came back from Londonderry. In the evening I'll see you farther."

"If I only could find a boat," Gervase said: "I could never reach the fleet by swimming now."

"I've been thinking of that," she answered; "there's a bit of a coble lying in the cove, but the oars are gone and it must be leaky as a sieve, for it had been lying there all the summer."

Gervase caught the idea eagerly. "Anything that will keep me afloat; I care not what it is. Mistress Graham, we'll save the city between us."

"There ye go," she said, with a smile of gratified vanity. "Ye could never make the two miles in yon crazy tub, but I'll see through the day if I can't turn my hand to caulking her myself. I've seen it done and I think I can try it, but what you'll do for oars I know not. However, the tide will help you and you'll manage somehow, never fear. It will be a great day when ye meet Sandy in the Diamond, and tell him I helped you through."

Throughout the day Gervase remained undisturbed in the cottage. A patrol had been stationed a little distance further along the shore, but they had not again visited the house. Two or three times he heard their shouts as they passed at a distance. Mistress Graham had kept her promise, and as well as she was able, had patched up the little boat, which she dragged into the water and left floating in the cove. By using one of the planks which had been left in the little craft as a paddle, she hoped that he would be able to make his way to the ships. All was now ready for his journey, and it only wanted the help of the darkness to allow him to set out.

It was a bright moonlight night when they went down to the beach together. There was not an air to ruffle the surface of the water, and they could see very plainly a couple of miles away the riding lights of the ships at anchor. The patrol that had been in the vicinity of the cottage during the day had apparently been withdrawn, for they had not been in sight since sundown. Gervase found the coble more than half full of water, which took him some time to bale out, and when he was ready to start he wrung the hand of the kind-hearted woman warmly. "I have no time to spare," he said. "God reward you for all your kindness! You had better go back to the house now, for if I should be discovered it would only bring you into trouble. I hope we'll meet under better fortune. Farewell."

He pushed off, and sitting down amid ships began to make his way slowly from the shore. The woman returned to the door of the cottage, where she stood watching till the black speck was swallowed up in the darkness.

CHAPTER XVIII.

OF HOW GERVASE REACHED THE SHIPS.

THE coble was a poor sea boat and very heavy for its size. The piece of timber that Gervase used was a wretched substitute for an oar, and while the tide carried him rapidly down he could see that he made little progress towards the ships. If he should drift past them it was impossible that he could ever make his way against the current, and he must be carried out to sea. Fortunately the night was clear, and the wind blew in fitful airs, coming from the shore. Notwithstanding his utmost exertion the boat hardly seemed to move, and when he looked round it was already two hundred yards from the shore. He knew that he was still far from being safe from pursuit. He could still easily be seen from the shore in the broad moonlight, and once observed his pursuers would have no difficulty in finding a boat in which they might easily overtake him. He put his heart into every stroke, till the perspiration began to run from his brows and his arms ached till he could almost have cried out for the pain. But he was making his way, however slowly; he could now see the vessels and the yards with the sails flapping idly against the masts. Over the water came the sound of a bell, perhaps calling up the watch, and for the first time he realized how near he was to safety. But the boat seemed to him to go more slowly, and to have grown more difficult to move. Then he looked down and saw that the water was almost up to the thwarts. There was nothing for it but to abandon the paddle and bale out the water, which proved a long and laborious task. When he had accomplished little more than half the work, he saw that a little more delay would bring him opposite to the ships and still far from being within hail. Again he seized his paddle and strained every nerve to make up the way he had lost. His mind was almost distraught with fear; he worked like one possessed; nearer indeed, he came, but Oh! how slowly. The boat would not move in this sea of lead; his muscles were beginning to refuse to act, and to his eyes the sea had grown red, like a sea of blood. His last hope was dying in his heart. To be so near the end of his journey, to have passed through such perils, and to have failed after all—the thought was maddening. Still he would not give way, and he knitted his brows and set his teeth hard. Then as he bent forward the paddle slipped from his hand, and went floating away astern. With a despairing cry, weakened as he was, he fell down in the bottom of the boat, and covered his face with his hands. It was all over; he was beaten at last, and had failed as the others had failed before him. For a minute or two he lay overcome by his despair; the sense of hopeless failure swallowed up every other feeling. The thought of present danger did not present itself to his mind; he had seen too many brave men meet their death in these latter days not willingly to adventure his own life lightly. His head reeled, his mouth was parched, and his eyes throbbed with an intolerable pain. Then almost without knowing what he did, he rose to his feet and tried to call out. At first he could not articulate the words, but his voice died away in a feeble murmur. How near he seemed! the spars stood out plainly against the sky, and the lights were burning clear and bright. He thought once he could hear the sound of the mariners calling as they lay out on the spars of the brig that was riding nearest to him.

Again he called out—"Ship Ahoy!" and this time his voice came strong and full, but though he stood and listened there was no response to his shout. A third time he called out, and then to his inexpressible delight he heard a hoarse voice coming over the water, "Ahoy! what boat is that?"

Rising once more to his feet he called through his hands, "Help! Help!" and sank exhausted in the bottom of the boat, incapable of making any further effort. He waited anxiously but there came no further response, and the little boat went drifting down with the tide. He began to fear that they had not heard his second call. Then—hours after it seemed—he heard the measured sweep of oars and the sound of voices coming nearer. But for his life he could not raise himself above the gunwhale;

his strength had left him, and he was as feeble as a child.

But they had caught sight of the little craft where it tossed about in the space of moonlit water, and in a minute or two the ship's boat was alongside. Gervase was trying without success to answer the questions the mate of the brig was putting to him. Divining at a glance his condition they lifted him into the boat, and one of the seamen with kindly pity threw his rough jacket over him as they rowed to the brig. He lay in the bottom of the boat utterly helpless and unable to move; but his heart was full of inexpressible emotion, for he had accomplished his work and saved the city.

He remembered rowing round the brig and seeing the words "Phoenix of Coleraine" painted in large white letters on the stern, but he fainted away as they lifted him over the side of the boat, and knew nothing more till he found himself lying in the round-house of the brig.

"What piece of goods have ye got there, McKeller?" the master said, standing by the shrouds, and looking over the bulwark as they lifted Gervase aboard.

"As fine a lad as ever I saw in my life, but thin as a whipping-post—a messenger I think, from Londonderry. Gently, my lads, easy with his head. Six feet two of manhood, and I guess a rare good one with his whinger if he had his senses about him."

They carried him to the round-house, and laying

him on the floor, poured a dram of aqua-vitæ down his throat, but for a long time he showed no sign of life. Then they noticed the letter where it was secured.

"You were right, McKeller," said the master, as he handed the case bottle to the mate, "the youngster comes from Londonderry, and he brings the message with him. Mayhap 'twill stir up the Colonel at last, and I trust it will, for the sake of Tom Robinson and my sister Marjorie. My God! what that young fellow must have come through; and a gentleman too, as I judge by the gewgaws on his finger."

"Ay," answered the mate drily, "and you have given him a pint of pure spirits by way of welcome. You'll hardly hear about Tom Robinson for a while after that."

"Never fear; these long-legged fellows stand a lot of moistening. I wouldn't for half my share in the good ship Phoenix have missed hearing the lad's hail this night; he never would have lived through a night in the boat—but he's beginning to come round."

Gervase showed signs of returning consciousness. His first action was to feel for the precious letter, and then he opened his eyes and looked round him with a gaze of vacant inquiry. "Where am I?" he said.

"Why, just aboard the brig *Phoenix*, Andrew Douglas, Master, hailing from Coleraine, and bound with the help of God, for the port of Londonderry;

and among your friends if you are what I take you to be. Now don't trouble your head but just take a drop more of this." The kindly shipmaster put the bottle to his lips and insisted on his drinking.

"Ye'll kill him," said the mate; "ye think that everybody has the same stomach for strong waters as yourself. It's food he wants, I'll warrant, not drink."

"And food he'll have," cried the master excitedly, "when I've brought back the colour to his cheeks, and he'll be on his legs in a twinkling. Here, Jack, you skulking rogue, set out the best there is on board, and make us a bowl of punch, for by ——, I'll drink the health of the bravest fellow I've clapt eyes on for a twelvemonth."

"You would drink with less provocation than that," said the mate, lifting Gervase to his feet and helping him to a seat. "Now ye can tell us the news from Londonderry, lad, if it's true ye come from there."

"I came thence to-day—yesterday," said Gervase. "They can hold out no longer. Where is Colonel Kirke? I must see him immediately."

The master looked at his mate with a broad grin on his face. "Faith ye'll not see the Colonel to-night, nor early in the morning either. If he's not abed by this time and as drunk as a lord, he's on the fair way to it, and swearing like a dragoon with a broken head. He's a terrible man in his cups, is Kirke, and they keep it up rarely on board the *Swallow*. I love the clink of a glass sometimse myself, but—hoot! there's no use talking. If you're able, spin us your yarn while they're getting you something warm, for you must want a heap of filling out to look like the man you were."

Gervase told his story shortly as well as he was able, interrupted repeatedly by exclamations of wonder and horror by the captain and the mate, and when he had finished they sat staring at him open-mouthed.

"That is the tale as briefly as I can tell it," said Gervase, "and you will not wonder that I would put the letter in Kirke's hands with all the haste I can. Next Wednesday there will not be a scrap of food in the city, and if you wait till then you may lift your anchors and go back to where you came from. For God's sake, tell me what you are waiting for?"

"Till Kirke has emptied his puncheons," said the mate bitterly.

"Not a soul on board the fleet thought it was going so hard with you, but you had better see Leake, who is a plain-spoken man with some authority. I hear he is all for making up the river, and your story will help him to move the scarlet-coated butcher who is but half-hearted in the business."

"Colonel Kirke I must see first," said Gervase; "my message is to him, and when he reads Walker's letter he can hesitate no longer. All that is wanted is the wind and the tide. There need be no fear of the guns, for in Londonderry we have learned what they can do."

The skipper had said nothing, but sat leaning his head on his horny hand. Then he seemed to awaken from his fit of abstraction. "And poor Tom is gone, you tell me? He was a younger man than myself by half a score of years, and as likely a fellow as ever lived when I danced at his wedding nine years syne. A putrid fever, you say. Odds, I would like you could have told me how it is with Marjorie and the young ones."

"He chanced to be of my regiment," said Gervase, "and that is how I came to know his end. But many a brave fellow has fallen into his last sleep yonder, and all for want of a little manhood here."

"For God's sake tell me no more of your story," said the master, "but even fall to on the boiled beef, and don't spare the liquor. For myself, please Heaven, I'll drink the taste of your yarn out of my mouth, though belike it will take a hogshead at the least to do it."

The master was as good as his word; while Gervase and the mate sat down at the lower end of the table, he produced a great bottle from a locker, and poured out a large measure of spirit, which he drank at a draught without any dilution of water. He filled the glass a second time and drank it without a word. It was clear that he was determined to drown his grief, and as Gervase glanced at him from time to time in amazement, he went on steadily until the bottle was nearly empty. The mate said nothing, only shaking his head as though the sight was not a novel one and remonstrance was out of the question. "He'll maunder a bit by-and-by," he said in an undertone, "and then he'll turn in; 'tis the way of him—he's a good Christian and a rare seaman, but liquorish. We've all our faults and he was born with a thirst. Surely ye haven't finished? why, man, I thought ye were starved yonder, and ye haven't done more than nibble at the good meat!"

"Try the punch," said the master, by this time some way in his cups, with his face shining like a furnace; "try the grog, and never mind McKeller; I have to do his drinking and my own as well, and 'tis devilish hard work, let me tell you. No man can say that Andrew Douglas ever shirked his duty."

"When it came in the shape of rum puncheons," said the mate. "Now ye'll just turn in, and I'll see that the young gentleman is made comfortable."

The master was induced to retire with a good deal of difficulty, while Gervase and the mate sat down to a long talk together, as the result of which Gervase came to the conclusion that all his difficulties were not yet over. Then he turned in and forgot all his troubles in a sound and refreshing sleep.

CHAPTER XIX.

OF A STORMY INTERVIEW.

GERVASE slept soundly that night on board the *Phoenix*, and in the morning the mate insisted on his making use of his shore-going suit, into which Gervase was able to get with some difficulty. When he came on deck the day was bright and cloudless, with a warm sweet air blowing from the north-west and the sea hardly broken by a ripple. The ships lay at anchor near them; the *Dartmouth* with her rows of guns showing through the open ports; beyond lay the *Swallow* and a little further away the *Mountjoy*, both of which vessels Gervase had seen before.

But his first glance was toward the city lying far up the river, and he was filled with joy when he caught sight of the crimson flag still flying from the Cathedral Tower.

The master was early astir and met Gervase on the deck, with his red face freshly shaven and clad in his best suit which had been brought out for the occasion. He was very contrite over his last night's potations, and made many polite inquiries as to how his guest had passed the night. The anxiety of Gervase to be put on board the *Swallow* to deliver his message to Kirke, was so great that he could hardly restrain his impatience during the breakfast to which the master and himself sat down together. But they had assured him that the Colonel had not slept off the fumes of his last night's excesses, and that of all men he was the least approachable in the morning. It was necessary to find Kirke in good humour; so Gervase stifled his impatience, though his feelings were so strong and so bitter that he doubted whether a less fitting messenger than himself could have been found for his errand.

"Ye'll just tell him your plain story like a plain man," said the mate, "and leave the rest in the hands of the Almighty. I know ye'll find it hard to shorten sail, but 'tis the only way ye'll make the port after all."

"I don't understand the matter at all," Gervase answered. "Here am I with a message to yon sluggard that should make his ears tingle for the duty he has neglected and the days he has wasted in useless waiting. One would think 'twas a favour I was begging at his hands. When His Majesty hears——"

"Tut, man, His Majesty—God bless him! will never come to know the rights of it. Just put your pride in your pocket and take as a favour— when ye get it—what should come to you by right. I don't see myself that the thing is as easy as ye make it. A ship's timbers are dainty enough, and yon boom's an ugly sort of thing; not to speak of the cannon in the forts and the channel—that's ticklish at the best of times."

"When a kingdom's at stake, one might run a little danger without being foolhardy."

"I'm not saying that he mightn't and I would willingly try it myself if I had the chance, but you must make allowances. I hear they had a parson aboard there the other day who gave them some plain speech and got a flea in his ear for his pains. Fair and softly will carry for many a mile. I'll go with you myself and maybe put in a good word if I can. The boats are ready and we'll be alongside in a twinkling."

As they rowed towards the *Swallow*, which carried Kirke's flag, Gervase's mind was full of the way in which he should deliver his message, while Douglas sat beside him pouring his homely counsel into his ear. It was evident that the latter stood in no little dread of the commander who had won for himself an unenviable notoriety for cruelty and severity, and was clearly doubtful of the reception that awaited an envoy who knew so little regarding the character of the man with whom he had to deal. But Gervase had determined that if all else failed he would speak out his mind without any fear of the consequences. He had not undertaken this perilous journey and faced so many dangers to shrink from plain speech if that would serve his purpose.

The master of the *Phoenix* on the news being

brought that Kirke would receive them immediately in the gunroom, was like to have turned tail incontinently and left Gervase to face the redoubtable soldier alone. "The boatswain yonder is an old crony of mine," he said, "and we don't often have a chance of a quiet word. I wish you all luck, but I think I'll step forward and have a bit of speech while you do your errand."

"By your leave, but the General must see you both, Master Douglas," said the man who had brought the message; "if you don't come now I'll have to fetch you by the ears by-and-by. He hath ten thousand blue devils tearing his liver this morning, so that we cannot bind or hold him. But you have seen the General after a wet night with a head wind in the morning."

"I was a fool to come aboard," Douglas muttered. "Speak to him fair and soft, Mr. Orme," he continued, taking Gervase by the arm, "if ye would have the tyke listen to ye, but for God's sake don't cross him."

"I'll tell him a plain story that wants no gloss," Gervase answered. "You need not be afraid that I shall speak outside my commission. Now, sir, I am at your service."

"He'll get a flea in his ear," muttered Douglas, letting go his arm, and dropping behind. "Send me well out of this."

When they entered the gunroom, Gervase saw a small knot of officers seated at breakfast, which was nearly over. At the head of the table was the man he had come so far to seek and who carried the destiny of the city in his hands. His dark brow was blotched and seamed by excesses, his eyes were prominent and bloodshot, and his jaws, heavy and coarse, gave to his face an expression of ferocity and obstinacy. He lay back lazily in his chair, his throat divested of his cravat, and his richly-laced waistcoat unbuttoned and thrown open. For a time he did not seem to notice the new-comers, but continued his conversation in a languid way with the gentleman who sat on his left hand. Gervase who had come into the centre of the room, stood silent for a minute or two, waiting for some sign of recognition, but Kirke, studiously ignoring his presence, never once looked up. Then Gervase stung into action by what seemed merely studied insult, quietly came forward and laid Walker's letter on the table.

"I was charged, sir, to deliver this into your hand without fail at the earliest moment. It brooks of no delay."

"And who the devil are you, sir?"

"A humble gentleman who with some peril to himself has succeeded in escaping from the city and finding his way thither. But the letter I carry will tell its own tale."

"They might have chosen a messenger with better manners," said Kirke, taking up the missive, "but these citizens know no better."

"These citizens, sir, have set you a lesson which you have not been fain to follow," cried Gervase, disregarding all the hints he had received and giving vent to the indignation that had become ungovernable. "For nine weeks they have served His Majesty as king was never served before; spent themselves in his service; seen their wives and children dying before them; and now they want to know what you have done and what you purpose doing?"

For a moment or two the general, who was not accustomed to such speech in the mouth of a rough seaman, as Gervase seemed, sat astonished and aghast. Then he leapt to his feet and pushed over the chair he had been sitting on. "God's wounds! I'll teach you to use such words to me if there's a yard-arm on the ship. Who are you that dares to question me in my own vessel. You hear him, gentlemen, you hear him, by——"

"They have heard us both, sir, and I wish His Majesty could have heard us also," cried Gervase, who saw that there was only one way to deal with the hectoring bully of whom most men stood in awe. "They have heard us and they may judge between us. I hold the King's commission like yourself, and can answer for my conduct in any fitting time or place. But this matter is of more importance than your dignity or mine. The salvation of some thousand lives depends upon it, and the last hold of His Majesty upon Ulster and Ireland. Colonel Walker hath bidden me place this letter in your hands without delay. I have only done my duty, and am no whit afraid of you or of any other man living."

Gervase had spoken quietly and with a fine glow on his cheeks. The gentlemen at the table who had preserved an expectant silence, looked at one another with a chuckle of amusement as Kirke broke the envelope without a word. In the reading he glanced once or twice at Gervase, and when he had finished he threw the paper with an oath across the table. "Read that, Leake," he said. "This parson in the buff coat thinks that round shot can be cooked like peas, and that a ship's sides are harder than stone walls. To hear him one would think that we had no more than an hour's sail to find ourselves at the quay, with meat and mutton to fill these yokels' bellies."

The gentleman to whom he had thrown the letter, a bluff, red-faced sailor, with a frank brave look that met you honestly, read the letter in silence, and then spread it open before him. "You had better hear what the young gentleman has to say. Colonel Walker seems to trust him implicitly, and I should like to hear how he came from the city. 'Twas a bold feat and deserves a better reception than you have given him."

"My reception hath not closed yet," said Kirke savagely. "But I am ready to hear what he hath to say, and if I find him tripping, fore God——"

"I have faced death too often during these three weeks," said Gervase gravely, "to fear the threats of any man, and I will speak what is on my mind boldly——"

"And briefly, for I am not a patient man."

"We in the city trusting to the expectation of speedy succour from England, have made our defence as I think defence was never made before. We have lost seven thousand men; those who remain are but living skeletons, stricken with sore diseases. We are distraught with our afflictions, and almost fear rather to live than to die. We can do no more. On Wednesday morning there will not be a pound of meat in the magazines, and the last stronghold of faith and freedom in Ireland will have fallen. And this is what they say yonder and—and what I say here. In the Lough are ships and men and food and guns, and a water-way to the city walls. A little courage, a bold push, and the boom that you seem to fear would snap like a thread. And they know not how to use their guns. We who have listened to their music for months have ceased to fear them."

"And the boom," cried Leake; "how know you that?"

"This I know, that there never was wood yet that could resist the edge of an axe if there were strong arms to will it. You have long boats and men courageous enough to try it. With your leave I'll show them how it can be done myself."

"By Heaven, the lad is right. If we were once past Culmore——"

"There is no great danger there," said Gervase, feeling that he had met a spirit as bold and resolute as his own, "their balls fly as innocent as wild duck. Let the frigate hold by the fort, so that under her shelter the smaller vessels may pass unscathed."

"We want none of your lessons," cried Kirke; "you have listened to sermons so long that you have caught the trick of preaching yourself."

"My sermon is not yet finished, General Kirke," continued Gervase, disregarding the hint the friendly sailor gave him, and determined to unburden his mind once and for all. "You have lain here and done nothing for us. The king, I am told, hath sent you an urgent message that the relief should be undertaken without delay. To-day you may carry out his commands; to-morrow you may return to England and tell him your cowardice hath lost him a kingdom. The lives of the starving souls yonder will be on your head. These are bitter words, but I speak them out of a full heart, and if you will not listen to me now, His Majesty will hear me presently, for as God is my witness, I will carry my story to the foot of the throne."

"You will carry it into the Lough with a shot at your feet," cried Kirke, purple with passion.

"You dare do nothing of the sort, sir, here in the sight of these gentlemen and in the full sight of the people of England, who will soon know the whole matter. I am the ambassador of the governor who holds the city for His Majesty, and it is by his authority that I speak the words that I have used. I am a gentleman like yourself holding His Majesty's commission, and owing you neither respect nor authority."

Kirke leaped to his feet, his face swollen red, and his eyes blazing with a fierce passion that overmastered his speech. He caught up the scabbard of the sword that lay beside him and attempted to draw the blade. Then Leake, who was sitting near Gervase, caught the outspoken envoy by the shoulders, and while Kirke still stood swearing incoherently, hurried him out of the gun-room. When they reached the deck he clapped him on the back with his broad palm, and cried with enthusiasm, "I like your spirit, my lad; that was the way to stand by your guns and rake him fore and aft. But it was ticklish work, let me tell you, to tackle him that way. He has got the wolf's tusk in his mouth (he learnt that in Tangier) and likes to see a pair of heels dancing in the air. But you've done the trick, I think, this time, and the old *Dartmouth* will have a chance of trying her ribs against the iron yonder. Now, clear your mind a bit and just tell me your story like a sensible lad, for you've got some common sense, and let me see if I can't make some use of your knowledge after all."

"I've been a weak fool," said Gervase, "to forget myself when so much depended on my discretion. I've ruined the best cause in the world."

"You have done nothing of the sort, sir, if I can lay a ship's head by the compass. You have carried your point and the burghers yonder will hear the roaring of our guns before the day is out. The general hath been told what we dared not tell him in plain speech that there is no mistaking.

Now let me know how matters are in the city, and what men and guns they have in the fort yonder at Culmore."

Then Gervase told his whole story soberly and plainly, without colour or exaggeration, but with such truth and effect that his hearer was so lost in admiration that he never interrupted him till he had drawn his tale to a close. Then he swore many oaths, but swearing with such honest and kindly feeling that Gervase forgave him, that such brave fellows were worth putting their lives in peril for, even if it did not profit His Majesty a farthing. And then he questioned Gervase searchingly, his eye scanning him narrowly all the time, about the forts between the city and the castle of Culmore, and where the cannon were posted and what was the weight of the guns. "Now," he said, in conclusion, " get you back with Andrew Douglas, who is an honest man and a good mariner, and you'll see what you will see. If there should be a little more wind and more northing in it, I'll stake my reputation we'll try of what strength yon timbers are, and you and I will get our share of the glory.' Glory, lad! That stirs the blood. That thought about the long boats was a shrewd one, and I have an idea of my own about the way to draw their teeth at Culmore."

Douglas was waiting for Gervase in the boat of the *Phoenix*, and welcomed him with a grim smile as he took his place beside him. He said nothing, but motioned to the two sailors to push off and row to the brig. When they got out of earshot, he burst into a hoarse cackle of laughter that grated unpleasantly on Gervase's overstrung nerves.

"I wouldn't have missed it," he cried, clapping his brown hands on his knees, "for a puncheon of rum. Man, ye gave it to him finely, and ye talked like a book straight up and down. A good wholesail breeze all the way and lying your course as straight as an arrow. It did my heart good to hear you. And he couldn't get in a word—never a word, but stared at you out of his red bulging eyes, and choked about the jaws like a turkey cock strangling in a passion. You're a well plucked one and no mistake. I had thought to see you, as he said, at the end of the yard-arm."

"Yon swaggering bully is an arrant coward," said Gervase, "and I wonder how he came to be chosen for a work like this. For all his bluster I saw that he was quailing, and I was determined that he should hear the truth for once in his life."

"He didn't hear a third of it, but I'm thinking he heard as much as was good for him. Will they move, think ye?"

"Leake says——"

"He's a man at any rate; I'd like to know what he says."

"That we'll see what we'll see. He thinks my speech hath done little harm, but I know not whether it hath done any good. God grant that it hath."

"Amen and Amen to that. Now let us go aboard, and let us see whether your adventure has taken away your appetite."

CHAPTER XX.

OF HOW THE GREAT DELIVERANCE WAS WROUGHT.

ON their regaining the deck of the *Phoenix* McKeller manifested great anxiety to hear the result of the interview, and the master had a greatly interested audience as he proceeded to describe the scene with many embellishments and quaint touches of his own. What seemed to have struck him most was Kirke's helpless rage, and the speechless anger he exhibited at the attack upon his courage and capacity.

Gervase lay against the bulwarks listening without a word; his eyes were fixed on the square tower of the Cathedral rising through the pall of smoke that overhung the city. In thought he saw the haggard gunners on the war-torn battlements, and the sorrowing crowd pouring out from the morning service. His mind was filled with the horror and misery of it, and his heart was bitter within him. He suddenly started and cleared his eyes as if he could not trust his sight; then he looked again. "Merciful God!" he cried, "the flag is down."

The little knot of men round him turned to look too, and they saw with sinking hearts that the flag, the garrison's token of defiance, was no longer waving on the Cathedral tower. A great silence fell upon them all—a silence in which one heard the lapping of the water about the bows and the distant scream of the sea-birds, startling and shrill.

"God's curse light on all traitors and cowards!" cried McKeller.

Then they saw two jets of fire spurt forth from the tower, and a little later the sullen roar of the ordnance, and the hope came into their hearts that it was only in sign of their dire extremity that the garrison had hauled down the flag. And they waited and watched, and again they heard the thunder of the cannon pealing from the tower. Then above the crown of smoke they saw the crimson flag run up the staff, and they knew the city was still inviolate. An involuntary cheer broke from the crew of the *Phoenix*, which was taken up by the other vessels, and a minute or two afterwards the *Swallow* fired a salvo in response.

"They have awakened up at last," cried the master. "Now we'll even go below and try the boiled beef, and mayhap a runnel of grog."

"Not a drop of grog," cried McKeller, "but what boiled beef you like. The wind is freshening from the north, and the Lord may want sober men for this day's work."

The captain was not destined to join in their midday meal; hardly had they sat down and hardly had McKeller, who generally acted as chaplain by reason of his superior gravity, finished the long grace by which the meal was introduced, than a messenger came from Kirke, that Douglas was to hasten with all expedition on board the *Swallow*.

"The more haste the less speed," cried the Captain, to whom the summons was by no means a welcome one, and who had no taste for a further interview with Kirke. "I'll have to answer for your speech, Mr. Orme, I'm thinking. I wish McKeller there was in my shoes."

"You were still good to McKeller," laughed the mate, "but this time you'll have to do your own business."

"I hope," said Gervase, "that this time it means business and not more speech. And I think it does. Bring us the news, Master Douglas, that you are to lift your anchor, and I'll not forget you as long as I live."

"Please Heaven, you may look for your night-cap in Derry to-night."

"With a sound head to put it in."

"The boat is waiting, and so is the General," added the mate.

The captain hurried out of the round-house, and Gervase and the mate sat down to finish their midday meal with but little appetite for their repast. The conversation between them flagged, and then the mate went out and presently returned with his prayer-book under his arm, from which he began to read in a low monotonous tone, following the words, like a backward schoolboy, with his forefinger. He never looked up but sat with his rough unkempt head bent over the book.

Half an hour passed in this way, when they heard the sound of the boat alongside and the Captain's voice shouting to get the mainsail set.

Presently he burst into the cabin, his face all glowing with excitement and his small blue eyes dancing in his head. He ran forward and caught Gervase in both his arms, "It's come at last, dear lad, 'tis come at last. Your speech hath done it, and we'll moor by the quay to-night with the blessing of God. This is no time for books, McKeller, no time for books. The Lord be praised! We're up the river in an hour. Browning and myself and the old *Dartmouth*, with Leake to give us the lead."

Gervase and McKeller were on their feet shaking one another by the hand. They could hardly believe the good news. Then, overcome by his feelings so long pent up, Gervase burst into tears and sobbed aloud. The captain stood aghast, but the mate laid his hand on the young fellow's shoulder and said with rugged kindliness: "I like you all the better for your tears, Mr. Orme; you have shown that you can do a man's work, with a man's heart under your jacket; 'twill do you good,—rain on the parched grass, as the book has it. Now, you old sea dog, what are you staring at? Go on with your story and let us know what we have to do."

"I'll clap you in irons for a rank mutineer," laughed the captain. "Lord love you, when I got aboard Kirke was like a lamb; not a damn in him, but all 'By your leave' and 'At your pleasure'. The council of officers had resolved to attack the passage that afternoon, the wind and the tide being favourable, and the messenger, that being you, Mr. Orme, having brought news that rendered their instant moving imperative, and more stuff of that kind. I could have laughed in his face, but for the cruel white and red in his eye. I don't like a man to have too much white in his eye."

" Go on with your story."

The *Dartmouth* goes first, and draws the fire at Culmore; we go on with what speed we can till we get to the barrier. That must give way by hook or crook, and then up the river. A good day's work, I'm thinking, but the little *Phoenix* will do her share if Andrew Douglas be alive to see it."

" With the help of God we'll all see it," cried the mate. " This will be a great day for all of us."

"Serve out a measure of rum to every man-jack on board, and get under way with all the haste ye can. In a quarter of an hour ye'll see the little *Phoenix* slipping through the water like a seagull. Come, Mr. Orme, and lend a hand with the weapons. I take it you are well used to them."

Gervase followed the captain on deck where the men were busy with the halliards, and all was lively confusion and disorder. The seamen were already swarming on the yards of the *Dartmouth*, and the long boat of the *Swallow* was in the water, with the carpenters hammering upon the rough barricado with which they were protecting her sides. The wind which from the morning had been blowing in quiet airs from the north-west, had gone round to the north and had freshened somewhat. In the summer sky there was hardly a cloud; the waves leapt and flashed in the sunshine, and the vessels were beginning to plunge at their cables in the livelier sea.

By the time that Gervase had finished his scrutiny of the cutlasses and muskets, and had seen to the loading of the three guns that the *Phoenix* carried, McKeller and the men had the vessel under sail. Then the windlass was manned, and it was only when the anchor had been lifted, and the little vessel was slipping through the water that Gervase felt their work was really begun and his task was about to be completed. The captain himself had taken the tiller, standing square and firm, with his coat thrown aside, and the sleeves of his shirt rolled up and showing his brown, muscular arms.

"There goes the *Dartmouth*," he cried to Gervase, who was standing near him, "well done, and seamanly. And the *Mountjoy*—she has the lead of us, being weightier and more strongly timbered. I don't grudge it to Browning; he's a good fellow and a gallant seaman. We've sailed together ere now. And the old *Jerusalem*—she'll come up when the eggs are boiled. We'll have to knock once or twice before they let us in."

The *Dartmouth* led the way with her ports open and the iron muzzles of her guns all agrin, the white sails on her lofty spars swelling out under the freshening wind. She did not wait for her consorts, but held her way steadily toward the river's mouth where the castle of Culmore guarded the entrance. The *Mountjoy* outsailed the *Phoenix* much to the chagrin of Douglas, and three cables' lengths already divided them. The men leaned over the bulwarks watching the fort where they could see the soldiers hastening to the guns, and could hear the drums beating the alarm. As yet the *Dartmouth* was not within range of the cannon, but already a round shot or two had come skipping along the water and had fallen short. As they drew toward the river's mouth the breeze had grown lighter, and Gervase feared that the afternoon would set in a stagnant calm. But they had the tide with them, and the wind blew fairly up the river.

"There's the music now," cried Douglas, as the guns of the fort flashed along the ramparts; "there's a hole in the royal yonder, but 'twill take more than that to turn old Leake. Will he never let them hear him?"

The *Dartmouth* was already within range, but she held on her way gallantly, never answering the fire that was poured upon her. Again and again the guns of the fort flashed out, and the frigate's canvas was torn by the shot, but her spars remained untouched. Still Leake held on steadily, his guns still silent and his men sheltering themselves as best they could behind the bulwarks. Only when he came within close range so that every shot might tell, his guns spoke for the first time. Again and again the living sheet of flame leapt from the open ports, and the great shot went crashing into the fort. As the fire of the enemy slackened perceptibly the seamen set up a great cheer which, was caught up by the men of the *Mountjoy* that had now come nearly alongside and was holding its way up the river. Lying abreast of the fort and within musket shot the crew of the frigate plied the fort with cannon and with small arms, while the *Mountjoy*, followed by the *Phoenix*, came drifting slowly up channel past the castle and safely out of range of its guns. Then the *Dartmouth*, her work being done, was moored in the bend of the river above Culmore, while the merchant ships went slowly up the narrow and winding channel, and the men in the *Swallow's* long boat kept them company and bent to their oars with a will. The great guns in the earthen forts along the river gave them welcome as they came, and the musket balls went singing by their ears.

It was a sight to see Douglas at the tiller, with a broad smile on his face and the dancing light of battle in his eyes. Once or twice he laughed aloud as some of the smaller spars came tumbling to the deck. And now in the pauses of the great guns and above the rattle of the muskets, they could hear in the summer air the shouts of the citizens from the walls—shouts of triumph and delight. On that scene the chroniclers have dwelt with some pride and much pathos. Every man who could drag himself to the wall was gathered there that summer day. Gaunt and hollow-eyed; so hunger-stricken that they could scarcely stand, wasted by fever and by wounds, they took up the joyous shout of triumph. Stout soldiers gave way to tears upon the necks of their comrades. Their anguish and despair were swallowed up in the hope of present deliverance. Here and there little groups were kneeling as in prayer for the safety of those who were bringing them succour, and never was prayer more earnest offered to the God of battles.

Meanwhile the *Mountjoy* and the *Phoenix* were coming close upon the boom, and the forts on either side were plying them with shot. Douglas never moved. One of the seamen was struck down beside him, but he never turned his head. The wind was coming in little airs, but the tide was running hard. Gervase saw the *Mountjoy* through the smoke, a cable's length ahead, suddenly strike upon the wooden barrier that lay across the river. Then the gallant little vessel swung round and grounded in the narrow channel. A great cheer went up from the banks, while they saw the redcoats hastening to their boats to board the stranded ship. "Now, McKeller, see what you can do with the long gun," cried Douglas, as the mate with Gervase's assistance brought the cannonade to bear on the mass of men who were moving to the bank. But the master of the *Mountjoy* was a stout seaman and knew his work. Quickly his guns were brought to the landward side, and at the discharge the little vessel slipped into the channel again, and went floating toward the boom with the running tide. Meanwhile the *Swallow's* long boat under the boatswain's mate had been laid alongside the barrier, and the bluejackets were plying it with cutlasses and hatchets. Every man did his best that hour, and as the *Mountjoy* struck the boom a second time, the great barrier cracked and broke and went swinging up the river.

McKeller leapt upon the bulwarks regardless of the risk he ran, and waved his hat with fine enthusiasm: "God save Their Majesties," he cried, "and down with Popery."

Every man on board knew that the work was done and the city was saved. But the wind had fallen with the afternoon and it was a dead calm. Only with the tide the vessels came slowly up the river; then the long boats of the *Swallow* took them in tow, and with the setting sun the vessels came drifting into Ross's bay. It was ten o'clock at night when the *Phoenix*, Andrew Douglas, Master (and a proud man was he!), came to its moorings at the little quay close by Ship Quay Gate.

No man has such gift of speech as to describe the scene when the master stepped ashore and raised his hat in presence of the thronging crowd. Men and women went frantic in their joy. Falling upon each other's necks and wringing one another by the hand, they forgot that stern reserve that marks their race and people. Bonfires were lighted upon the ramparts, and the bells rang out a joyous peal, and all the while the unlading of the ship went on, till all men were satisfied, and the terror of the morning seemed like a dream that had passed away.

Gervase left the *Phoenix* unnoticed in the tumult, and made his way through the deserted streets to his old lodging. The door was lying open, but the house was deserted. Simon and all his family were in all likelihood among the crowd at the quay. Then he lighted his lamp and sat down to enjoy his golden dreams alone. His heart was filled with the thought of what he had done and of the reward he hoped to win.

He would call upon Dorothy in the morning — Dorothy, whose sweet face had kept him company through his perils, and the thought of whom had moved him in his dangers. She had told him that she loved him.

The darkness was gone and they had come into the sweet sunshine at last. And so he dreamed his dreams till Mistress Sproule returned laden with her spoils, and gave him a joyous welcome as to one who had come back from death.

CHAPTER XXI.

OF HOW THE VICOMTE MADE HIS GREAT RENUNCIATION.

On the following morning Gervase was up betimes. It seemed to him that a new world had opened out before him with boundless possibilities of joy and hope. For weeks he had been dragging himself about like one bent under the infirmities of age; to-day the blood of youth ran quick in his veins. With a pride that was pardonable, he felt that he had done his task manfully and performed his share in a work as memorable as any in his time. He had won honour for himself, and he had found the one woman who realized his boyhood's ideal. She was waiting for him now—waiting with that glad and joyous look in her steadfast eyes that had thrilled him at times when his grief had weighed upon him. She must know that the work he had undertaken was done for her sake, and that he would be with her presently to claim his reward.

Simon Sproule came to see him when he was seated at breakfast, a good deal shrunk and wasted, but bearing himself with his brave and confident air for all the troubles he had passed through. The young soldier was one of the linendraper's heroes, and Simon had come this morning to offer abundant incense at the altar of his worship.

"We are both proud of you, Mr. Orme, Elizabeth and myself. I heard the whole story from Andrew Douglas last night, and it was done like an ancient Roman, sir, but in no foreign or pagan spirit. It was a great feat and should be remembered for many a day."

"It will be forgotten in good time," said Gervase cheerfully, "and was no very wonderful business after all. But I am glad for your sake the fighting is over, for yours and your wife's and——"

"Do not mention them. Oh! I cannot bear it, sir. There were eight of them when you came back with the old captain, eight white-haired youngsters that gathered about the table and made music for me—and now there are but four of them. It was the judgment of God for their father's cowardice."

"I think you did your best, Simon," Gervase said gently.

"I did all that I could, and that was nothing; but it was the pretending that was my sin. I, who was made for nothing but to measure lace and lawns, should not have given myself over as a man of war, and boasted of deeds that I knew that I could not perform. It has broken their mother's heart, and I think it has broken mine. I cannot think they are gone; indeed I cannot. Why, I stood listening to their footsteps on the stairs even as I came into your room, and I heard them calling 'Daddy,' every one of them. But 'tis a sin to mourn."

"Nay, nay, man, weep to your heart's content, and tell them I said a man's tears are as manly as his courage. We must all face it some day."

"I cannot help it," said Simon, drying his eyes, "but you do not know what it is for a father to part with the red-cheeked boys he loved: we have come through a great tribulation."

"Thank God there is an end of it now. In a day or two there will not be an Irish Regiment north of the Boyne, and I hope we'll get back to the works of peace again. I myself will turn husbandman and beat my sword into a pruning hook."

"And marry the sweet lass by the Bishop's-Gate, and nurse your brave boys on your knee. You see we have had eyes, Mr. Orme."

"I do not know how that may be, but——"

"And," Simon went on, "if you will do me the honour to let me furnish you with the wedding coat, I'll warrant it of the finest—a free gift at my hands, for all your kindness to me and the boys."

"We must first find the lady," laughed Gervase.

"I think she is already found, and I know she is very sweet to look at."

In the forenoon Gervase found himself in the wainscoted parlour that was for ever associated in his mind with Dorothy Carew. He had dressed himself with some care, and looked a handsome fellow as he stood by the window looking out on the grass plot that he remembered so well. It seemed to him years since he had stood there; a whole life was crowded between that time and this—a life in which he had seen many strange sights and come through some memorable fortunes. Dorothy, he did not doubt, was still the same, but Macpherson, so rugged and so kindly, was gone, and the tragedy of his death came vividly before him as he stood in the room where he had first met the man by whose hands he had fallen. He was determined that Dorothy should never know the secret which could only bring her grief; this was the one secret in which she should not share. It was hardly likely that Jasper Carew would ever cross his path again—if he did it would then be time enough to think in what manner he should deal with him. In the meantime here was Arcady with the pipe and the lute, with the springtime crowned with the sweetest love, and care and sorrow laid aside for a season. His heart seemed to rise into his throat and a mist to cloud his eyes, as he heard a light footstep behind him. The gallant speeches that he had been rehearsing vanished from his memory, and he stood with his mind all blank as Dorothy came softly into the room, with her hand extended, and her eyes cast down. Her manner was awkward and constrained, though he did not notice it. He would have held her hand in his but she withdrew it gently and seated herself by the window.

"Dorothy, Miss Carew," he began, with an overmastering desire to take her in his arms, "my words have come true, the words I spoke that last afternoon when——"

"Yes," she said, "I remember."

"I said when we next met the joybells would be ringing. Listen, you can hear them now; the old time is all gone."

"Yes, it is all gone—and—and, Mr. Orme, I cannot say all that is in my heart. The city is ringing with your great exploit, but I knew it all. All the night I watched you as you floated down the dark tide. Oh! it was a gallant deed; no man ever did a braver. You did not tell me what was in your mind, but I felt and knew it. I knew you would not fail."

"I want no other reward but to hear you say that. But you must not praise me overmuch, for I have done nothing but my plain and simple duty. When I look back on it, it has seemed an easy thing to do. There was no risk like what I ran with Sarsfield's troopers, when you—nay, I had not thought to have awakened that memory."

"I have not forgotten that either," she said, "I was a girl then, but I am a woman, and I think a very old woman, now," she added with a sad smile. "I owe you a great deal since we first met. I shall never be able to repay you, but when we part, and perhaps I shall not see you again, I shall remember your kindness as long as I live."

"We have not parted yet," said Gervase, trying

to take her hand. "Dorothy, I have come here to speak what I have not dared to say before. Nay, nay, you must listen to me, for all our life depends on it. From the first moment that we met, I have had one thought, one hope. I have watched you in silence, for it was not a time to talk of love. Every day on duty, every night on guard, you have been with me consoling and sustaining me. I have no words to tell you all that I would tell you. I have reproached myself for my selfishness. While others were overcome with their misery, I went about with a light and joyous heart; it was enough for me to be near you, to feel your presence, to serve you with my life. Dorothy, I love you."

"Oh! I cannot hear you," she cried, rising to her feet and hiding her face in her hands; "it is wrong for me to listen to you."

"Nay, nay, my best beloved, you shall listen to me," he went on, with all a lover's gentle but fierce insistence. "You have spoken words that you cannot recall. All the night in the river and in the woods they rang like music in my ears, and kept my heart from failing in me. I knew you loved me."

"I will not hear you," she cried; "they were weak words and wicked. I had no right to speak them."

"But they were true," he said, with no clue to her meaning, "and I will hold you to your words. I dare not let you go; there is nothing stands between us and nothing will."

"Everything stands between us." Then with a great effort she calmed herself and went on gently, "My words were wrung from me, I should not have spoken them, but I stand by them—they were the truth. I do love you. Nay, you must hear me out; you must not come nearer, now nor ever again. When they were spoken I had no right to speak them; I was the betrothed wife of Victor De Laprade."

He stared at her incredulously.

"I was alone; there was no one to whom I could go for advice. I was only a girl; I did not know my own heart. Then the Vicomte de Laprade was struck down unfairly by my brother to whom he had given back his fortune and—and I thought he was going to die. What reparation I could make, it was my duty and my will to make. I had not thought of love—or you. Oh! why did you speak to me?"

"Nay, but, Dorothy, this means the sacrifice of your life. De Laprade is generous. He will not ask——"

She turned to him with a look of pride in her tearful eyes. "He will never know, for I shall stand loyally by the word that I have given him. I shall school my feelings; I shall subdue myself; I shall rise above my wayward thoughts. And you will help me. You will say, 'Farewell, my sister', and think of me always as a sister you have loved and is dead."

"But consider——"

"I consider all. When he lay there dying, faithful, loyal, as he is, I thought I loved him and I brought him back to life. My love, worthless as it is, is precious to him, and there is one Carew who keeps her word at any cost. Speak no more to me of love. You demean yourself and me. I belong to another."

"Oh! this is madness," Gervase cried, knowing in his heart that he could not change nor turn her. "There is no code of honour in the world to make you give your life to one you do not love. Such marriage is no true marriage. You are mine by every right, and I will not let you go."

"There was a time when I should have liked to hear you talk like that, but it will never be again. I shall give him all duty and honour, and in time, perhaps—you will help me to bear my burden, Gervase Orme, nor make it heavier for me? I see my duty clearly, and all the world will not drive me from it."

Gervase took her two hands, feverish and trembling in his own. He saw there was no need for further argument; he could not change her.

"I have no gift of speech to show you what you do. Your will has been my law and I shall try to obey you utterly. God knows I loved you, Miss Carew, and still love you. But you will hear no more of me nor my importunate love; there is room abroad for a poor soldier like myself. And De Laprade is a gallant gentleman and worthy of his splendid fortune. I can say no more than that I envy him with all my heart."

He drew her to him unresistingly, and kissed her on the forehead. There was nothing lover-like in the act; it was simply in token of sorrowful surrender, and she recognized it as such. She did not dare to raise her eyes to his but kept them bent upon the ground; he could see the lashes were trembling with unshed tears.

"I knew," she said, "you would speak as you have spoken. It was my duty to see you; it is very hard. You will go now?"

"I will go, Miss Carew, and I ask you to remember that through life, in good and evil fortune, you have no more loving and loyal friend than Gervase Orme, your faithful servant. Time will not change nor alter me. It was too great fortune for me to deserve it."

Before she could speak he was gone, and she heard in a dream the door close behind him. One of his gloves had fallen to the ground and was still lying at her feet. She caught it up and pressed it passionately against her bosom. She was now able to read her own heart in all its depth and fulness; standing there with her eyes fixed on the door through which he had departed, she saw the greatness of the sacrifice she had made. She felt that moment that she stood utterly alone, closed out from all love and sympathy. She had believed that she had become resigned, and that she had succeeded in mastering her feelings, but they had burst out afresh and with a fervour and passion that terrified herself. "Oh! God," she cried, "how I love him!"

Throwing herself in the chair from which she had risen, and burying her face in her hands, she gave way to her sorrow, feeling all the while that she dare not reason with herself, for however much she suffered she determined that she would not break her faith. She would bring herself to love De Laprade; love him as she honoured and admired him, the loyal and courteous gentleman, who treated her rather as a goddess than as a woman.

She did not hear the footsteps coming from the open window; she was thinking at the moment of how she could meet her betrothed with an air of gaiety. Then a hand was laid lightly on her shoulder and she looked up. De Laprade was standing over her, with a pleasant smile playing about his lips. His face was pale and his voice trembled a little when he spoke, but only for a moment; otherwise his manner was free and pleasant, with something of his old gaiety in it.

"I am a dull fellow, Cousin Dorothy," he said, "but a dull fellow sometimes awakens, and I have aroused myself. I have been sleeping for weeks, I think, with dreams too, but poof! they are gone. You have been weeping—that is wrong. The eyes of beauty should ever be undimmed."

She did not answer him, and he sat down on the chair beside her, taking Orme's glove from her lap where it lay, and examining the embroidery critically. "Monsieur Orme is a pretty fellow, and I have much regard for him. I am going to make you very happy, my cousin."

"I am not——"

"Nay, I know what you would say. But I have a long story to tell, so long that I know not how to begin, nor how to make an end. It will be easier by what you call a parable."

Dorothy looked at her lover curiously. For some time his old manner of jesting with something of gay cynicism about it had disappeared, but all at once it had returned with something else she did not recognize. He could not have learned her secret, for she had guarded that too carefully, but her woman's instinct warned her that perhaps after all he had guessed the truth.

"There was once," he went on, "a prodigal who spent his youth in his own way; he drank, he diced, he knew not love nor reverence; no law, but that poor thing that men call honour. But it was well he knew even that. So far, he did not think, for he had no mind nor heart. He only lived for pleasure. Then he found that he had spent his fortune, burst like a bubble, gone like a dream, and his friends—they were many—left him to beg with his outstretched hands, and turned their faces as he passed them on the way. But he had grown old, and loved pleasure and the delights of riotous living. Then there came to him a great good fortune—to him unworthy, beggared, disgraced. He seized it eagerly and he thought—what will men think?—that he would again be happy. It was not to be. He carried with him the stain of his early riot, the shame of his sinful life, the thoughts that will not die, the habits, even, he could not alter. His fortune hung heavily about his neck and pressed him down to the ground. He knew that it was of priceless value, but it was not for him. Then being a wise prodigal, he said: 'I am selfish. This cannot make me happy. I will place it in the hands of another who will know how to use it rightly, and so rid me of my load.' And he gave the treasure to another, and then went away and the world saw him not any more. There, my cousin, is my story. Monsieur La Fontaine must look to his laurels."

"You are jesting with me, Victor; I do not understand your parable."

"It must be that I shall speak more plainly. My story must have its moral."

He still held Orme's glove upon his knee and was unconsciously plucking to pieces the lace with which it was embroidered. But neither of them noticed it. Dorothy was waiting breathlessly for what was to come, and determined on her part to refuse the generous offer De Laprade was about to make.

"It shames me to think I was an unwilling listener but now, and I heard, not all, but enough. The window was open and I heard before I could withdraw. But I had known it all before and was only waiting."

"You shall not wait," Dorothy cried impetuously. "I am true and loyal."

"I never doubted you, but I am not. I am inconstant as the wind, and change my mind a hundred times a day. Fortune, not love, is my goddess, the fickle and the strange. I am out of humour already and long for change. Your city chokes me, a bird of prey mewed up among the sparrows. You must cut the silken thread and give me my freedom, *ma belle*."

"I shall never," Dorothy said, disregarding the words and thinking only of the spirit that prompted them, "I shall never forgive the weakness I have shown. Indeed you have my regard and my esteem, and some time I hope you will have my love. I shall keep my faith, truly and loyally. I shall not change."

"Then I must help myself when you will not. You are cruel, my cousin, and force me to speak. I, Victor De Laprade, a poor gentleman, having found that in all honour I cannot marry Dorothy Carew, here declare that I am a pitiful fellow and leave her to go my own way, hoping that she will trouble me no further with her importunity. Now, that being done, let us be friends, which we should never have been had you married me."

"This is like you, Victor," she said sadly; "I am a pitiful creature when I measure myself with you."

"You are a woman, my dear; I have served them long and bought my knowledge dearly. But you are better than most of them," he added with a smile, "for some that I have known would have held me despite all that I have said. I was not made for your Shakespeare's Benedict, I think it was."

"Oh!" she said, "but I cannot treat your words as serious; you are but playing with my weakness. I will not let you—how can I, a woman, say what I should say?"

"You should say: Monsieur le Vicomte, I am happy that you have discovered yourself in time. You are free—go—farewell?"

"But I cannot say that."

"Then I shall do it for you. My cousin," he went on, more seriously, "my mind is made up. To-morrow I start again on my pilgrimage, and you are as free as air. Do not think that your words have pained me, for I have long known that I was unworthy and I myself almost desire to be free. We cannot live twice."

"You are too generous."

"By no means. I am only a prodigal; even this treasure I could not keep, but I must let it slip through my fingers with the rest. Now I shall leave you to think upon what I have said. Do not judge me hardly."

"I shall think of you always as the best gentleman in the world. Oh! Victor," she cried, as though interrogating herself, "why cannot I love you?"

"Because, my dear, I would not let you. There is but one thing more to do and then I leave your cold North for ever to seek my fortune elsewhere.

'Et je m'en vais chercher du repos aux enfers.'

I shall send you a peace-offering that I know

you will receive as much for my sake as its own. And now I kiss your hand."

He had borne himself throughout with a cheerful gaiety, never once complaining or reproaching her, but placing himself in the wrong as though he were to blame for her inconstancy. She knew that he was only playing a part and that he was suffering while he jested; that he was making his sacrifice in such a way as to avoid giving her pain. She reproached herself bitterly that she had been unable to control her heart and guide her wayward feelings. It was true she had been loyal in outward act but her heart had been a traitor to her vow. She was not worthy of so much heroic sacrifice; she was but a Carew after all, with the taint and sin of her race; she, who had cried out for loyalty and truth. She had boasted of her strength and constancy, and this man who had laughed at virtue had shown a sovereign strength that put her quite to shame. What had been done would never be undone; her weakness, her want of faith, her treachery of affection, had been made plain to the two men whose regard she esteemed the most in the world. Yet all the time she had tried to follow the path of duty; she had striven to do what was right and trample her inclinations under foot.

And so she sat and thought while De Laprade went out to complete the great work of his renunciation. He smiled bitterly to himself as he passed down the street, wondering what sudden change had taken place within himself that he had surrendered so easily what he had so earnestly desired to obtain. He knew that he loved Dorothy Carew as he had never loved before, and that he had never loved her half so well as that moment when he bade her farewell. He was unable to recognize himself or the new spirit that had prompted this stupendous sacrifice. "If," he thought, "I was inviting him under the walls to a repast of steel, I should be acting like a sensible fellow anxious to cure my wounded honour. But that is not my humour. I think I have lost all my manhood. Oh! my cousin, you have taken from me more than you will ever dream of. It was hard to bear, but now that it is done it will not have to be done again. A year ago I had not given up so easily, but the battle is to the strong. Orme will make her happy."

Gervase was surprised to see De Laprade entering his room, and though he bore him no ill will, he would have preferred that he should not meet him. He had not yet faced his bitter disappointment and resigned himself to the sudden fall of his house of cards. He had come home to realize what his rejection meant for him, for he had been so certain, so blindly certain, of Dorothy's love, that she had seemed a part, and a great part, of his life. The cup of happiness had been dashed from his hand when it was already at his lips; he was still smarting and sore, and it would be idle for him to attempt to offer congratulations to his successful rival. He was not magnanimous enough for that. But he wished him well and wished that he would leave him in peace. He took De Laprade's hand without ill-will but with no great show of cordiality.

"I could not leave your city, Monsieur Orme," said De Laprade, "without bidding you farewell. We have been friends, I think, and done one another some service in our time."

"Your departure is sudden; I had not heard——"

"Only an hour ago I found that I must leave. We strolling players live at large, and shift our booth a hundred times a year."

"When do you return?"

"I disappear for ever," answered Victor with a laugh. "Your country suits me not; your speech is barbarous, your manners are strange, and your climate dries the marrow in my bones. I want sunshine and life and pleasure. Your blood runs slowly here."

"It has been running fast enough for nine weeks," said Gervase, with a grim humour, though feeling in no mood for jesting.

"Ay, you fight very prettily, and you not among the worst, but phlegmatically. I have heard the story of your journey, but I did not come to talk of that."

"I am glad of that at least. I have heard nothing else all day, and 'twas no great feat when all was said."

"Perhaps. Your people are proud and cold and lack sympathy. But I want sympathy."

"Vicomte de Laprade," said Gervase, "I am in no mood for playing upon words. I tell you that I am but now bearing a great trial, the nature of which no man can know but myself, you, perhaps, least of all. I sincerely value your friendship; I have seen your goodness of heart, but it is best that you should shorten this interview. With all my heart I wish you all good fortune, though I shall not see it. I leave by the first ship for Holland."

"We shall see, my friend, we shall see, but I think not."

"How?"

"I said but now you were phlegmatic. I was wrong—you are too impetuous. There are many things which you must put in order before you set out, and perhaps you will never take ship at all."

"I do not understand you, sir."

"Mr. Orme, I know you think I am laughing at you, but it is only a trick that I have, and I am in no mood for jesting any more than yourself. I know you think me a coxcomb, a trifler who hath no depth or height of feeling. But I am come here to speak serious words. I had hoped to marry Miss Carew," he continued softly, looking Gervase full in the face with his eyes fixed and bright, "but that is past. I found that she loved a better man and a worthier than myself, and that I—perhaps that I did not love her as she deserved to be loved. With a deep sense of honour, duty merely—mistaken duty—she would have remained steadfast and allowed me to mar her happiness. I tell you—why should I not speak it?—I loved her too well to marry her, and she is free to give herself to the man she loves. I owe this speech to her, for she hath suffered, and I would not add to her sorrow."

The two men had risen to their feet, and before Gervase knew De Laprade was holding him by the hand, with the tears running down his face.

"God knows," said Gervase, steadying his voice, for he felt himself visibly affected by the other's excessive emotion, "you are a far better and stronger man than I am. I could not have given her up."

"I am a weak fool," said De Laprade, with a forced laugh. "But I know that you will make her happy. You must not tell her of my weakness else—There, the comedy is played out and the curtain having fallen, leaves me a sensible man again. As I have said, I depart to-morrow, to return never again, but I shall hope to hear that all goes well with you. And meantime remember Victor de Laprade, who will not forget you."

"Why," cried Gervase, "should my happiness be gained in your loss?"

"That is past," the other said simply. "You will see Miss Carew when I leave you. She will reproach herself, and you will comfort her, for she is only a woman after all, and will find happiness and consolation. You will sometimes think of me when I am gone and perhaps—perhaps she may name one of her boys after her poor kinsman who by that time will have found rest."

When the evening came down it found Gervase Orme alone with a great happiness and a great regret.

The curtain rings down and the players pass

from view while the humble showman to whom this mimic stage has been a great reality, wakens from his dream, rubs his eyes and goes about his business. He has lived for a while in the stormy days of which he has written—days in which men made heroic sacrifices and performed most memorable deeds, the memory of which still stirs the languid pulses of the blood. Not the muse of history has been his companion; not his is the lofty task to write the story of his people with their valour, their endurance and their intolerant pride; it was only his to tell an idle tale for weary men by winter fires. The men and women of whom he has written did their work for good and evil, and in due time went the way of all flesh.

Simon Sproule again blossomed out in the sunshine of prosperity, and the archives of the city show that he was elected an Alderman, and did his duty faithfully, which cannot be said of all men. And though history is silent on the subject, there can be little doubt that his wife stimulated his civic ambition, inspired his speeches, and kept him in excellent order. There are still Sproules in the North Country who look to Simon as the head of the race, and when touched by family pride they tell the story of his gallant deeds in the memorable siege. But they will find the true history here.

Jasper Carew fell with many a better man on that day when the fate of the kingdom was decided on the banks of the Boyne. He was seen heading the gallant charge of Berwick's horse on Hanmer's men coming out of the river, and as the smoke and dust closed on the broken ranks, he went down and was never seen again.

Of Gervase Orme there is little more to tell. He married the woman he loved, and had sons and grandsons, and served his king like a good and loyal subject. There are certain manuscripts extant which speak of these things, and an escritoire filled with precious letters which came too late to hand to use in this narrative. Especially interesting are certain letters relating to the search after and discovery of a great treasure. But of all the memorials I think the most precious is that portrait in the gallery, of which I have spoken—the portrait of Dorothy Orme taken some two years after her marriage. Above the picture there hangs a rapier, whether by design or by accident I know not, which they tell you vaguely belonged to a kinsman of the lady, who had served in Ireland with Rosen, and fell a year or two afterwards, a gallant gentleman, on the slopes of Steinkirk. He had a history, but they do not remember it; not even his name. *Sic nobis.*

THE END.

MARK TWAIN'S JOAN OF ARC

PERSONAL RECOLLECTIONS OF JOAN OF ARC. By the Sieur LOUIS DE CONTE (her page and secretary). Freely translated out of the Ancient French into Modern English from the Original Unpublished Manuscript in the National Archives of France, by JEAN FRANÇOIS ALDEN. Illustrated from Original Drawings by F. V. DU MOND, and from Reproductions of Old Paintings and Statues. Crown 8vo, Cloth, Ornamental, $2 50.

One of the most delightful books of the time. It is read with keen enjoyment, and its leaves will be turned over again many times in delicious reminiscence of its fascinating episodes and its entrancing digressions.—RICHARD HENRY STODDARD, in *N. Y. Mail and Express.*

Vivid, abounding with life and color, with pathos, with humor.... A story to be intensely enjoyed by all lovers of the Maid and of good reading.—*Advance*, Chicago.

BY THE SAME AUTHOR:

New Library Editions, from New Electrotype plates. Crown 8vo, Cloth, Ornamental, $1 75 each.

THE ADVENTURES OF HUCKLEBERRY FINN. Illustrated.

A CONNECTICUT YANKEE IN KING ARTHUR'S COURT. Illustrated.

THE PRINCE AND THE PAUPER. Illustrated.

LIFE ON THE MISSISSIPPI. Illustrated.

TOM SAWYER ABROAD—TOM SAWYER, DETECTIVE, and Other Stories, etc. Illustrated.

THE AMERICAN CLAIMANT, and Other Stories and Sketches.

The print and form of the volumes are excellent, the binding is serviceable and artistic, and altogether the handsome set of books pays the tribute to the novelist that it should.... He is a man to have on one's shelves, somewhere near Thackeray.—*N. Y. Tribune.*

PUBLISHED BY HARPER & BROTHERS, NEW YORK

☞ *The above works are for sale by all booksellers, or will be mailed by the publishers, postage prepaid, on receipt of the price.*

By JOHN KENDRICK BANGS

THE BICYCLERS, AND THREE OTHER FARCES. Illustrated. 16mo, Cloth, Ornamental, $1 25.

> The farces are crowded with comic situations, brilliant repartee, and wholesome fun.—*Brooklyn Standard-Union.*

A HOUSE-BOAT ON THE STYX. Being Some Account of the Divers Doings of the Associated Shades. Illustrated. 16mo, Cloth, Ornamental, $1 25.

> Well worth reading. . . . It is full of genuine crisp humor. It is the best work of length Mr. Bangs has yet done, and he is to be congratulated.—*N. Y. Mail and Express.*

MR. BONAPARTE OF CORSICA. Illustrated by H. W. McVICKAR. 16mo, Cloth, Ornamental, $1 25.

> Mr. Bangs is probably the generator of more hearty, healthful, purely good-humored laughs than any other half-dozen men of our country to-day.—*Interior, Chicago.*

THE IDIOT. Illustrated. 16mo, Cloth, Ornamental, $1 00.

> "The Idiot" continues to be as amusing and as triumphantly bright in the volume called after his name as in "Coffee and Repartee."—*Evangelist, N. Y.*

THE WATER GHOST, AND OTHERS. Illustrated. 16mo, Cloth, Ornamental, $1 25.

> The funny side of the ghost genre is brought out with originality, and, considering the morbidity that surrounds the subject, it is a wholesome thing to offer the public a series of tales letting in the sunlight of laughter.—*Hartford Courant.*

THREE WEEKS IN POLITICS. Illustrated. 32mo, Cloth, Ornamental, 50 cents.

> He who can read this narrative of a campaigners' trials without laughing must be a stoic indeed.—*Philadelphia Bulletin.*

COFFEE AND REPARTEE. Illustrated. 32mo, Cloth, Ornamental, 50 cents.

> Is delightfully free from conventionality; is breezy, witty, and possessed of an originality both genial and refreshing.—*Saturday Evening Gazette, Boston.*

PUBLISHED BY HARPER & BROTHERS, NEW YORK

☞ *For sale by all booksellers, or will be mailed by the publishers, postage prepaid, on receipt of the price.*

By A. CONAN DOYLE

THE REFUGEES. A Tale of Two Continents. Illustrated. Post 8vo, Cloth, Ornamental, $1 75.

    A masterly work.... It is not every year, or even every decade, which produces one historical novel of such quality.—*Spectator*, London.

THE WHITE COMPANY. Illustrated. Post 8vo, Cloth, Ornamental, $1 75.

    ... Dr. Doyle's stirring romance, the best historical fiction he has done, and one of the best novels of its kind to-day.—*Hartford Courant*.

MICAH CLARKE. Illustrated. Post 8vo, Cloth, Ornamental, $1 75; also 8vo, Paper, 45 cents.

    A noticeable book, because it carries the reader out of the beaten track; it makes him now and then hold his breath with excitement; it presents a series of vivid pictures and paints two capital portraits; and it leaves upon the mind the impression of well-rounded symmetry and completeness.—R. E. PROTHERO, in *The Nineteenth Century*.

ADVENTURES OF SHERLOCK HOLMES. Illustrated. Post 8vo, Cloth, Ornamental, $1 50.

MEMOIRS OF SHERLOCK HOLMES. Illustrated. Post 8vo, Cloth, Ornamental, $1 50.

    Few writers excel Conan Doyle in this class of literature. His style, vigorous, terse, and thoughtful, united to a nice knowledge of the human mind, makes every character a profoundly interesting psychological study.—*Chicago Inter-Ocean*.

THE PARASITE. A Story. Illustrated. Post 8vo, Cloth, Ornamental, $1 00.

    A strange, uncanny, weird story,... easily the best of its class. The reader is carried away by it, and its climax is a work of literary art.—*Cincinnati Commercial-Gazette*.

THE GREAT SHADOW. Post 8vo, Cloth, Ornamental, $1 00.

    A powerful piece of story-telling. Mr. Doyle has the gift of description, and he knows how to make fiction seem reality.—*Independent*, N. Y.

NEW YORK AND LONDON:
HARPER & BROTHERS, PUBLISHERS

☞ *The above works are for sale by all booksellers, or will be sent by the publishers, postage prepaid, on receipt of the price.*

www.ingramcontent.com/pod-product-compliance
Lightning Source LLC
Chambersburg PA
CBHW031422230426
43668CB00007B/400